A Long, Dark Shadow

A Long, Dark Shadow

Minor-Attracted People and Their Pursuit of Dignity

ALLYN WALKER

University of California Press

University of California Press
Oakland, California

© 2021 by Allyn Walker

Cataloging-in-Publication Data is on file at the Library of Congress.

ISBN 978-0-520-30634-9 (cloth : alk. paper)
ISBN 978-0-520-30636-3 (pbk. : alk. paper)
ISBN 978-0-520-97369-5 (ebook)

30   29   28   27   26   25   24   23   22   21
10   9   8   7   6   5   4   3   2   1

To those who accept themselves,
to those who are working on it,
and to those who accept others,
even when it's hard.

Contents

Acknowledgments

I am thrilled that my discussions with minor-attracted people (MAPs) have a physical "home" and platform, in the shape of the book you now read. This book was a collaborative project in the sense that the book would not exist without the courageous and forthright people I spoke with as well as the mentorship I've benefited from. I extend my sincere thanks to Lila Kazemian for having the confidence that I could successfully collect these data in responsible and rigorous ways, and for guiding my initial analyses. I thank Valli Rajah, Karen Terry, Cynthia Calkins, Patrick Lussier, and Evan Mandery for their helpful comments on my data collection process, drafts, and initial thoughts about these topics.

Luke Malone generously helped with my study recruitment and framing. Prominent members of the MAP community provided invaluable assistance with my pilot study, such as Richard Kramer of B4U-ACT, while Nick Devin and Ethan Edwards of VirPed helped me develop my recruitment plan. There were others who publicized my study on the VirPed and B4U-ACT forums, effectively vouching for me and my study.

Data collection and transcription was supported by two awards via John Jay College and the CUNY Graduate Center: a Doctoral Student Research Grant and the Arthur and Elaine Niederhoffer Memorial Fellowship. Additional travel funding was supported by multiple awards from the Graduate Center, to present study findings at conferences. I worked on this book during my time at the University of Utah, Penn State Wilkes-Barre, and Old Dominion University, and I thank each of these institutions for providing me with support.

I thank Maura Roessner at the University of California Press, for her vision and support in bringing this book to fruition. I thank Michael Seto and other, anonymous reviewers for their comments on my proposal and sample chapters, and two reviewers, including Jill Levenson, for their encouragement and for their thorough reads of the full manuscript. Fellow UC Press author Joseph Fischel provided feedback on multiple chapters. Madison Wetzell provided helpful editorial assistance.

The writing of this manuscript would not have been possible without the encouragement of my colleagues and friends who helped me talk through ideas: from Utah, Robert P. Butters, Kort Prince, Erin Becker Worwood, and Christian Sarver; from Pennsylvania, Lizzie Hessek, Shara Donohue, and Zane Winey; and from New York, Celinet, Laura, Colleen, and Maggie.

I am especially grateful to my family for their unending support. Vanessa Panfil has helped me write this book not only through her encouragement but also by reading numerous drafts and providing insightful comments. I also thank my parents, Marcie and Frederick Walker, and my sister, Rachel Walker Bowman, for their continuous care, support, and belief in me.

Prior publications that have utilized these data include "Understanding Resilience Strategies among Minor-Attracted Individuals," published by CUNY Academic Works, and "'I'm Not Like That, So Am I Gay?' The Use of Queer-Spectrum Identity Labels among Minor-Attracted People," published in the *Journal of Homosexuality.*

Finally, to the 42 participants of my study, I am indebted to you all. Thank you for your courage in trusting me with your experiences and for your willingness to advocate for yourself and others. I hope my words do yours justice.

Preface

When I began my first job as a social worker, if you told me that in five short years I was going to be researching minor-attracted people's experiences with facing stigma, I would've called you absurd. At the start of my career in social work, I was working as a counselor for victims of sexual assault. Some of my clients were children; some others were adults who had been victimized when they were young. I would leave work at night enraged by what I had heard during the day, wishing I could do something more for my clients, wishing more than anything that I could have prevented their victimization.

Back then, if you had talked to me about minor-attracted people, I would've automatically assumed you were talking about someone who had committed a crime. This is partly because I working with crime victims, keeping the topic of crime almost constantly in my mind. But this was—and still is—also a typical assumption. We generally don't place a distinction between people who are attracted to minors and people who have committed a sexual offense against a child. Stigma against people who were attracted to minors, then, was not something I ever expected to be something I would advocate against. If anything, I would probably have advocated for greater stigma.

Although my interests in preventing crime and helping victims never went away, over time, they began to be joined by other understandings about crime and justice. As part my job counseling crime victims, I facilitated a support group for incarcerated women who had been sexually assaulted. This was my first direct experience with the criminal processing system, and I realized how ineffective the system was at actually *helping* victims and survivors of sexual assault. Multiple women in the support group coped with their victimization through drug use and had been incarcerated due to drug-related offenses. Police, courts, and prisons failed these women. I would leave work these nights furious not just at individuals but at systemic injustice.

Over the next few years, I became more invested in advocating against the way our society treats individuals who have broken the law. I interned for an organization that visited prisons and reported to state representatives on the conditions inside. I volunteered for a nonprofit aimed at reforming harmful police practices. Eventually I found long-term work with an organization that partnered with my city's government to make changes to our court system. As time went on, I became increasingly frustrated by the injustices I heard about in my work and volunteer positions, and less sure that small steps to reform could ever be enough to fix the system. In short, I became convinced that police and prison abolitionists had the right idea. But I kept hearing the same arguments against abolition. One of the big ones was "But what about pedophiles?" That question was apparently meant to indicate that some people are born bad, that some people inevitably commit crime and will always need to be incarcerated, that their predatory inner nature is a threat to us all, and without police and prisons, we are all doomed to be victimized by them. The question always seemed to trip up abolitionists. "Well," we would say, "we'll always have *some* need for prisons." Even those of us who were against incarceration could not deny the assumed threat caused to society by the evil "pedophile."

It wasn't until years after my social work career started that I first learned about the existence of people who are attracted to minors who have never committed an offense against a child. Suddenly the pattern of "truths" I believed I understood about these people—their supposed lack of morality, the inevitability of them becoming offenders—unraveled around me. I stopped assuming that their attractions meant something about their behavior, and I began asking questions. These questions developed into the research that has informed this book.

In an era where more attention is being paid to police violence than ever before—including through, for example, Black Lives Matter organizing, #SayHerName campaigns, and calls for defunding the police or outright abolishment—I am seeing and hearing more arguments for abolition all the time. These arguments ask us to imagine a society in which police and prisons are no longer considered necessary, because people receive the support that they need from others before they commit a crime. This would mean divesting from the criminal processing system and, importantly, reinvesting the money that had previously gone toward policing and incarceration instead into communities and in people. Through this investment in communities, society would engage in preventing offenses instead of merely reacting with punishment. A necessary step toward building this kind of society must involve letting go of our fatalistic beliefs that some people are beyond help. Instead, we must ask ourselves how our society is currently structured to impede people from accessing the help that they may need. Abolitionists believe that police, courts, and prisons are part of a societal structure that inhibits people from accessing support, thus producing more crime.

Minor-attracted people are among those who are imagined to be beyond help. Even many people who advocate against policing and prisons continue to believe that we need societal protection from these individuals. Yet when it comes to individuals who are attracted to minors, my research shows that they, too, are being kept from help—help that could lead to prevention against child sexual abuse. Within the pages of this book, along with describing how minor-attracted people strategize not to commit sexual offenses, I explore how they have been subjected to stigma, and I advocate against it. Because of this, and because we link so tightly in our minds a connection between attractions to minors and sexual offending, I worry that my readers will think I am somehow downplaying sexual abuse against children, or that I am even trying to normalize it.

Nothing could be further from the truth. My former clients' stories reverberate in my mind to this day, and still I find myself the social worker who wanted to prevent their suffering. No one can prevent the abuse they already experienced, but we can prevent abuse from occurring in the future. Prevention does not come from stigma, police, or prisons, but from support and understanding. I hope this book can help to spread this much-needed understanding as an important first step in prevention.

Introduction

Who Are Minor-Attracted People?

I met Cameron[1] at my first B4U-ACT workshop. He seemed nervous, but then so was I. Cameron introduced himself as a student, like I was. He had a handsome smile, and a soft-spoken, self-effacing demeanor that made me feel comfortable around him almost instantly. He explained to the group that he was there because of his studies in psychology. He was interested in learning more about minor-attracted people (MAPs)—maybe even in providing services for them in the future. He and I spent the day in a hotel conference room near Baltimore, Maryland, with 50 or so other individuals—about half of them MAPs, the other half therapists and researchers. B4U-ACT provides these annual workshops as part of the organization's efforts to remove barriers to mental health care for MAPs interested in therapy. Accordingly, workshop participants were there to learn from one another, although the researchers and therapists—often thought of as "experts"—learned far more than the MAPs, who generously shared their stories with us. Cameron and I spent most of our time listening rather than speaking.

I walked away from the workshop unsure why I had been so nervous to be there. Thinking back on it now, though, it seems obvious: this was my first time being in a room full of people who were open about being sexually attracted to children. B4U-ACT uses the term MAPs, rather than the term "pedophile," to decrease stigma against this group, but the stigma follows them nonetheless. Although I hadn't been worried for my safety in attending the workshop, I had grown up as we all do: with stories of pedophiles being vilified, characterized as predatory and evil. I must have taken on some of that fear, somewhere down the line.

A year later, I attended the next B4U-ACT workshop, decidedly less nervous this time. By then, I had been engaging in interviews with

MAPs for my research for about a month, and after my experience at the workshop the previous year, I was more aware of what I would be walking into. I recognized Cameron, who seemed just as nervous this time around. Early into the day's discussion, I found out why, when he came out to the group as a MAP. He talked candidly about how his attractions to minors affected his life, about the stigma he felt, and the secrecy he needed to maintain in order to function. He told the room: "I felt like I cast a long, dark shadow."

Cameron's need for secrecy was so great that even in a room full of people who shared his attractions, as well as sympathetic others, he had not felt comfortable enough to come out the year prior. In fact, he had kept his attractions a secret not only from those in the room that year but also from most individuals in his private life. Cameron later told me that there were only three people in his personal life who knew he was attracted to minors—his partner and two friends. Although it pained and exhausted him to be "perpetually in the closet," the risk to his personal and professional life was too great.

Given the nature of his sexual attractions, Cameron's choice to keep his attractions a secret from conference attendees and his own family and friends is understandable. The word "pedophile" conjures several distinct images in the contemporary imagination. Perhaps a faceless man behind a computer, or a stranger lurking in a dimly lit corner. We imagine that they all are predators of small children, prowling in playgrounds or online, waiting to strike. This assumption causes us to decry pedophiles as dangerous, as monsters, as sex offenders and child molesters. This assumption kept Cameron from disclosing his attractions to others. This assumption, I argue throughout the book, propagates the danger to children that we all fear.

. . .

Cameron, who was in his 30s when I met him, is one of many MAPs I spoke to as I collected data for this book. He experienced attractions to children as young as eight. Like my other research participants, Cameron struggled with these attractions for a number of reasons, never behaving inappropriately with a child but knowing that society vilifies those who share these attractions, whether or not they act upon them. My research participants were all minor-attracted people who refrained from any sexual contact with minors, all of whom were dedicated to living lives free of offending. This book is about them: how they form identities as minor-attracted individuals, how they cope with the stigma they face from society, and how they strategize not to commit offenses.

A POPULATION SHADOWED

Cameron spoke about the shadow he cast, but his is not the only shadow of relevance to this book. As a society, understandings about this population have been shadowed by moral panic, leading to numerous misconceptions often accepted as fact. For decades, our mental image of minor-attracted people—or, as we have called them, "pedophiles"[2]—has been of individuals lurking in the shadows of back alleyways, playgrounds, and internet chat rooms, waiting to prey on children. Societal misconceptions about minor-attracted people create problems for individuals like Cameron and the other participants of my study. Furthermore, I argue that these misconceptions simultaneously place children at risk of harm. Accordingly, I explore several myths and realities about minor-attracted individuals below, in an attempt to shed some light on this obscured population.

Misconception 1: All Pedophiles Are Offenders

Misunderstandings about people who are attracted to minors begin with common usage of the term "pedophile." In daily language this word is frequently used interchangeably with "child molester." Even news outlets broadly considered to be credible sources typically the use these terms as if they were synonymous. In fact, as I was writing my first draft of this introduction in April of 2019, I heard CNN reporter Anderson Cooper posing a question about voting rights to Pete Buttigieg, a candidate in the Democratic presidential primaries. He asked, "People like the Boston Marathon bomber; people convicted of sexual assault, rape and other things; pedophiles...what do you think...should they be able to vote?"[3] This usage implies that pedophiles are necessarily criminals. Presumably, when Anderson Cooper used the word "pedophiles," he used it as a shortened term for "people who have committed a sex offense against a child."

The problem with Anderson Cooper equating pedophiles and sex offenders is that they are two entirely distinct groups. Although pedophilia indicates an *attraction* to children, it does not indicate anything about an individual's *behavior*. But if you were unaware before you picked up this book that the term "pedophile" is not synonymous with "sex offender" or "child molester," you are not alone. When I give talks to groups about the research I've conducted, I generally provide the definition of "pedophile," pointing out that it does not indicate sex-offending behavior. At this point, I've come to expect phones to come out of people's pockets. It's not uncommon for me to see multiple incredulous attendees Googling whether the definition I've given is correct. (It is.) This includes scholars within the field of criminology. Indeed, news media is not the only source using the term "pedophile" as another term for "child molester": even criminological research frequently uses language equating pedophilia with offending behavior,[4] demonstrating how far misunderstanding and stigma about pedophiles extends. Hundreds of academic articles, many written since 2015, feature such phrases as "the crime of pedophilia" and "victims of pedophilia." Nearly all articles about pedophiles are from a criminal justice– or psychology-related source, demonstrating that most academic writing about pedophiles focuses on this population as offenders or as mentally ill.

The absence of a behavioral implication in the definition of "pedophile" is backed up by research. Although there are currently no agreed-upon estimates of the percentage of pedophiles who have committed sexual offenses against a child, due at least in part to the hidden nature of the population of pedophiles,[5] we do know that not all pedophiles commit sexual offenses.[6] In fact, some research suggests that only a small proportion of people who are preferentially attracted to children have been convicted of sexual offenses against minors.[7] In addition, evidence from multiple studies has shown that many to most of those who do commit sexual offenses against children are not pedophiles.[8] These individuals are not preferentially attracted to minors.[9]

Misconception 2: All People Who Are Attracted to Minors Are Pedophiles

Just as it is common to assume that all pedophiles are sex offenders, so too is it a common assumption that all people attracted to minors are pedophiles. In 2017 a special election was called in Alabama for the U.S. Senate seat previously held by Jeff Sessions. The Republican nominee was Roy Moore, a former Chief Justice of the Supreme Court of Alabama. Upon his nomination, multiple women accused Moore of sexual assault and other sexual misconduct, when he was an adult. Some of the women had been minors at the time of the alleged incidents, including a woman who had been 14 at the time and multiple women who had been 16 years old. In response to the allegations, the media collectively referred to Moore as a pedophile. Here the media again may have been looking for a shorthand way to indicate that he had committed a sex offense against underage girls, for which "pedophile" would be the wrong term to use, but this term was also wrong for a second reason: "pedophilia" refers to a specific age range of attraction.

Although it may be true that a person attracted to minors is a pedophile, this is not always the case. Above, I referenced the definition of "pedophile."[10] The definition, according to the American Psychiatric Association,[11] specifically refers to individuals over age 16 who exhibit a preferential attraction to *prepubescent children*. In other words, pedophiles are attracted to children who have not yet begun to go through puberty; generally around age 11 and under. Clinicians frequently distinguish between pedophiles and hebephiles, the latter of whom are preferentially attracted to children in the beginning phases of puberty, typically from the ages of 12 to 14.[12] Ephebophiles are a third set of individuals attracted to minors; these are people with a preferential attraction to minors in the late stages of puberty (usually between the ages of 15 to 19).[13] However, researchers and other sources disagree over use of the term "ephebophile,"[14] as well as which age ranges best fit which definitions.[15] In addition, people who are attracted to minors themselves use a range of terms to describe themselves in terms of their attractions, including (but not limited to) pedophile, hebephile, and ephebophile, although the age ranges they are attracted to may or may not fit the clinical definitions of these terms. These terms are all in contrast to "teleiophile," which refers to an adult who is attracted to other adults.[16]

Why does it matter whether someone is a pedophile or a hebephile? Overgeneralizing and referring to individuals who are attracted to minors as pedophiles further promotes misunderstanding about this population, pulling us toward our colloquial understandings of "pedophiles" as child molesters. In addition, as discussed in Chapter 1 of this book, individuals who are attracted to minors frequently describe themselves using terms that denote the age of the individuals they are attracted to—in other words, some refer to themselves as pedophiles, and some hebephiles—so understanding the differences in the terms promotes an understanding of these individuals' experiences.

To account for the disagreement over definitions, as well as to be inclusive of individuals attracted to all age ranges of minors, I use the terms "minor-attracted person" and "MAP" throughout the majority of this book. "Minor-attracted person" is an established umbrella term that can refer to all individuals preferentially attracted to children. In addition to its usefulness in describing individuals preferentially attracted to minors of any age, the term "minor-attracted person" has also been identified by the MAP-led group B4U-ACT as a phrase that is preferable to the term "pedophile" due to its less-stigmatizing nature.[17] The question that may naturally arise is, "Why should we want minor-attracted people to feel *less* stigma?" This brings me to my third key point.

Misconception 3: Stigmatizing MAPs Protects Children

While I was preparing to interview MAPs for the project that would become this book, I reached out to journalist Luke Malone. A story of his had run on the popular NPR show *This American Life*—it dealt with MAPs who were supporting each other in their efforts to cope with their attractions to minors,[18] and I had been in the beginning stages of planning my research with MAPs when it aired. Luke agreed to meet me for coffee, and he gave me invaluable advice for getting in touch with MAPs for my research. Then he gave me advice of a different kind—about the reactions of the general public toward hearing narratives about MAPs. He told me about the hate mail he's received. One exchange in particular sticks out in my mind. Someone had reached out to Luke to argue that because his *This American Life* story encouraged empathy toward MAPs, the story was dangerous to minors. This person told Luke: "You have to think about the children."

I have since encountered similar responses to my research. It's standard to treat empathy toward MAPs and the safety of children as if the two concepts oppose each other so profoundly that they cannot both exist. Common logic seems to dictate that if we treat MAPs with empathy and compassion, we are somehow condoning sexual abuse against children. Therefore, the argument that we should "think about the children" reveals a philosophy that to keep children safe, MAPs need to be shamed for their attractions.

There are two main problems with this assumption. The first is that shaming people for their attractions won't make their attractions go away. Of course, an argument can be made that there is value in temporarily shaming people for negative *behaviors*—criminological theory emphasizes the benefit of shame in response to criminal acts, if the criminal actor is successfully reintegrated into society afterward.[19] Hence, there could be social benefit to shaming people who commit crimes against minors, as this could change the behavior of these individuals in the future.[20] If the goal in shaming people is *behavioral* change, however, shaming people for their *attractions* to minors is ineffective. Again, we see here the misunderstanding of pedophiles as sexual offenders. If society shamed only MAPs who commit crimes, that could, according to this theory, have an effect on offending. But society does not only shame MAPs who commit crimes—it shames *all* MAPs. Therefore, presumably the goal is to convince MAPs that they should not be attracted to minors, and in doing so, to change their attractions entirely. Attempting to change the attractions of MAPs is a futile enterprise, however. Researchers and theorists in multiple fields have begun to acknowledge that, among those who are preferentially attracted to minors, this attraction tends to endure across the lifespan. Whereas it used to categorize MAPs as mentally ill, the fifth edition of the *Diagnostic and Statistical Manual of Mental Disorders*[21] has categorized pedophilia as a "sexual interest."[22]

Other researchers have gone further than the American Psychiatric Association, conceptualizing attractions to minors as a sexual orientation. The definition of this phrase is contested: while media watchdog organization GLAAD[23] and other LGBT organizations define sexual orientation in terms of attraction to a specific (or multiple) sex(es) or gender(s), others see the distinction about attractions toward gender as arbitrary and argue for an expansion of our understandings of sexual orientation. For example, sexologist Charles Moser[24] has proposed that sexual orientation does not need to be defined by gender but can instead be categorized by multiple other characteristics that distinguish sexual orientation from other sexual interests. These characteristics include attraction, relative permanence, fluidity, early age of onset, and importance to the individual. While all of these are relevant to sexual orientations toward a given gender (or multiple genders), these characteristics also have relevance to orientations that are not characterized by gender.

Applying Moser's definition, there is evidence showing that attractions to minors can be considered a sexual orientation. Psychologist Michael Seto[25] has identified pedophilia alternately as a "sexual age orientation," and a "chronophilia," pointing to numerous similarities between attractions to minors and attractions to either the same or another gender. His work shows that MAPs' attractions and trajectories mirror those of other sexual minorities in terms of the age when individuals first become aware of their attractions, their sexual history, endurance of attractions over time, and experiences of romantic feelings in addition to sexual attraction. MAPs often report becoming aware of their attractions to children during adolescence, a trend that is typical of other sexual minorities.[26] MAPs also report feeling romantic attachments to those they are attracted to, in addition having sexual feelings for them, which is consistent with the discourse surrounding other sexual minorities,[27] providing further evidence for the existence of a sexual age orientation.

Two arguments are commonly applied against labeling attraction to minors as a sexual orientation. The first is that using the term "sexual orientation," a term that generally gets invoked when discussing queer communities, cannot apply to MAPs because children cannot consent to sex, whereas relationships between consenting queer adults are morally permissible. Allow me to be clear: this book does *not* promote sexual contact between adults and minors. My point here is *not* that children can consent to sex, nor do I suggest that sexual contact between adults and minors could be beneficial to children in any way. Rather, my objection to this argument is that the fact of children's inability to consent to sex is irrelevant in the application of the term "sexual orientation" toward attractions to minors. If our definition of "sexual orientation" is about attraction to a certain group that develops early, remains relatively consistent across the lifetime, and is important to the identity of the individual, evidence shows that this applies to MAPs. The fact that MAPs are attracted to a group with whom they cannot morally or legally engage in sexual activity does not mean that they lack a sexual orientation toward minors. Again, this comes back to attraction versus behavior. A person's sexual orientation does not determine their behavior—it only determines their sexual interests.

The second common argument against using the term "sexual orientation" to describe attractions to minors is related to, but slightly different from, the first. This argument says that calling attractions to minors a sexual orientation sets MAPs up for comparisons to queer communities, which presents a danger to queer people. This argument is harder for me to oppose—in fact, I can't say I disagree with it. If an enduring attraction to minors constitutes a sexual orientation, and if queer populations are individuals with non-normative sexual orientations, certainly MAPs apply under the large queer umbrella. What, then, does this mean for other queer communities, who have for ages been subjected to accusations of sexual violence and child predation[28] based on ignorance and hate?

As a queer person myself, this question haunts me. And yet it is perhaps the fact that I am queer that gives me meaningful understanding of others who are treated with suspicion and stigma based upon a sexual orientation that cannot be changed. I can't begrudge other queer individuals who do not want to be associated with a population assumed to be child molesters; however, it is also important to realize that unfounded and reductive historical claims of queer individuals' supposedly predatory behaviors mirror today's assumptions about MAPs. It is a common belief in today's society that minor-attracted individuals are all offenders, which is a flawed assumption that contributes to stigma felt by MAPs. The tendency of queer communities to distance themselves from MAPs indicates either agreement with that erroneous belief or a willingness to prioritize the wellbeing of *some* queer people at the expense of others.

Ultimately, shifting away from the conceptualization of attractions to minors as a mental illness and shifting toward their conceptualization as a sexual orientation indicates that attraction to minors is neither treatable nor curable—indeed, if it is not an illness, it cannot be cured. In fact, before the American Psychiatric Association[29] moved to call pedophilia a "sexual interest," sexuality theorist Augustin Malón[30] critiqued its former categorization, calling it "a diagnosis in search of a disorder." In addition, sexual orientation change efforts (SOCE), also known as conversion therapy or reparative therapy, have been condemned by many as ineffective.[31] Although this type of "therapy" is specifically denounced (and in some jurisdictions prohibited by law)[32] when applied to LGBT individuals, there is no evidence that it works to cure attractions to minors either—indeed, research has yet to substantiate any treatments that might supposedly change the attractions of MAPs.[33]

If the first problem with the assumption that shaming MAPs makes children safe is that shaming MAPs can't change their attractions to minors, the second problem is that shaming MAPs for their attractions alone may actually put children in *more* danger. If we really want to "think about the children," it is possible that treating MAPs with empathy is the *key*. This suggestion may seem counterintuitive: again, common wisdom says that if we don't place stigma and shame upon MAPs, we normalize their attractions and promote offending. However, because shame is not used to target only *offending* MAPs, and because MAPs cannot be "cured" of their attractions, shaming them is an ineffective method of keeping children safe.

Instead, shame may have the opposite effect. The stigma associated with experiencing sexual attractions toward minors is so severe that it may affect how MAPs cope with their attractions. Where can someone go for help if they realize they are preferentially attracted to minors? The taboo against sexual attraction to children is societally ubiquitous—who could trust their parents to be understanding? Their siblings or friends? An adult romantic partner? In the absence of support from friends and loved ones, where can MAPs turn for help if they feel tempted to commit a crime? Do mental health providers even know enough to provide help, given society's current misperceptions about MAPs?

The effect of shaming not only MAPs who commit offenses, but MAPs in general, means that MAPs are societally confused for sex offenders and therefore might have very few options for help-seeking, even in the event that help is necessary to prevent themselves from committing a crime. Taking into consideration the fact that our social environment provides so few resources for MAPs to access help, the resilience of my study sample, in terms of coping and in terms of non-offending, is remarkable. This resilience is a key topic in my research, and I share my participants' coping methods and strategies for non-offending throughout this book.

INTERVIEWING MAPS ONLINE

I was an adult with a full-time research job by the time I first learned about the existence of MAPs who do not commit offenses against minors. In that moment I was stunned. Why hadn't I considered before that people with these attractions may not be offenders? I began asking more questions: How do non-offending MAPs strategize to resist committing offenses? How do they cope with their attractions, and with the stigma they face? Finding few answers in available research at the time, I decided to ask non-offending MAPs themselves.

I conducted semi-structured interviews with 42 MAPs across the globe. Most of these interviews took place over the phone or over text-based chat, although some were through video chat or in person. As I was interested in speaking only to non-offending minor-attracted people, requirements for participation in my study were that my participants had to be 18 years or older, preferentially or exclusively attracted to individuals under the age of 18, and that they had never committed a crime involving sexual contact with a minor.[34] The MAPs I interviewed, and whose narratives are presented throughout this book, range in age from 19 years old to their mid-sixties, with the majority in their twenties and thirties. Exactly half of the sample lived within the United States; the rest of the population lived internationally, spread across six continents. The majority were men, although three were women and one was agender. In terms of race, the sample was almost homogenous: the vast majority (90%) were white. Slightly less than half of my sample was exclusively attracted to minors; the rest were preferentially attracted to minors, with some attractions to adults as well. More information about my sample is available in Appendix A, and further information about my research methods is in Appendix B.

Although it is unlikely that participants' characteristics are representative of all individuals who are preferentially attracted to minors, they do seem to be largely representative of the groups from which I recruited them.[35] I met most of my participants through two online peer support groups for MAPs: B4U-ACT and VirPed. Both of these groups were created to help MAPs get emotional support and to help them not to commit an offense. B4U-ACT was developed in 2003 as a partnership between MAPs and mental health professionals. Their original goal was to provide mental health services to the MAP community through a crisis hotline as well as referrals to care providers. However, various barriers arose in the development of the hotline and referral list, and B4U-ACT shifted its mission to eliminating barriers between MAPs and mental health care. B4U-ACT currently operates two online peer support forums: one for MAPs and another for family members of MAPs. At the end of my data collection, in mid-2016, B4U-ACT had about 100 online participants. The group also hosts annual workshops for MAPs, mental health care providers, researchers, educators, and students. B4U-ACT encourages empirical research about MAPs by collaborating with researchers to assist with study recruitment and the development of research instruments.

VirPed, which stands for Virtuous Pedophiles, is an offshoot of B4U-ACT. Founded in 2012, VirPed provides a peer support forum for MAPs,[36] although researchers, journalists, and other members of the public are permitted to join. As of the end of my data collection period in 2016, more than 1,500 individuals were members of the VirPed forum, which is split into topics such as requests for support and advice, discussions of various aspects of members' lives, and broader discussion about the experiences of MAPs in therapy, the nature of pedophilia, and recent research about MAPs. VirPed also operates a chat service for members wishing to converse and access support in real time. While VirPed leaders are willing to promote research recruitment efforts on the forum, research collaboration is not a main focus of the group. The VirPed website provides information for the general public about pedophilia, including research articles and other media on the subject, but the forums are reserved exclusively for members. To join the forum, individuals must submit an email to the moderators,[37] introducing themselves and requesting membership.

The main difference between B4U-ACT and VirPed is that VirPed takes a solid stance about sexual activity between adults and children, stating that it is fundamentally wrong. B4U-ACT has declined to take a moral stance on the issue, instead choosing to focus on creating a dialogue between those with varying moral opinions. VirPed began as an offshoot of B4U-ACT and was created as a response to the B4U-ACT's lack of taking such a stance as an organization.[38] B4U-ACT, however, clearly states on its website that the protection of children is part of its mission and that MAPs should abide by the law for the sake of children and themselves.[39]

During interviews I asked participants questions about how they formed identity, ways in which they experienced and coped with stigma, what motivated them not to commit an offense against a child, and how they strategized to resist offending, among other topics. The topic of stigma weaved its way through multiple sections of my interview, as it affected identity formation, coping, and strategies to keep themselves from committing offenses. As such, stigma is a main theme throughout this book.

DUAL FOCI

The primary goal of this book is to explore ways of thinking about MAPs that may better protect children from harm. Indeed, my own research participants told me during interviews that they were interested in speaking to me out of an interest in protecting children. What's been lost in this discussion so far, however, is a focus on experiences of MAPs for the sake of their own wellbeing. We have been conditioned to see MAPs as criminals or (in the words of multiple research participants in my study) as "ticking time bombs." But these are real human beings who happen to have attractions that they never asked for, that they typically do not want, and that they cannot get rid of. Their daily struggles include many more than resisting an interest to act on their attractions: MAPs often face futures with no chance of romance, sex, or love, and on top of that, society sends them constant messages telling them that they are monsters for experiencing unwanted attractions. I am therefore writing this book with two main foci—the prevention of child abuse and the promotion of wellbeing among MAPs—because protecting children is important, because MAPs are people who deserve compassion, and because these foci are not contradictory.

With these aims in mind, I have structured this book to explore the experiences of MAPs, as constructed by my participants' narratives. Chapter 1 examines their varying identities as they relate to their attractions toward minors as well as the circumstances under which they formed these identities. Chapter 2 describes their decision processes about whether or not to tell others in their lives about these identities and their experiences in doing so. Chapter 3 explores strategies for coping with their attractions to minors and the resulting stigma that they face. Chapter 4 looks at how they have strategized not to commit offenses and their motivations for living as non-offenders. Chapter 5 takes an in-depth look at one particular strategy for both coping and to resist committing an offense: seeking out mental health care. This chapter explores my participants' motivations for seeking out mental health care, as well as their experiences in speaking with providers. Chapter 6 explores main takeaways from each of the chapters.

For the interested reader I also include two appendices: Appendix A details participant characteristics and Appendix B covers research methods with further information about how I successfully recruited this population and conducted the study. It is my hope that this book will further our understandings of a group of people that has been living in shadow for too long.

1. "Am I a Monster?"

Forming an Identity as Minor-Attracted

Hugo can recall feeling drawn to children who were younger than him since he was 11 years old. In our conversations, he described experiencing a strong pull toward friendships with elementary-age children throughout his middle school years. Once he was in high school, Hugo began to recognize that he was attracted to boys who were slightly younger than he was, although this didn't initially strike him as particularly odd. He recalled, for instance, finding freshman boys attractive when he was a sophomore. As he grew older, however, he found himself attracted to younger and younger boys. This eventually worried him, and when he realized he was having sexual thoughts about young boys, he felt profoundly disturbed. He told me that at this point he began to question what he was feeling, asking himself, "Oh, man, what is this?...Am I a monster? What the hell?"

Hugo and his siblings were raised by their father in a religious community, the Church of Jesus Christ of Latter-Day Saints. The LDS church is famously conservative. Writings by elders describe "serious transgressions" that can lead to excommunications include, for example, "homosexual relations," "transsexual operation," and "false swearing."[1] Although Hugo had close relationships with his father and brothers and a strong connection to his church, given the restrictive environment in which he was raised, he did not feel able to share his growing concerns about the attractions he was experiencing with anyone else. As a result, these attractions made him feel alone. Hugo's growing sense of alienation was heightened by the fact that he had never before heard of an individual who shared these attractions who had not committed a sexual offense. Hence the questions he was asking himself about his attractions made him wonder if he was monstrous: a child molester waiting to happen.

Hugo's anxieties reached their peak at Christmastime when he was 17. He was going on a trip with his father and at the airport Hugo saw a boy of about 12. The boy caught Hugo's attention—he recalled thinking the boy was "super cute." At that moment Hugo realized his fears were true. "Oh, shit," he thought. "I think I'm a pedophile. I think I'm attracted to kids." He felt devastated upon his confrontation with this knowledge about himself. In that moment, Hugo recalled he "didn't really want to live." Although Hugo overcame his feelings of not wanting to live, he explained his reasoning for these negative feelings in our interview. "Just for a while I thought I was the only one," he told me. "It was just so silly but I definitely felt that way." I asked him: "You felt you were the only what?" He replied: "Like, person who was attracted to kids who didn't act on it."

Hugo explained: "I just felt like I was combating it alone, you know? I felt like—it was difficult because it was a hard thought to have, I don't know if I fully believed it or not, but I definitely had the thought at times . . . [that it would be] impossible for other people to have the same feelings." Eventually he found VirPed, an online community of thousands of MAPs who are committed to non-offending. He connected with others who shared his attractions, which made him feel less alone and supported by others who understood. They even helped encourage Hugo to come out to his father, which was a supportive experience for him as well.

·   ·   ·

Saying that Hugo's experiences in forming his identity as an adolescent were different from most others' would be a dramatic understatement. Yet it was common for the participants in my study to detail similar narratives during our interviews. As MAPs begin to recognize themselves as having a prevalent attraction to minors, frequently in adolescence, they do so within a societal context of widespread fear, hate, and suspicion toward those who share their attractions. The ways in which my participants came to terms with their attractions and put words to them were affected by this stigma, which frequently set the stage for the ways they would attempt to cope with their attractions and remain resilient to offending.

Developmental psychologists, particularly Erik Erikson, have conceptualized identity formation as a key task of human development.[2] In assuming the task of identity formation, an individual examines their own personal values, beliefs, and goals, and tries on roles to determine who they are and how they fit within society. If an individual does not form a strong sense of identity during adolescence or young adulthood, thought Erikson, they would experience an identity crisis or "role confusion," leaving the individual struggling to find themselves. Although the task of forming identity extends to most adolescents and young adults, the process looks different for different individuals. Distinct consideration has been given to the development of identity among sexual minorities, who historically have formed their identities within a context of social stigmatization of the very identities they have developed. MAPs share atypical sexual attractions with other sexual minorities, as well as the associated stigma, making early scholarship about identity formation among sexual minorities especially relevant.[3]

This book's introduction discussed the societal assumption that all MAPs are offenders, as well as the possibility that the stigma attached to attractions to minors may contribute to offending by this population. This chapter investigates how MAPs develop their own identities, taking the context of stigma into consideration. People's coping skills can be heavily influenced by their own identities.[4] Therefore, the ways in which MAPs form identity have implications for their own wellbeing as well as for their motivations and strategies to remain resilient to committing offenses.

SEXUAL IDENTITY LABELS

Before I discuss how MAPs form their identities, these identities *themselves*—that is, the words that minor-attracted individuals use to describe themselves—should be explored. Prior to conducting interviews, I had expected my participants to identify as MAPs, or perhaps as pedophiles. In reality, the number of different labels that they employed to portray themselves in terms of their attractions was staggering. My participants were contemplative and introspective about their choice of words to describe their attractions, and they frequently explained at length the thought process that had gone into this choice. These labels signified various aspects of their attractions—from the age of the individuals they were attracted to, to the gender(s) to which they were attracted, to how prevalent these attractions were for them. Their decisions about which labels to use were also determined by societal perceptions about these words and understandings (factually accurate or not) about their meanings.

Age of Attraction

The majority of study participants labeled themselves using terms that signified their age of attraction (AoA). Age of attraction refers to the age range of those an individual is attracted to. Participant AoAs ranged widely—from one year old to late adulthood—but the average AoA was between 8 and 14 years old. My participants referred to themselves using clinical labels signifying their AoA, including "pedophile," defined by the American Psychiatric Association as exhibiting attractions toward prepubescent children, generally under 11 years old;[5] "hebephile," indicating attractions to children in the early phases of puberty, often between the ages of 11 and 14; and "ephebophile," indicating attractions to adolescents, often between the ages of 15 and 19. Many used the term MAP (or minor-attracted person) to indicate preferential attraction to minors of any age. Other labels signaling AoA were sometimes (though less commonly) cited by participants, such as "pedohebephile" (attracted to both prepubescent and pubescent children), "paedosexual" (an alternative term for "pedophile"),[6] "parasexual" (atypical sexual attractions), and "achronophile" (lacking age preference).

"Too much baggage": Wrestling with stigmatized identity labels. Significantly, despite my choice to use the term MAP throughout this book, only 14 of my participants used the term "minor-attracted person" to refer to themselves. Somewhat surprising to me at first was that 21 of my participants self-identified as pedophiles. In interviews, those who identified as pedophiles shared this fact with me self-consciously, sometimes apologetically, frequently seeming concerned that I would confuse labeling themselves as a pedophile with an admission of committing a sexual offense. I got this impression because after telling me that they self-identified as a pedophile, they often quickly pointed out that their use of this label did *not* mean that they were a sex offender. For instance, when asked about labels that he used to identify himself, Strand referred to himself as a pedophile and immediately (and with no further prompting) added: "I consider myself that in my attractions, but not my actions." He, like others, felt it was important to make this distinction to me right off the bat. Clearly he was used to misunderstandings about the meaning of the term.

The distinction between "MAP" and "pedophile" held significance for my participants. "I'm not too afraid to call myself a pedophile," Hugo told me—an indication that others in fact were quite hesitant to do so. Indeed, as this quote suggests, many of my respondents who fit the clinical definition of a pedophile (in other words, those in my study who were preferentially attracted to prepubescent children) noted a reluctance to self-identify as such due to stigma associated with the term. Conversely, the term "MAP" provided some distance from the stigma accompanying the word "pedophile." As Kevin told me, "'minor-attracted' is a better euphemism; it comes across more positively due to the stigma associated with pedophilia." He used both the terms "pedophile" and "MAP" for himself, but as someone who had experienced "guilt" and "torment" over his attractions to minors, Kevin appreciated that "MAP" provided what he considered to be a more positive term for his sexuality.

Even those who used the term "pedophile" to describe themselves indicated a certain degree of conflict in doing so. For example, Avery stated that "the description of 'pedophile' I see when I open up a dictionary describes me, though other people seem to use that term differently," referring to the common notion that "pedophile" is equivalent to "child molester." Bryan noted that "the term 'pedophile' has too much baggage," indicating that although he felt the term was an accurate fit with his attractions, its use still made him uncomfortable due to others' associations with it. Stigma associated with the term "pedophile" was so pervasive that it colored my participants' own perceptions about the meaning of the term as well. When I asked Shawn how he defined himself in terms of his attractions, he declined to use any labels that would denote his age of attractions. However, further into our conversation, he referred to himself as a pedophile. When I asked Shawn about this, he backtracked, stating, "Well, maybe that was the wrong choice of words. Words mean something, and specifically a pedophile is somebody who collects photos of young children...I don't collect photos." As no scholarly nor clinical definitions of pedophiles include any mention of the collection of photos, Shawn's statement reflects a colloquial understanding rather than any official classifications of pedophilia. His account is indicative of the stigma and misunderstanding that MAPs face when forming their own identities and disclosing them to others.

Due to the high degree of stigma associated with the term, those who identified as pedophiles often talked of reclaiming the word, or of an interest in educating others about the difference between pedophilia (a sexuality) and sex offending (an action). Vincent explained:

> At first I was really not into [using the word "pedophile"] at all, but that's I think mostly just because I, like most people, associated that with abuse. With committing crimes and hurting people. And I kinda

thought, well, you know, maybe we should rebrand. (laughter) We better come up with another way to describe ourselves, because that's
always going to kinda creep people out to use that word. But I posted
about this on VirPed and got a lot of negative reactions. Everyone's like
"No, that's the right word. People are just using it wrong, and it's better
to take back the word." And I guess over time I've come to agree with
that. It just took some getting used to, to kind of get that old idea of
what it meant out of my head.

Although Vincent previously felt ashamed by the term "pedophile" due
to the societal tendency to link it with sex offending, he now felt that the
word "pedophile" needed to be reclaimed to decouple the two concepts.
Neil, who at age 21 was one of my youngest participants, also spoke about
taking back the word. "I read that 'queer' was used in the past as a slur and
has been mostly reclaimed by now," he told me, "which . . . gives me hope
that words like 'pedophile' can be reclaimed as well."

Exclusivity. Study participants also took the exclusivity (or lack
thereof) of their attractions to minors or a particular age range into
account when they decided which labels fit them best, although often
they found that no single label fit them well. While the clinical definitions of words like "pedophile," "hebephile," and "ephebophile" suggest
mutually exclusive groups, the labels employed by those in my study
suggested overlap. That is, some of my participants who regarded themselves as pedophiles were also attracted to individuals in the hebephilic
age range, while some who identified as hebephiles also had attractions
to prepubescent children. In addition, many who identified themselves
as MAPs, pedophiles, hebephiles, or ephebophiles were also attracted to
adults.

Of the respondents, 27 described themselves as "nonexclusive"—in
other words, they were attracted to both adults and children. This was
in part to resolve a mismatch between their sexual identity labels and
the predetermined age parameters given to these labels by clinicians.
Inversely, those who considered themselves "exclusive" were usually
solely attracted to minors. Nonexclusive individuals generally felt weaker
attractions to adults than to minors. Although three of my participants
were equally attracted to individuals of all ages, none of them were
primarily attracted to adults. Harper, who is attracted to both girls and
women noted: "I'm kind of like a bisexual person who's like 90% into one
gender and 10% into the other. . . . Except for me, it's age, not gender—the
gender's consistent." Harper used both the terms "minor-attracted per-

son" and "pedophile" to describe herself, although her attractions fell into both pedophilic and hebephilic age ranges: her AoA was from 8 to 14. She described her attractions to adult women as "less intense" than her attractions to girls, although at the time of our interview she was in a long-term relationship with a woman her same age.

Brooke also drew a comparison between nonexclusivity and bisexuality, noting that she had heard bisexual people express confusion over straight or gay individuals having a specific attraction to one gender; similarly, Brooke did not understand why age might factor into someone's attractions to another person. Some participants noted that they could be attracted to adults, but only if they were relatively young (or if they appeared young). For example, Robin (who was primarily attracted to boys ages 13 to 18) and George (who was most attracted to boys ages 10 to 15) both specified they were also attracted to "twinks": in other words, young or young-looking, slim, adult gay men. Zach, who was primarily attracted to girls in the age range of 11 to 15, said he had a "decent degree of attraction" to younger-looking adult women, in some cases up to 30 years old.

MAPs who are attracted to both males and females can be attracted to different age ranges within each gender. For instance, Xavier reported being attracted to girls between the ages of 2 and 17 but to boys between the ages of 2 and 9. MAPs may also be attracted to only one gender of minors but to both male and female adults (or vice-versa). Lucas reported attractions to girls from the ages of 4 to 9 as well as adult men and women. Charlotte similarly disclosed attractions to adult men and women, although her attractions toward minors were only toward girls. Some respondents noted a different intensity of attraction to each age range and gender. For example, Robin mentioned attractions to mainly teen boys, with a secondary attraction to younger boys and occasionally also adult men and women. And while Victor felt sexual attractions to boys between 7 and 12 years old, he also noted having attractions to adult women, although these attractions were not sexual in nature.

My participants also made the distinction between romantic and sexual attractions regarding their age of attraction. Some respondents reported having only romantic attractions to older individuals, while having sexual attractions to children. For example, Dominick, who identified as a pedophile, said he had sexual attractions to males ages 6 to 15 as well as "nonsexual attraction to males about ages 16 to 45, but nothing as strong as those in my main age of attraction."

Types of Attractions

Although research about MAPs has tended to focus on sexual offending, and therefore on attractions toward children that are specifically sexual in nature, very few individuals in my study indicated feeling only sexual attraction to children. In contrast to Victor, who described his attractions to adults as "emotional" rather than sexual, many of my participants described their attractions to minors as romantic or used other nonsexual descriptions for their feelings. Most respondents reported experiencing attractions toward minors that were romantic, aesthetic, physical, emotional, sentimental, or based on a desire for friendship. Mitchell, who is attracted to teenaged boys, told me: "The attraction is not just sexual, but also emotional. I feel like I fall in love, and feel like a few times, that has happened, although I never let the boy know that I felt that way about him." The majority of the time, my participants said that they had these feelings in *addition* to sexual attraction, although some said these feelings were in *place* of any sexual attraction.

The MAPs in my study found deep importance in this distinction between sexual and other types of attractions to minors. They were often frustrated with what they saw as a societal presumption that attractions toward children among MAPs must be entirely sexual in nature. Neil told me: "Sometimes, I feel like it's impossible for me to truly convey my feelings, that I'll never be able to make [teleiophiles] understand how much love means to me." For Neil and others, being a MAP meant facing a life without the possibility of ever experiencing a fulfilling romantic life, which they grieved over. Thus participants emphasized their feelings toward minors other than mere sexual attraction during our conversations.

To illustrate the range of feelings that MAPs may have for children, those in my study who were equally attracted to both adults and children stated that they had the same feelings in all respects toward all age groups. Tyler, for example, told me: "I could look at somebody in their thirties and be attracted to them, and then I could look at somebody prepubescent or maybe somebody 12, 13, 14 and have just completely identical feelings to the attraction I had to somebody who's in their twenties or thirties." When describing their attractions, participants frequently recounted imagined scenarios involving developing a friendship with a child, holding hands, or falling in love, rather than sexual fantasies. For example, when I asked him about his attractions to minors, Lee said: "I would say there is sexual attraction as well but for me it's more of an emotional attraction. It's kind of silly but it's more of a romantic kind of feeling, more like I would like to be with them and have a relationship and hold hands, and those kinds of things."

Lee identified as an exclusive pedophile, with no attractions to adults of any sort. Because experiencing a romantic relationship was something he wanted, he had tried to make himself be attracted to adults and worked on expanding his attractions toward adults for years in therapy, but found he was unable to do so. For a while, Lee thought he might be able to have a relationship with an adult woman, but eventually he gave up on this idea. Nonetheless, he still deeply wanted to fall in love, but all of his romantic fantasies were about girls between the ages of 8 and 12. He knew that this was unrealistic: after telling me about these interests in love and romance, he remarked: "It's a very, very childish way of thinking about this." He was embarrassed by these attractions.

Along the same lines, Aiden told me: "I have more of a romantic attraction.... More romanticized, versus objectified. So, I tend to have more of a romantic notion of it. Like, wanting to be their boyfriend and have a relationship with them." Aiden developed feelings for boys that he described similarly to a crush, making him feel shy around them. Like Lee and Neil, Aiden recognized that he was not going to have the kind of relationship he wanted. He said that being minor-attracted was "tough to deal with" because "any time I see like adult relationships or anything like that, it's a reminder of what I can't have." He added: "Even if I see like two adults like holding hands in the streets? It just reminds me that I can't ever have that."

To convey that their attractions to minors went beyond sexual interest, some of the participants used the terms "boy-lover" (BL) and "girl-lover" (GL) for themselves. Like the term "MAP," the respondents explained that these two labels carried less stigma than the word "pedophile." However, while "MAP" was generally considered a neutral label, some of my participants were opposed to the use of BL and GL. Noah argued that terms such as "boy-lover" and "girl-lover" were euphemistic terms meant to romanticize sexual activity between adults and minors and to "downplay the sexual aspect of their desires." Notably, however, individuals who referred to themselves as "boy-lovers" or "girl-lovers" within my study did not express distinct beliefs with regard to the morality of sexual relations between adults and children when compared with those who employed different labels.

Queer Identity Labels

In addition to labels signifying age and type of attraction, study participants also used labels to indicate the gender(s) they were attracted to. While such labels as "boy-lover" and "girl-lover" do fall into this category, many participants (especially those attracted to the same gender as themselves) used labels that are commonly associated with queer communities, such as gay, lesbian, bisexual, queer, or homosexual. My participants commonly combined these terms with terms designating their AoA (e.g., "homosexual pedophile" or "bisexual hebephile"), although some preferred to use these queer-spectrum terms without labeling themselves by their AoA at all.

The decisions of MAPs about whether or not to use queer-spectrum labels for themselves are based around a variety of factors. Generally, participants who used these labels were attracted to individuals of the same gender or multiple genders. Brooke did not often use labels to convey her AoA but did use the term "lesbian" for herself. "I have considered myself a lesbian for quite some time," she told me. "I am attracted to girls and women [of all ages], and being a woman who's attracted to women, there's a pretty simple word for that. So, 'lesbian' works." Brooke considered being attracted to minors as one of multiple facets of her sexual orientation. She also felt ties to the larger lesbian community, which further informed her decision to use this term for herself.

Many of those who used queer-spectrum labels for themselves felt that they belonged with queer communities in part because they believed their attractions to minors were, in and of themselves, tantamount to a sexual orientation. Gene told me:

> There's a lot of debate about whether pedophilia is a sexual [orientation]....[Sigh] I think that...I think that for me, I really have gotten to the point, quite a long time ago, where I almost see that as a moot point. A lot of people really get hung up on the orientation thing. And I go, okay, well, we have all these criteria for what is an orientation... the fact of the matter is, this is what I'm attracted to. You can't change— even the professionals who have been working with this for a long time, [they] can't cure it; you can't change it. Once somebody is like that, they're gonna always be like that. It's what I'm attracted to. I didn't choose it. I can't change it. I'll always be this way. So...for all intents and purposes, it's an orientation. I'm oriented towards kids. I'm not oriented any other way and never will be....I'm going to die that way.

Gene, like many other MAPs, had actively attempted to change his attractions toward minors and found he was unable to do so. For him, attraction to minors was a sexual orientation because of its immutability and the fact that he did not choose it—two narratives common to other queer identities.

In a text-based interview, Bryan added that he felt he was "born with an orientation (and I do consider it a sexual orientation, whether by nature or nurture), that I didn't ask for, and no one in their right mind would want to have in this society and culture. [Being attracted to minors] means that, based on my own personal assessment, I will never have this specific fulfillment of my primary orientation (As I was told by one therapist, 'You can't have what you want, so you'd better get used to it')." Bryan had accepted that his orientation was toward minors. However, contrary to the argument that labeling attractions to minors an orientation would mean suggesting that sexual contact between adults and minors is morally permissible, Bryan accepted that his sexual orientation did not mean that acting on his attractions would be in any way acceptable. Notably, none of my participants who described their attractions as an orientation used this to suggest that sexual relationships between adults and children should be accepted.

While many participants used labels commonly employed by queer communities to communicate something about their attractions to minors, others used queer-spectrum labels to obscure the fact that they were attracted to minors. As Neil told me, "I like that 'queer' is so inclusive and thereby also 'unclear,' which makes it more difficult for people to attack someone who identifies as queer." Neil liked to use the term "queer" for himself because its meaning was flexible enough that it allowed him to openly and accurately identify as such, without creating suspicion that he was attracted to minors.

The belief among some participants that their attractions toward minors constituted a sexual orientation is no doubt a controversial one. Indeed, as noted in the introduction, both queer communities and the scholarly literature on the subject diverge regarding whether MAPs can be considered queer and whether minor attraction can be considered a sexual orientation. My study participants diverged in this debate as well. While many referred to their attractions to minors as a sexual orientation, others felt it could not be considered as such. Harper, who identified as a lesbian and dated adult women, told me that she believed it was "dangerous" to refer to her attractions toward young girls as a sexual orientation. Even Neil, who at the time of our interview described himself as both gay and queer, initially felt badly about doing so. He explained that when he first began identifying as gay: "I started to feel guilty because I felt if I can't come out as gay, then that's not honest, but if I *am* honest and [I say] that I'm a MAP *and* gay, then this will give gay people a bad [reputation]...because gay people are often seen as, like, 'evil pedophiles.'" Neil recognized the historical struggles of queer communities in fighting perceptions that they were child molesters. In a twist of irony, Neil felt guilty for calling himself gay because of these struggles, although he himself is part of a current effort to fight perceptions of MAPs as inherently dangerous to children.

While Neil decided to use the terms "gay" and "queer" for himself despite awareness of the efforts of queer communities to disassociate themselves from MAPs, many MAPs who are attracted to their own gender reject these labels for themselves. As Mitchell detailed:

MITCHELL: To use clinical terminology, I would call myself a hebephile: homosexual hebephile, I guess. And I also call myself a boy-lover.

AW: So you use the term "homosexual"?

MITCHELL: Mm hmm. Just because I'm attracted to the same gender. I'm not attracted to females at all.

AW: Gotcha. Do you ever use the term "gay" for yourself?

MITCHELL: Well, I, I, every once in a while, I think, should I call myself gay? But I haven't, mainly because I think they, my impression is, certainly everything I've read, the gay community would reject me. So I guess I don't want to be part of a community that would reject me.

It surprised me that Mitchell used the term "homosexual" for himself. As a queer person in my 30s, the word "homosexual" brings to my mind, and the minds of many of my peers, an age in which being gay was thought of as a mental illness: the term "homosexual" is inextricably linked to the American Psychiatric Association's *Diagnostic and Statistical Manual.* The DSM used this term to describe a "sociopathic personality disturbance" in its first edition in 1953 and continued to list it as a mental disorder until 1973.

Mitchell had been involved in a gay Christian group in the 1990s and had felt supported by them as a gay man. However, once he came out to them as minor-attracted, they excluded him from the group. Mitchell and others felt that queer communities would reject them because of a societal trend toward accepting queer individuals: if the LGBTQ community were welcoming toward MAPs, they would risk losing that acceptance.[7] Some participants who were attracted to the same gender rejected queer-spectrum labels for other reasons. For example, some male participants who were attracted to boys sometimes felt that they should not be regarded as gay because they were not attracted to traits typically defined as "masculine," which they felt was a requirement of gay identity. Others were resistant to refer to themselves as gay because they felt their experiences were too disparate from those generally encountered by gay men.[8]

Overall, labels used by participants to describe their sexual identities were the result of careful consideration. The language used to describe these identities was developed by weighing ages and genders of attraction, level and type of attraction, and exclusivity or nonexclusivity. This was all against a backdrop of stigma that colored their knowledge and beliefs about themselves and other MAPs. The next section describes the process experienced by participants in developing these identities.

THE IDENTITY FORMATION PROCESS AMONG MAPS

Hugo, whose background I described at the beginning of this chapter, had experiences that hinted at his attractions from a young age, but he did not fully realize he was minor-attracted until he was 17. The experience of feeling different in some way, but not connecting it to a sexual identity until much later, is nearly universal among MAPs. This experience of making these connections was rarely described as an epiphany; it generally unfolded as a gradual process. In Erik's words, "there wasn't a lightbulb moment. It didn't just happen overnight. It was just sort of—I just became aware." The process of forming an identity as a MAP looked different for each participant, but there were commonalities among their experiences. These patterns are significant because the ways in which MAPs form their identities have consequences for their self-esteem, mental health, and available support systems. Such consequences in turn can affect how MAPs cope with their attractions as well as how they strategize not to commit offenses.

For the participants in my study, the process of realizing that they were attracted to minors, either primarily or exclusively, was generally described as both confusing and disturbing. This mirrors the literature on identity formation among lesbian, gay, and bisexual individuals. Social stigma about being minor-attracted, similarly to social stigma about being attracted to individuals of the same gender, can shape these sexual minority identities as unthinkable—as an identity held by other, lesser, or perhaps morally corrupt individuals—not one that people could imagine as a possibility for themselves. Because these identities are often inconceivable as applying to oneself, the process of connecting one's attractions to a sexual identity becomes a process that occurs over time.

Scholars have developed models of the identity formation process among sexual minorities, specifically gay and lesbian individuals, since the 1970s.[9] These models conceptualize multiple stages in the formation of gay and lesbian identities. Early models were constructed taking into consideration a historical environment of rampant stigma and showing a pattern of growth from early experiences of feeling different, to identity confusion, to identity assumption, to commitment to the identity. Because these early models focused on the effects of stigma on sexual minority identity development, their structures are perhaps more relevant today to MAPs than to sexual minorities who are afforded more general cultural acceptance in the global north.[10] I structure the rest of this chapter largely around the experiences of MAPs in relation to stages of identity formation identified in sociologist Richard Troiden's[11] work because my participants' experiences reflect, in a similar order, the stages identified in his model. Although many comparable stages emerged in my data, my participants encountered shared experiences that were unlike those faced by lesbians and gay men. These are explored as well.

Importantly, just as Troiden noted that not all gay men and lesbians experience the stages of identify formation as he conceptualized them, not all MAPs go through those outlined in this model either. Rather, these stages represent general patterns found from data with gay men and lesbians that I saw being mirrored in my data with MAPs. In addition, it's important to note that not all MAPs progress through each of the following stages. Many of my participants were still struggling with their identities at the time of our interviews. Given the stigma and loneliness felt by MAPs in today's society, this is hardly surprising.

Sensitization

In Troiden's model the first stage of identity development is "sensitization." In this stage an individual has "perceptions of being different from same-sex peers" but does not connect these perceptions to their sexuality. These feelings of being different in the early lives of gay men and lesbians are often based around gender-nonconforming behaviors; however, Troiden wrote that the specific experiences encountered were less important than the meanings attached to them—for example, after forming identities as sexual minorities, queer individuals often reinterpret these early experiences to be signs of gay/lesbian identity.

Although participants in my study did not generally talk to me about early experiences with gender nonconformity, they nonetheless frequently discussed with me experiences that they pointed to as precursors to their sexual identities. These experiences, rather than being gender-related, were age-related—that is, participants often described feeling "stuck" at a certain age, or like their development was in some way "stunted." These feelings often centered around two types of occurrences: experiencing some form of adverse event in childhood or adolescence, or wanting to go back to their childhood or adolescent years in some way. Multiple participants spoke about incidents that they experienced as traumatic in their childhoods, connecting these events to their identity as a MAP. Such incidents were generally brought up when I asked participants about how they realized that they were attracted to minors.

However, these incidents rarely took the forms focused on in research about childhood experiences and pedophilia, such as experiencing childhood sexual trauma.[12] In fact, the crises participants described could often be considered commonplace. Nonetheless, these experiences were clearly significant to them. For instance, Aiden detailed childhood events that felt scarring to him when I asked how he realized he was attracted to minors. He explained:

> I had an issue happen when I was around 12 years old, where I had a girlfriend and then she broke up with me in a kind of a traumatic manner. Like in front of a lot of her friends and everything, and it was pretty traumatizing for me. And then within a few months I fell in love with my best friend, who was male, when we were both 12.…He was, you know, he was experimenting with me, but I was in love with him. And so, we were kind of sexually active for about six months to a year and then he moved away, and I never saw him again.

Embarrassment surrounding a public breakup at age 12 and separation from an early adolescent love interest are somewhat banal "traumas." Even sexual experimentation at age 12, while perhaps an out-of-the-ordinary occurrence, may be more commonplace among males who have sex with other males.[13] Nonetheless, Aiden's narrative shows that he felt profoundly affected by these early experiences. He connected them to forming his identity as a MAP, telling me that he thought these occurrences "kept me stuck at 12."

Phillip similarly connected early painful experiences with his identity as minor-attracted:

> When I was 10 years old, which is right in the heart of my attraction, I moved from Connecticut to West Virginia. That's a huge culture shock, as anybody can obviously understand between Connecticut and West Virginia. And my father died within a couple of months of me moving to West Virginia. And so I lost everything. I lost…you know, my family was, like, upper-middle class in Connecticut and in West Virginia we began to lose everything.…In West Virginia we were not upper class.

Phillip experienced these dramatic changes of location, socioeconomic status, and the death of his father as deeply traumatic. He connected this to what he called a "growth problem"—a feeling that he was unable to move beyond past childhood social development stages. Notably, he also described to me a vague memory of experiencing potential sexual abuse as a child. He said:

> I don't have any real recollection of any kind of abuse, but at the same time, I do have some kind of idea in my head, not just in my head, but like about something that may have happened. And I'm not so sure that it didn't happen. I brought it up to [my sister] and she kinda said she had the same idea....But I mean, but I don't know. Honestly I could lie to you right now and say, yeah, I was molested as a kid, so that's why I'm fucking crazy [and therefore attracted to minors]. But I don't know.

Surprisingly to me, Phillip connected his rapid period of transition in childhood to his attractions to minors more than he did the potential abuse he experienced.

Multiple participants had a specific name for this feeling of being "stuck" or "stunted." Erik, Aiden, Bryan, and Desmond all mentioned feeling that they had "Peter Pan syndrome" in that their interests and manner of thinking lined up more closely with children than adults. Bryan described this as "an aspect of my psychology (the hating myself as an adult, the forever wanting to go back to being a boy), that has been constant and in the forefront of my mind as long as I can remember. It has shaped my perception of reality, no matter how much, on a logical level, I realize that this is maladaptive. I hope that makes sense. I suppose a psychologist would call it 'psychosexually stunted.'" Bryan told me that his mother was highly complimentary of him when he was a young boy, but once he hit an awkward stage of adolescence, she stopped complimenting him, which was made him feel grotesque. He believed that this "stunted" his development and gave him "a psychological desire to want to be a boy again."

"Peter Pan syndrome" manifested in different ways, depending on the participant. It was common for my participants to tell me about interests in childhood toys, games, or activities, or for them to talk to me about an ongoing fantasy in which they went back to childhood. Desmond said that he wished he could be a child again, because "it's so much easier. No responsibilities, no worrying about what other people think of you or whether or not you're doing something right. I'm almost 36 and I have no clue how to be an adult!" While Desmond's childhood interests were focused on the difficulties of adulthood, Zach and Erik both talked to me about interests in childhood activities. "I honestly feel, identity-wise, on the inside, I never really grew up past [young adolescence]," Zach told me. "I still love doing the same things I've always done socially. I love things like just hanging at the mall, going to amusement parks, concerts, doing all the creative stuff I was doing back then." Similarly, Erik said, "I feel like a child myself. I kind of almost feel like I never grew up once I got to about 12. You know, I still have a big box of Lego. I still play with all my old video games." Although Zach and Erik did not feel that their interest in childhood activities was a *cause* of their sexuality per se, they at least thought it was relevant and perhaps that it was a latent indicator.

Of course, many adults enjoy going to amusement parks, malls, and playing with video games and Legos. Many adults have also had adverse, or even traumatic, experiences in childhood. Clearly, not all of these adults are MAPs. Similarly to Troiden's writing about the importance of sensitization among gay individuals, the importance of my participants sharing these experiences with me was not because of some intrinsic relevance between enjoying relics of childhood and being attracted to minors but because of the connections that these participants made between the two.

Identity Confusion

Troiden characterized the "identity confusion" stage of gay and lesbian identity formation as the stage in which individuals realize that their feelings or behaviors are different from those of their peers. Confronted with this realization, Troiden said that gay men and lesbians become confused. During this stage, gay individuals may begin to realize that their feelings or behaviors can be categorized as "homosexual," although they do not at this point assume that label for themselves, as gay and lesbian identities are dissonant with prior self-images. Compounding this confusion is the stigma attached to same-sex attractions, which was ubiquitous at the time of Troiden's writings (and clearly still pervasive to this day).

According to Troiden, gay men and lesbians could deal with their identity confusion in one of four ways: by *denying* that their feelings and behaviors are consistent with homosexuality, by enlisting professional services to eradicate (or *repair*) their "homosexual" feelings, by attempting to *avoid* their "homosexual" feelings themselves, or by *accepting* an identity of gay or lesbian (thus moving into the next stage of identity formation). In my conversations with MAPs about how they realized they were minor-attracted, nearly all of them recounted a pattern of experiences similar to those Troiden identified as identity confusion. This pattern typically emerged during adolescence (although, as with other sexual minorities, there was some variation in the age when this occurred).

Denial. My participants commonly recalled noticing in their teen years that their peers were attracted to older individuals, while they were attracted to same-age peers or younger. As they aged, the age of individuals to whom they were attracted remained the same (or in some cases, fell). As Erik told me:

> I went to an all-boys school, and there was a teacher who I guess was mid-thirties, and she was, I guess what you'd stereotypically call attractive. And being in a group of all-boys-school sort of teenagers, she was obviously mentioned, and I never really saw the appeal. I just didn't get why she was interesting to them. She was just another teacher to me. And that was probably the first sort of clue that I had that I thought maybe I'm not interested [in adult women]. I did find myself looking at the year seven [sixth grade] boys coming in and I would understand that they were attractive. But by [the time they were] about 14, 15, I was starting to notice that as they got older I wasn't interested in them anymore. And the new boys coming in, I was interested in some of them. And I thought, "Well, maybe I'm just gay." Well, that's not an issue; my parents have always been very open-minded, luckily for me. 'Cause I know that others have not had that; been so fortunate. But it was when I started to grow up, and realizing that the boys, as they got older, I was losing interest in [them]. And I wasn't really looking beyond that first year of 11, 12-year-olds. So, that's really, probably when I first had an inkling, but I never really pieced it together until I was well out of school.

For Erik, although he was aware that he was attracted to different individuals when compared with his friends, this preference did not strike him as being particularly odd until later in life. In other words, Erik was in denial.

This was a common experience among my participants: recognizing some kind of difference but not connecting that difference to being minor-attracted. Avery told me:

> It's hard to say when I realized exactly. I remember in high school that feeling that many of the middle school girls were much cuter than the girls in my class but I didn't think it was strange at the time. I guess the first time I realized that my sexuality was really odd was when I was about to graduate high school. I volunteered at an elementary school for my senior project. I found a bunch of girls there really attractive.... It was strange because I figured I ought to be too old by then. I was 18

so I was technically an adult....I don't think I was immediately anxious. I knew it was weird, but I've always been a little weird, so I didn't let it bother me.

Avery's attractions to minors did not make him feel immediately different. He described his attractions as "odd"—that is, he knew that his attractions to young girls were outside the norm, different from attractions that his peers had experienced. Nonetheless, he was able to shrug them off, to deny to himself that his feelings were consistent with a sexual attraction.

Troiden wrote that gay men and lesbians were able to deny that their feelings were "homosexual" for a variety of reasons, including a lack of awareness that homosexuality existed and/or what it meant, and because societal stigma induces secrecy and shame regarding homosexuality and contributes to a lack of accurate information about the subject. Troiden published this in 1989, when queer individuals were more likely to be thought of as "disease-spreaders" and "criminals"[14] than the positive representations that are much more widely available today in the global north.

Similarly to gay and lesbian individuals in the 1980s, MAPs today have a distinct lack of role models in the media. During their youth my participants rarely encountered depictions of minor-attracted individuals in the media, with the notable exception of sex offenders. My participants expressed that they were unaware that adults could primarily be attracted to children and therefore did not consider it a possibility for themselves. Neil, who was about 16 when he began to recognize that his attractions to boys might mean he was a MAP, told me: "I first thought that I [was] the only person in the world [who was] attracted to boys. I thought there was no one else because I just had never heard of it. I thought, like, pedophiles are only attracted to girls, and also that they are very old and ugly and stuff like that." Because of a lack of societal information about MAPs, Neil, like others in this study, did not think he could be one himself. Upon recognizing that there were other individuals attracted to minors and that their own attractions put them in a similar category, my participants were often terrified, associating their attractions with those of child molesters.

Fear of being a "monster" or turning into a child molester were common anxieties for participants at the time that they first realized that they were primarily or exclusively attracted to children. Hugo asked himself if he was a monster when he began to question his attractions. A Finnish participant, Cody, remembered divulging that he was a pedophile for the first time in an online forum and instantly feeling ashamed, believing that this made him similar to an infamous Finnish sex offender known as "Jammu-setä." "I took on everything, the burdens that come with the label. Everyone thinks you're a monster," Cody recounted. "Wait, is that how I'm supposed to be? Am I that already? Should I become that? I don't want to become that." Cody was so disturbed by his attractions that he worried they meant he was destined to become a sex offender.

The concept of being a "monster" was so prevalent that this exact word came up in my interviews with 17 different participants. Five participants reported feeling, when they realized their attractions, that they were (or would become) a "monster," while 14 participants discussed the societal perception that they were monsters. Many more disclosed anxieties upon realizing their attractions, believing that this meant in some way that they were destined to commit offenses. Societal narratives about individuals with attractions to minors who live their lives without committing sexual offenses against children are absent, raising the question of whether it is possible to reconcile attractions to minors and the development of a prosocial identity. Even among individuals who, upon realizing their attractions, were certain that they would not commit an offense against a child, remarked that they had been unaware of individuals with primary attractions to children who had not offended. "The only people I'd ever been aware of who felt the way I felt were in news articles, when they were in sort of jail," Erik noted. "So, and that made me kind of feel—I never really thought that I am going to be like them because I still realize that I don't have to. But it did get me down." Erik recognized that he was not destined to commit an offense against a child, but he still felt demoralized by the apparent association between sex offenders and MAPs.

A common recollection among participants who did not believe they would commit an offense against a child when realizing that they were minor-attracted was the idea that they were the only moral person with these attractions. Oliver conveyed this idea:

> I had the mentality perhaps that I was the only kind and caring one, and the other people out there were hurting and abusing kids. Which, in thinking back on it now, it doesn't really make much sense to me. I mean, statistically speaking, I wouldn't be the only nice one with these attractions. To me, it seems obvious now, but of course there would be other people born this way, who are not sociopaths or abusing children, but that's the mentality I had of it in my adolescence: that I was the only nice one and I was unique in that regard. But I didn't experience it as an urge or I didn't feel I was any danger to kids.

Oliver, much like Hugo, felt that he was not destined to commit a sexual offense against a child, despite common societal narratives describing MAPs as offenders. However, these narratives still had an effect on Oliver and Hugo, because the idea that there could be other individuals who shared their attractions and were committed to non-offending did not occur to them. Just as Troiden wrote in the 1980s that the stigma toward being gay led to a lack of accurate, accessible information for gay people to understand, so did MAPs in my study show that stigma led to inaccurate information about their ability to make a decision not to commit an offense against a child. Given that MAPs have a limited ability to access information about attractions to minors net of sexual offending, it is hardly surprising that MAPs would be in denial about their sexuality.

Avoidance. Another strategy for MAPs to deal with the stigma associated with their attractions is to engage in avoidance. Troiden described avoidant people as those who viewed their sexuality as unacceptable. Although Troiden named multiple strategies that gay and lesbian individuals engaged in to avoid identifying with these unacceptable feelings, the one most applicable to my participants was redefining their attractions as something temporary or situational. My participants often believed their attractions to be situational, and accordingly, they talked about their attempts to identify the situation that caused them. Some who spoke about feeling "stuck" in adolescence or childhood felt that was the cause of their attractions. Philip, who had told me that his father died early in his life, said: "I think, you know, part of me thinks that maybe that's part of the reason.... Because that's right at the age, right there. [Sigh] I mean, that's right at the age I'm interested in, so I don't know." Isaac revealed to me that his father and grandfather had both committed sexual offenses against children, and he presumed that he had learned from them that attraction to children was "normal." My participants brought up the work of sexologist James Cantor and his colleagues, mentioning whether or not they possessed characteristics that MAPs have been found more likely to exhibit (e.g., left-handedness, below-average IQ, or childhood sexual trauma)[15] than teleiophiles (individuals attracted to adults).[16]

One common theory debated among participants related to whether attractions to minors were caused by mental illness. Despite a shift in the scientific community toward a conceptualization of attractions to minors as a sexual orientation,[17] participants themselves were split between those who regarded their attractions as a sexuality or sexual orientation (as described earlier) and those who regarded them as a problem or an illness. Three participants—Strand, Tony, and Tyler—consistently referred to their attractions as their "problem" during interviews. Others lamented this viewpoint, criticizing authorities such as the American Psychiatric Association for including "pedophilic disorder" in the DSM, given that they had previously come under fire for problematizing "homosexuality" in similar ways.[18]

Repair. Among study participants who felt, at one time or another, that they had a mental illness, it was not uncommon for them to seek out professional assistance in getting rid of these attractions. Troiden referred to this behavior among gay men and lesbians as "repair." "Reparative" therapy—also known as conversion therapy or sexual orientation change efforts (SOCE)—is now thought of as ineffective for gay and lesbian individuals and has been outlawed for minor LGBT individuals in many locations across the United States. Nonetheless, it remains legal for MAPs. Multiple participants had tried various techniques to "cure" themselves of their attractions, including hypnotherapy and smelling ammonia when thinking about children, among other strategies. My participants' experiences with mental health professionals, including seeking help to reduce or remove their attractions to minors, are described in Chapter 5.

Identity Assumption

Troiden described the "identity assumption" phase as the stage of gay and lesbian identity formation in which the individual begins to self-identify as a "homosexual." During this stage the individual begins to seek out contacts with other gay and lesbian individuals and takes on the task of managing stigma. Troiden categorized the individual during this stage as not "accepting" a self-identity as gay or lesbian but as "tolerating" it. The interactions with other gay and lesbian individuals experienced during this stage would determine whether the individual would accept the label for themselves.

Seeking out contacts with other MAPs was indeed an important step for many of my participants. Victor told me that introducing himself to MAPs when he was 23 had a profound effect on his life:

> On Wikipedia I saw a group: "Virtuous Pedophiles." The name stood out since the word "virtue" is used a LOT in my church, and seeing it with the word "pedophile" made me think: "Huh, what?" So I learned about them, and after weeks of hesitation I sent them a [message] requesting to join....I armed myself of courage and one night I wrote it all on my introductory post...and cried like a little girl while doing it. At the end of the post I was begging for help. I wanted to know if a normal life was possible, if I was such a bad person as I saw myself....I

wanted all the answers right away and needed emotional support…
they told me to calm down and relax, that it's not the end of the world,
that they went through that alone and congratulated me for being brave
to join the conversation at my age. They all offered me helping hands.

Victor credited joining VirPed with raising his self-esteem. This helped
him tolerate his attractions to minors—he was able to see that others who
shared this identity label could be friendly, supportive, and accepting,
and most important, that they could live good lives.

A major difference between Troiden's model and my participants'
experiences is that among gay men and lesbians, this stage marks the
point at which people engage in romantic and/or sexual relationships
with one another. Among my participants that was generally not the case
(and indeed not the point, since gay people are attracted to each other and
MAPs are not). What unites my participants is not sexual interest in each
other, but sexual interest in minors who are typically below the legal
age of consent. My participants had never committed a child molestation offense and were firm that they would never do so. Thus, this stage
introduced a hardship unlike those that gay men and lesbians encounter:
for the majority of respondents, the knowledge that they were minor-
attracted meant facing a dramatically different life than the one that they
had previously expected. For those exclusively attracted to minors, this
meant a lifetime lack of romantic and sexual relationships with any individual to whom they could be attracted. Aiden told me that this feeling
of loneliness became amplified with age: "[It's hard], you know, the idea
of not having a significant other in an adult relationship. Like, having an
adult that I, you know, grow old with and can spend time with. I feel very
alone. And don't feel like I'll ever be able to have that. I know I can't ever
have what I want, so it just creates a division in me. As far as I want an
adult relationship but I'm not attracted to adults."

In addition, respondents faced constant shame regarding their attractions. Although many recognized that they would never act on their
attractions and were able to neutralize guilt as a result, others were constantly reminded of societal opinions of people like them. When Cody
first realized that he was primarily attracted to minors, he started noticing characterizations of pedophiles in the media:

> Everyone was hunting pedophiles and others were cheering. That's how
> it conveyed through the papers and TV, anyway. Every time I saw one
> of those news [stories], I wondered what [my parents would] say if I (I
> was about 15 then) would tell them that I'm attracted to kids. The dudes
> in the papers were always old dudes, 40–50 years old with beards.

Then I just kinda thought that it was hopeless. As soon as you have the label of "pedophile," you're done. You're no longer a target for empathy. You're a monster and it is your civic duty to kill yourself before you touch a kid. No matter what age, no matter where. No matter how you convey it. Done.

Negative societal images of individuals with attractions to minors are so ubiquitous that the VirPed forum has dedicated an entire section to "comment awards," which are sarcastic rankings of the most vitriolic comments aimed at MAPs online. West, a VirPed member, was able to laugh at these comments. Others avoided the comments sections in online articles and YouTube videos about MAPs, even when the article or video was not demeaning to MAPs, because the comments sections would invariably contain malicious messages. Indeed, in the years since I stopped conducting interviews, I've kept contact with some respondents on websites like Tumblr. In 2018, however, Tumblr began systematically deleting accounts that showed support toward MAPs, including my own. They did, however, allow many "anti-MAP" accounts to remain open, including those with posts tagged as "MAP Positivity," bedecked with emoji hearts, telling adolescent MAPs to "kill yourselves."

Psychologist Vivienne Cass[19] wrote that for gay men and lesbians who accepted their identities (which occurred at the end of the identity assumption stage, if the individual made supportive contacts with other gay and lesbian individuals and was able to successfully navigate encountered stigma), "you are quite sure you are a homosexual and you accept this fairly happily." It would be difficult to assert that the same is true for MAPs who have accepted their attractions as part of their sexual identity. Depression, anxiety, and suicidal thoughts were common among my participants, even among those who were not concerned about posing a threat to children, even among those who could shrug off the stigma, even among those exclusive MAPs who accepted that they would lead lives without experiencing sexual or romantic satisfaction. Many of my participants continued to experience some or all of these mental health issues at the time of interviews.

Commitment

Troiden described the commitment stage as the stage in which the individual becomes comfortable identifying as a gay or lesbian individual and adopts "homosexuality" as a lifestyle. Key facets of this stage are "self-acceptance" and "comfort with the homosexual identity and role."

This stage is the hardest to apply to MAPs, although there were some participants in my study who certainly accepted their sexuality more than others.

Despite the negative feelings with which most participants wrestled regarding their attractions to minors, some succeeded in managing their anxiety regarding their attractions. Strategies used by respondents to cope with these negative feelings are explored in Chapter 3. These individuals recognized that they were not going to be a threat to children and have succeeded in separating in their mind their feelings from potentially harmful actions in which they have committed not to engage. For instance, Brooke, Felix, Klaus, Lucas, and Zach all described being relatively unfazed by the stigma associated with their attractions, understanding themselves well enough to know that their attractions would not necessarily determine their behaviors. To this point, Felix explained: "Yes, I'm attracted to children. So what? I'm not going to hurt anyone...I wouldn't take advantage of anyone. I wouldn't manipulate or coerce. No, I'm not a rapist. I like trying to be a good, ethical person."

Part of the commitment phase as Troiden described it involved synthesizing one's sexual identity with other parts of the individual's identity. A few of my participants exemplified this through discussions about their identity labels. Brooke, for instance, did not feel that her identity as a MAP was any more important than any other facet of her identity. "I would say that 'minor-attracted' is an accurate description [of myself]," she told me, "although I don't generally claim it as an identity label, if that makes any sense as a distinction." She further argued that "it's not a primary identity, I guess. It's something that describes me, just as I am a prescription lens wearer." Avery provided a similar account:

AW: So what does identifying as a pedophile mean for you?

AVERY: Well, I just feel like it's not really me "identifying" as one. I look at the facts of the situation and feel that the term "pedophile" most reasonably applies to me.

AW: Ooh. Is there a label you identify with more?

AVERY: Not in regards to my sexuality. But I guess if there was a label I would most identify with it would be me being a mathematician.

Neither Avery nor Brooke felt particularly stressed about their attractions toward minors. This could in part be explained by the fact that neither of them was exclusively attracted to minors, and they had both had romantic and sexual relationships with adults. For MAPs who did not have to worry about the loneliness aspect of being attracted to minors, and especially for those who could pass as teleiophiles, it stands to reason that they would be more comfortable with their attractions than others.

A final common task in this stage, according to Troiden, was coming out to others who are not sexual minorities. More of my participants than I expected had come out to at least someone in their lives. I explore this more in the next chapter.

UNMAKING "MONSTERS"

The narratives provided by the study participants reveal a great deal of variety in the experiences of MAPs in forming identities and coming out. Although these experiences were diverse, almost all of them were influenced by stigma in some way. Even the labels that participants used to refer to themselves reflected societal reactions about attractions to minors. Many respondents were uncomfortable with the term "pedophile," despite its potential accuracy to describe their attractions, because of a collective misunderstanding about the meaning of the term. Most individuals understood that the term referred to attractions rather than actions, but they were often hesitant to align themselves with the term out of concern that others would regard them as child molesters.

As I first engaged in the data analysis for this chapter, I was surprised to find that their processes of coming out to themselves and to others frequently mapped onto the identity formation processes of gay and lesbian individuals as identified by Troiden and Cass before him. As a queer and trans person myself, I've been struck by the stigma that was attached to the LGBT populations who came before me. The work done by activists in these communities to address this stigma has resulted in me being able to feel a positive sense of self today. I often ask myself who I would be if I had been subjected to that kind of stigma. While there are very obvious differences between gay and lesbian populations in the late twentieth century and the MAP community now, the forms of stigma they have been subjected to are glaringly similar. Examining and describing the parallels between the identity formation process among lesbian and gay individuals in the United States when Troiden and Cass engaged in their own research, and MAPs today, was unavoidable to me.

For most of my participants, the process of coming to terms with their attractions was fraught with anxiety. The vast majority of respondents had never, before realizing that they were minor-attracted themselves, considered the possibility that individuals with attractions to children may be distinct from child molesters. As a result, in realizing their attractions, these participants often echoed societal concern and worried that they may become sex offenders themselves. It is not surprising, then, to note that participants came out to very few others, if any. Despite the fact that a majority of respondents received supportive or neutral reactions from those to whom they came out, the risk of rejection that they faced was real and ongoing, and it had serious implications for their lives. Chapter 2 explores participants' experiences with staying closeted from others and coming out in more detail.

2. "Leading a Double Life"

Staying Closeted and Coming Out as a MAP

For years after becoming aware that he was exclusively attracted to preteen girls, Jeremy hid this truth about himself from all others. He had spent the majority of his life denying that he was a pedophile, as he now identifies, by "blocking it out"—refusing to think about it, even to himself. When he finally recognized that he was attracted to children, rather than adults, he was overcome with feelings of guilt and shame. Seeking a reprieve from his pain, Jeremy decided to pursue counseling. "I guess when I first went," he said, "I wanted to somehow believe that it could somehow be cured or that [I] could somehow move on from this in a way that it wouldn't be an aspect of my life at all." In addition to hoping he could be cured of his attractions to minors, Jeremy said that he "wanted to get rid of the guilt, I wanted to talk to someone and just have it off my chest."

Jeremy had been in a graduate-level teaching program when he decided that he wanted help, so he sought help from a counselor at his university. Unfortunately, the counselor was disturbed by Jeremy's disclosure of his attractions. As Jeremy put it, his counselor "reacted quite badly to it," especially given that Jeremy had plans to become a teacher. The counselor gave Jeremy an ultimatum: leave the program or "otherwise they would...tell the teacher's college that I was attracted to kids." Although Jeremy had never felt that he was "even remotely close to being a danger [to children] in any way," he understood why his counselor believed he was unfit to become a teacher and complied with his counselor's insistence that he leave the program. Jeremy's counselor left a door open for him to continue on his path to become a teacher, however, saying that if Jeremy could find a new therapist who could cure him of his attractions to minors and vouch that he had been cured, he would be allowed to return and learn to teach.

On the advice of his school counselor, Jeremy sought out a new therapist. This therapist worked with sex offenders and approached Jeremy's treatment as if he were, as Jeremy put it, a "ticking time bomb." He used techniques common to conversion therapy with Jeremy, encouraging him to write down his fantasies about children and then to use ammonia inhalants (otherwise known as smelling salts) to "try and give [his] body a shock"—that is, to train his body to associate his fantasies with discomfort. Jeremy struggled with this invasive therapy. He also had to contend with a new task of lying to friends and family about why he had quit his teaching program. Although Jeremy had pushed himself to disclose his attractions to multiple counselors, he still felt shamed by his attractions to minors and could not confess to his family and friends that he was a pedophile. Around this time he reached a breaking point: he developed a plan to end his life.

Jeremy was close with his parents and wanted to minimize the pain they would feel upon his death. "I had sort of planned it all out," he explained. "And obviously I didn't want to leave my parents in the dark. I feel like the worst thing you can do if you kill yourself is leave everyone wondering why or what happened." Although he did not want to tell them about his attractions to minors, Jeremy felt obligated to let them in on his plan, so he sat them down. As he recalled:

> I can't remember whether I mentioned I was suicidal first or just mentioned that I was attracted to kids first. But sort of both came up eventually. I said, this is what's been going on in my life, I want you to know I'm attracted to kids, and I'm planning to kill myself in a few months' time. That was pretty much the short of it. There wasn't too much more. My parents, of course, reacted pretty badly to the suicidal part. Yeah, so for them that for them was a lot worse than me being attracted to kids. And they're quite strongly religious, so…we just talked about praying about it and trusting God and all that…I think it was what I needed. And I'm still here, so obviously it worked.

Jeremy's parents did not focus heavily on his attractions to minors, a reaction that he attributed to their religion, but it was a relief to him that he was able to acknowledge them out loud to important people in his life. His parents encouraged him to stop going to therapy, which they felt was doing him more harm than good.

Jeremy's conversation with his parents was a turning point in his mental health. "I feel that…how they reacted was pretty good," he told me. "Especially for them and knowing sort of how deeply religious they are, and how much they struggle with people being gay, and that kind of stuff. They basically, they said, 'We'll always love you regardless, whether you're gay or you're attracted to kids, whatever.... We're your parents. We'll still love you.'" Since coming out to his parents, the topic had rarely been revisited, but he said that they occasionally bring it up and express that he should work harder at "getting rid" of his attractions through prayer. Nonetheless, by the time of our interview, Jeremy had come to accept his attractions, and most of his large family was aware of them. He had even told his flatmate and described that conversation as "pretty chill." At the time of my interview with Jeremy, he identified as being in good mental health.

·   ·   ·

One of the first questions I asked my participants during interviews was what being attracted to children meant for them. A common response to this question was that it meant having a secret from almost everyone important in their lives. As Desmond said, his attractions to minors meant "that I have to live a double life, because I could never reveal to anyone that I'm actually attracted to kids." Tyler used that phrase in his answer to the same question—that it meant "leading a double life." As in Jeremy's case, many participants did not feel that they could tell their friends and family about their attractions to minors, for various reasons—frequently because they did not want to visit the shame they were experiencing on others. Whether it was necessary for Jeremy's counselor to compel him to leave his graduate program is debatable, but Jeremy's decision to tell his counselor and his therapist about his attractions to children indisputably had major consequences for his education, career, and mental health. Moreover, his decisions to hide his attractions from his loved ones, and later to tell his parents, had similarly monumental consequences for his life.

During interviews I was careful not to use terms and phrases such as "closeted" and "coming out," out of concern that my doing so would be coopting a term used by LGBT communities. Nonetheless, my participants used such terms themselves. I therefore use them in describing their experiences throughout this chapter. Although "coming out" is often thought of as a onetime event, it can better be described as a continuum between being closeted from oneself to being out to all others,[1] as well as a process that continues throughout one's life, as one must constantly come out to new acquaintances in order to be fully out. Therefore, it would be misleading of me to report some number of my participants who had come out and who had not. MAPs may be closeted from themselves or any number of others. There are different risks and potential benefits associated with coming out to other MAPs, loose acquaintances, counselors, friends, or family, as well as risks and benefits to staying closeted from any of these. In interviews my participants talked to me in depth about their decision-making processes for coming out to others or staying closeted as well as their experiences with doing so.

Clearly, everyone in this study had come out to themselves: all participants had been identifying as minor-attracted before contacting me. While they all shared the experience of having come out to themselves, there was great variety in who else they had chosen to come out to. Some participants had told nobody else, or nearly no one, about their attractions.

"I CAN'T SAY HOW THEY WOULD REACT": DECIDING WHETHER TO COME OUT TO OTHERS

As I discuss throughout this book, societal opinions about MAPs are rife with condemnation, vilification, and fear. Accordingly, for MAPs, coming out to each new person entails new risk. Staying closeted from others, however, does not equate to the absence of hardship—only a shift in the type of hardship experienced. During our interviews my participants talked in depth about the meanings and consequences that staying closeted and coming out had for their lives. Their meanings for coming out and staying closeted show how fraught their decision-making processes are about disclosing their attractions to others.

Difficulties of Staying Closeted

While the majority of participants were out to at least someone, few were out to most—or even many—individuals in their lives. Remaining in the closet from others was a heavy burden for those in the study. This is consistent with LGBT individuals' experiences with being closeted—research has shown a variety of poor mental and physical health effects as a result of staying closeted.[2] Robin, who is attracted primarily to teen boys and young-looking adult men, talked about the weight of being in the closet on his life. He had come out to himself twice in his life—once as gay and, later, as a MAP. Being closeted as a MAP brought on particular frustration:

It's like I'm always in the closet, like, all the time, pretty much. I'm in the closet when I walk around. I'm in the closet when I'm in my private, like, masturbation sex life. And I was in the closet for a long time as a gay person. I was attracted to men my own age, or boys my own age when I was younger, and even in my romantic adult attractions and partnerships with partners, just people my...with men my own age in my twenties and thirties. I mean I'm 35 now, but I uh...y'know, I was in the closet for a while. I came out of that only to like find that I was actually in this minor attraction closet. That's pretty...it's pretty, pretty zonking.

For Robin, having come out to others as gay was an achievement: he had spent many years hiding his identity as a gay man and feeling ashamed by it. By realizing that he was closeted about his attractions to minors, that achievement felt taken away. Although he was actually out to a few others (including his therapist, boyfriend, and some friends), he felt demoralized over the fact that he was in the closest to most people in his daily life. I asked Robin what "zonking" meant. He defined it as an onomatopoeia that he made up for emphasis that didn't really have a definition. When I looked it up, though, I found that it has a meaning as both striking (as in physically), and exhausting. "Zonking" feels particularly apt to me here, as later in our conversation, Robin talked about how tiring staying closeted was, to the point of physical debilitation.

Aiden also found being closeted demoralizing. He spoke with some envy about what he considered to be gay people's relative ease in coming out, making comparisons based on sexual orientation. He explained:

[Being minor-attracted] reaches into every facet of my life. So it, just like any human sexuality, it hits everywhere. I consider it part of my sexual identity. So I mean, it's pretty much a part of me, just as much as sexuality is part of the human condition. I almost consider it like an orientation almost, or it's, like, an age-fixed orientation. Because it feels immutable. So I mean, I consider it part of my identity....I always want to, I have the urge to express it. You know, have sexual expression. Um, and be able to keep it as part of myself. Kind of like being out, like a gay person would be. Like, "uh!" Like, out of the closet, you know? But of course, I can't do that. So it feels repressed, and it feels like a secret that I have to keep from the world and that makes me feel ostracized and alone.

Aiden assumed that if he were gay, he would be able to come out. In today's society, not all gay individuals are able to safely come out. However, as a cisgender, white man, it is indeed comparatively more likely that Aiden would have the privilege of coming out without fear of stigmatization if he were, in fact, gay.[3] Nonetheless, as a white man who is minor-attracted, Aiden did not believe that coming out was a possibility, which increased his feelings of stigmatization.

Aiden wanted to feel accepted, but keeping his attractions a secret meant, to him, that he would never feel that way. "[My friends ask] me who I'm attracted to, or is that guy hot or is that girl hot?" he told me. "Or they'll [talk about] all of their relationships and, like, you know, there's so many things where I can't tell them the truth. I have to kind of just lie or like, pretend that I'm something, like I'm normal. You know, so the urge to tell them and just be honest is just very high, but I have to resist doing that. So, it's just, it's tough. On a day to day basis of just not feeling accepted." Staying closeted meant that even parts of Aiden's life that were supposed to bring him joy, like friendships, were stressful. He felt badly about keeping his attractions a secret (which to him was tantamount to lying), but he didn't feel he had a choice.

For some MAPs, the strain being closeted puts on relationships is too much to bear. Avery was nonexclusive in his attractions to minors, but although he had some attractions to adult women, relationships with them did not feel like an option.

AVERY: I feel that I'm restricted in being my honest self around people. I fear being in a relationship with someone. I either have to lie about my feelings to them or risk screwing up my life by being honest with them.

AW: Can you tell me more about what you mean by risking screwing up your life by being honest?

AVERY: Well, if you tell someone you're not really sure how they'd react. They could see you as a threat and then spread your secret to everyone you know.

Avery believed that keeping a secret as significant as his attractions to minors from someone he was romantically involved with would be wrong. Rather than coming out to a potential romantic partner, Avery felt the better solution was to avoid being in a relationship entirely. Later in our conversation, he took a dismissive attitude toward romantic relationships in general, saying, "There's more to life than that. Many relationships are awful anyways." Nevertheless, the topic of romantic relationships was significant enough to Avery that he brought it up early on in our conversation, perhaps suggesting that being in a relationship was more important to him than he let on.

Perceived Risks in Coming Out

As Avery demonstrated, the fact that MAPs experience hardship due to staying closeted does not necessarily mean that they feel coming out to others is an appropriate alternative. This is a common finding within research about LGBT populations as well.[4] While being closeted can necessarily mean holding a secret and not feeling accepted, coming out can make an individual much more vulnerable. My participants spoke about the various risks they faced if they decided to come out.

Facing judgment. My participants' primary fear about coming out to others was that their relationships would change for the worse upon their disclosure. Depending on who they came out to—family, friends, or others—they felt at risk of facing suspicion, fear, disownment, or being outed to others.

Harper was in seminary at the time of our interview, being trained as a leader in her faith. Although her denomination was comparatively liberal, she spoke about a fear of being judged by other members of her church community. Because of the large number of cases in which powerful religious leaders have abused children, Harper's church regularly engaged in conversations about child sexual abuse and about best practices for child protection. Although she shared in others' anger regarding abusers and she appreciated these conversations, she was devastated by the inaccurate use of the term "pedophile" that regularly accompanied them. She explained:

> In going through [a training program for everyone who works with children in the church] several times, and in the church in general, I've noticed a lot of misuse of the word "pedophile." "Pedophile" does not mean "sex offender"...most child molesters are not pedophiles, and most pedophiles are not child molesters. So you hear the word "pedophile," which is a word that accurately describes me, used in place of "people who abuse children," which are possibly rightly considered to be the worst kind of person that there is. That bothers me a lot...like, hearing people talk about pedophiles as being the same thing as a child molester.

Harper assumed that because members of her church did not understand the difference between pedophiles and child molesters, if she came out to them, they would similarly mistake her for a sex offender, and she would be forced to leave the seminary. She lamented:

HARPER: There are very few people who really do seek to understand rather than to judge.

AW: So you, you think that friends and family would be judgmental?

HARPER: I certainly do think so, yes. I can't fathom anyone I know being understanding about that.

Harper was concerned that that if she came out, not only would other members of her church assume she was a threat to children, but that her parents and friends would assume the same as well.

Noah was especially concerned about how his family would react. His reasoning for being nervous about their potential reactions was similar to Harper's.

NOAH: I have thought about coming out to my immediate family for the past few years, but I can't decide if it is the right thing to do. I don't know how they will react.

AW: How do you suspect they might react?

NOAH: I honestly don't know. They are educated, liberal-minded people, but they also hate child molesters. I can't say how they would react if they found out my brain was wired like a molester.

AW: And you're just worried they'd think it was wired like that, or do you think that it is, too?

NOAH: Well, if I was to tell them I was sexually attracted to children, I can only assume they would make the pedophile–child molester connection. And yes, I do think my brain is wired like a molester's. I would have sex with a child if I thought it was okay.

Like Harper, Noah was concerned that his family would make an assumption connecting "pedophile" with "child molester." The difference here is that while Harper was indignant that general society believes people attracted to children are equivalent to child molesters, Noah seemed to find this understandable, perhaps believing it himself. Although he indicated that he would engage in a sexual act with a child if he thought it were morally permissible, the dual implications here are that he had *not* committed any sexual acts with a child and that he did *not* think it was okay. Noah seemed to be missing the reality that he was, indeed, very different from a child molester. While he was confident that he would never engage in sexual activity with a child, he described his attractions as "dangerous" and found them significantly distressing. His shame over equating these two concepts may have been a further hindrance from coming out to other people.

Xavier similarly equated sex offenders with MAPs in his explanation about why he had not come out to his family. He told me that coming out "would destroy my life....My mom was—she was raped when she was seven. So she's got a really bad taste in her mouth about people like me. If I told her, she'd pretty much disown me. And my uncle, the same thing happened to him. My dad, he, uh, nothing like that ever happened to him, but he just hates people like that. My whole family would block me out. And the public would, too." Xavier believed he would be disowned by his parents and the rest of his family if he came out. He used analogous terms in his explanation to those that Noah used, essentially saying that people who rape children are "people like [him]." It is unsurprising that Noah and Xavier would choose not to tell their families about their attractions to children, given that they so strongly associate sex offending with the attractions they experience. Unfortunately, as Harper, Noah, and Xavier all indicate, it would also be unsurprising if those they wanted to come out to made similar associations.

Fear of being thought of as dangerous was common among my participants. Avery, who told me he avoided relationships with adults so that he wouldn't have to lie to a romantic partner, mentioned that he had considered at one point telling friends or family about his attractions to minors. He decided not to because he felt "it could just do more harm than good." When I asked him what kinds of reactions he thought he might receive from his friends or family, he said, "I think they would feel that I'm mentally deranged and dangerous." He added that his assumptions regarding friends' or family's potential reactions made him anxious, but since he did not plan to tell them, he just tried not to let these thoughts bother him.

Fear of suspicion or of being considered dangerous most commonly came up in interviews with participants who had regular current or prior interactions with children. Robin chose not to come out to his family for multiple reasons, including that he was not very close with his parents, but a more relevant reason was that he didn't want to frighten his brother. He explained:

> I have a niece and nephew that are four and two years old. I have no issues with attraction to my niece or nephew. Like, all I feel for them is like love and avuncular care, but the idea that like my brother would know that I was attracted to minors, or anyone would know I was attracted to minors, and then I was like in a care-taking situation with my godson—It's like nightmarish to me...it's a relationship with my brothers and with my niece and nephew that I cherish so much, [and] I don't want to do anything to jeopardize it. And I really don't know what to do about that, frankly, except to like not to say a word to anybody.

Robin's niece and nephew were not in his age of attraction, and Robin was not worried about them being in his age of attraction eventually either because he had never felt an impulse to commit a criminal offense against a child of any age. However, Robin assumed that if his brother (their father) knew of Robin's attractions to minors in general, he may feel uncomfortable with Robin spending any time with them.

Unlike many others, Kevin had plans to come out to his family and friends. However, he was delaying this eventuality for reasons similar to Robin's.

> KEVIN: I do have intentions, I think some point in the future to come out to my, uh, immediate family and close friends. Uh, but not at the moment....I think, I know it's going to be a very stressful period....I have stress about how those relations will be after I do tell them...
>
> AW: What do you, what do you imagine that they'll be like?
>
> KEVIN: I don't imagine I'll be completely cast out, I imagine it'll be a very difficult period. I believe my parents will still love me and we'll still be a relatively close family. Um, but I suspect there'll be a lot of awkwardness around me. Particularly if there's other children around, just always knowing what are they thinking about me? Do they trust me? And my mom is particularly quite fundamentalist religious so she's opposed to any form of sexual minority, sexuality, and everything. So there will be some difficulties there.

Although some of my participants worried about being disowned, Kevin did not have that fear. But he did think that his parents might question whether he could be safe around children. While he was preparing to face the probability that his parents would see him as untrustworthy, he wasn't prepared just yet. He told me he thought he would take another year to come out to them.

Erik also worried that he would be seen as dangerous to minors if he came out to others. He volunteered with a youth group, with children at the upper range of his age of attractions. He justified this by saying that working at the youth group decreased his "desires" but knew that if others knew he was attracted to minors, they would be uncomfortable with his volunteer work. He remained closeted from his family and friends because he didn't want them to "persuade [him] to leave" the youth group. Likewise, while Gene was out to most people in his life (due to being outed online), he was still not out to specific friends of his because he had spent time with their kids when he was younger. He emphasized that he had never acted inappropriately with their children, but even though their kids were adults by now, and had children of their own, he worried that if these friends knew he was attracted to minors, they would be somehow suspicious of his former behavior.

Safety risks. A less frequent, but possibly more distressing, concern shared by some of my participants was that if they came out, they could be physically victimized. My participants had heard stories about other MAPs who had been subjected to violence and some were afraid that coming out could result in a similarly dangerous situation. Elias illustrated this fear:

> Trying to keep my feelings from showing on my face causes me physical pain. People have been killed just for being falsely accused of being attracted to children…it's a witch hunt. I feel like I'm living in a dark age, but nobody else can see it. There was a guy named Bijan Ebrahimi in Bristol, England. Falsely accused, burned to death by a mob. Others have been hounded until they killed themselves. In the last three years or so I have been reaching out to people anonymously online. I get a lot of death threats.

Elias equated his distress over being closeted from those he was close to with "physical pain," but he worried too much about potential violence to come out to people he knew in real life. Coming out online had resulted in Elias receiving death threats—a common experience among my participants (see Chapter 3 on facing stigma). In addition, he could point to a specific and disturbing case of someone being killed due to accusations of experiencing the same attractions as Elias.[5]

While Elias had concerns about potential violence committed by an indistinct other, Cody was able to identify a specific individual he was afraid to come out to. When I asked Cody if he had told any of his friends or family about his attractions to children, he said:

CODY: Nope. Not planning on doing so any time soon either. I find it likely that I might end up telling it eventually if I end up in a relationship one beautiful day. Right now I don't feel like having gentlemen with axes visit me.

AW: And that's what you think would happen if you told?

CODY: My father might be a bit dangerous if I told him. On the other side, the information might actually be dangerous to my mother. She has a slightly fragile psyche, so she might become suicidal again. The highest risk (for me personally) in telling anyone would be the sizable risk that they'll tell someone. If information spreads, I could be denied jobs on that basis. It's legal to discriminate against people such as me, I don't belong to a protected class in Finland. Something that will 100% happen if I tell someone, is that I probably wouldn't be able to get over the thought of "this person owns me now."

Cody related a number of concerns in our text-based interview, including fear of being outed and facing financial difficulties, but the first one that came to his mind was a fear of weapon-wielding villagers knocking at the door, which he connected to potential violence from his own father. He also worried about the pain this would cause his mother.

My participants had other safety concerns beyond experiencing physical violence. These concerns included being outed. Robin, who was out to his boyfriend and a few other acquaintances, described the power that individuals hold over MAPs after they are made aware of their attractions.

ROBIN: There's this fear that it'll used by against me at some point.

AW: You still have that fear?

ROBIN: Totally. And it's a fear that if I tell anyone else, even if I tell some of my other guy friends... or if I tell anyone that I date that... if we have a horrible breakup, they could go on Facebook and tell everyone that I'm attracted to little boys.

AW: Yeah.

ROBIN: They could tell some of my roommates, or my friends or... like, the character assassination scenario, while probably not real, it feels that, I think, extremely fearful when I talk about it, because it can always be used against me.

Robin was afraid that anyone he told about his attractions to minors might someday decide to out him to other people. Being outed by others is a safety concern in that it can pose a risk to one's employment, housing stability, and other economic factors. In the United States, for example, states vary on whether employers, landlords, lenders, schools, and public and private businesses may discriminate based on sexual orientation. Even when states prohibit discrimination, it is unclear whether MAPs are legally covered by these protections. Many of my participants were therefore understandably concerned about employers or people they lived with finding out about their attractions.

Causing pain to others. Although MAPs worry about the effects of coming out on their own lives, they may also choose not to disclose their attractions to others out of concern for them. For my participants, coming out to themselves caused them significant pain, and they didn't want to inflict that kind of hurt on their loved ones. When I asked Charlotte what her identity as a pedohebephile means to her, she said: "It means that I'm always going to have a part of myself that prevents me from being totally open with everyone." Later in our conversation, I asked if she had ever thought about telling her family that she's attracted to minors.

CHARLOTTE: No. No. [Laughs] No, that is never going to happen.

AW: Okay. Can you tell me why?

CHARLOTTE: Maybe one day I just find that I really want to hurt them, I'll tell them. [Laughs]

AW: So you think it would really hurt them to find out?

CHARLOTTE: Oh, yeah. I mean, they wouldn't be able to process it. They wouldn't understand.

AW: I see. Do they know other things about your sexuality?

CHARLOTTE: Yeah, they do. They know that I'm attracted to [women] and they're not, they're not okay with that.

I got the sense that Charlotte suggested more out of sarcasm that she would tell her parents about her attractions to minors if she wanted to hurt them, to emphasize how much she felt it would pain her parents to hear about these attractions, than out of any actual possibility of her coming out to them for that reason. Charlotte was comfortable with her bisexuality, but her parents did not approve of that when she came out to them. Given that they weren't comfortable with her attractions to adult women, Charlotte couldn't imagine them accepting her attractions toward minors, and indeed she thought it would "hurt" her parents to know about them.

Floyd also believed that learning the truth about his attractions would cause his loved ones pain. I asked him to explain his decision not to tell friends or family about his identity as a MAP.

FLOYD: I feel there is no benefit to disclose where it would not be understood.

AW: And you don't think your friends or family would understand?

FLOYD: Correct. And feel it would be a burden they need not grapple with, as I feel it is my own experience to manage and be responsible for. Also, I feel that such disclosure would have long term unwarranted suffering on them.

Like Charlotte, Floyd felt that it would hurt his friends and family to know about his sexuality. He thus decided that it would be for the best if he concealed this information from them.

Tyler had a complex take on the effects that his coming out would have on other people. He had come out to one other person in his life but had no plans to tell anyone else. When I asked him about this, he said:

> I've thought about it. And the more I think about [it], the more I think [I'm] not going to. I think telling people, I mean, telling your family is one thing, but as far as telling friends I think it puts a weird pressure on them. Let's say hypothetically I tell somebody and then let's say hypothetically I fuck up and [commit a sexual offense against a child]. Like, just the effect that's gonna have on that person, it's like "Oh shit, I knew and I could have done something and I didn't," shitty person. I mean, like, obviously that's never going to happen, but I feel like that's the thought process they're going to have. Um, somebody is going to go, "Oh shit, I know this thing about him. What if he, what if he acts on it and then I'm complicit." That's why I don't think I'm going to tell anybody. They're always going to have that in the back of their head.

Tyler was worried that if he came out to someone, they would have an intense burden placed on them of having to feel in some way responsible in the event that he committed a crime. Tyler was not actually worried that he might commit a sexual offense, but rather he knew that *others* would believe that that was a strong possibility, given societal misunderstandings about pedophilia. Tyler wanted to protect others from this anxiety. I wasn't sure what Tyler meant about family being different and I asked him next if he might have plans to tell his family about his attractions. He stumbled a bit over his answer, telling me uncomfortably,

TYLER: Uh, no. I, I, I don't think so. My, my mother, my mother is, uh, really enjoying retirement and I feel like it would just fuck it up. . . . She wouldn't enjoy life anymore if she knew that.

AW: Oh, okay. You think [her reaction] would be really negative?

TYLER: Yeah. She was just a really wonderful mother and we still have a great relationship. And, you know, she's, she's proud of what I'm doing, and what I'm up to career-wise. Like, I don't want to . . . She's not going to be around forever, so I don't want—hell, if she lives to be my Grandma's age she'll be around for another 30 years—but, you know, I don't want those last 30 years to be plagued with something like that.

Tyler's feelings about this were intense to hear, as if having attractions to children were so shameful it would genuinely ruin another person's life. Tyler felt that if his mother knew about his attractions to children, she would no longer have pride in him, and indeed he went so far as to say that this knowledge would take away her happiness for the rest of her existence. Instead, Tyler kept his burden mostly to himself, including the burden of his mother's potential feelings, should she find out.

Although many participants viewed coming out to others as inherently risky, it should be said that their decisions about staying closeted and coming out likely have as much to do with the shame that they felt as the risks that they faced. Noah's and Xavier's narratives revealed a belief that their attractions made them akin to child molesters; those who felt their attractions would cause pain to their loved ones felt responsibility over that potential pain. Shame and perceived risks are likely interdependent; influencing each other as much as they influence decisions regarding staying closeted and coming out. The risks of coming out faced by my participants were enough to keep the majority of them closeted from *most* others in their lives. Nonetheless, most of my participants came out to at least *some* others.

EXPERIENCES WITH COMING OUT

While I have previously indicated that it would be misleading to make some kind of definitive statement about whether someone is "out" or "not out," my participants can be compared to one another in terms of who they were out to and how they had come out. Again, everyone in my sample was out to themselves, but they varied in whom else they had come out to. Out of the 42 participants in my study, 34 had come out to at least one individual whom they had a face-to-face relationship with (as opposed to only communicating online), including family, friends, classmates, or random acquaintances. Six participants had reached out over online forums to MAPs and/or other individuals, but by the time of our interview had not come out to anyone they knew personally. Although the pattern among my participants was to either be out only to people online or to people both online and in "real life," one of my participants (Shawn) was out to one real-life other (his therapist) but to no one online. I tell more of his story in Chapter 5. Only one participant (Noah) was closeted from all others, even choosing not to come out to others online—the single exception being for our interview.[6]

Although respondents differed in terms of whom they had come out to, they also differed in how candid they were upon coming out. While some were straightforward in their approach, explaining that they identified as minor-attracted, a pedophile, or other terms that could describe their identity, others hinted at it or were satisfied with their belief that friends or family suspected their attractions to minors. For example:

BRYAN: When I was 18 and came out to my parents [as gay] many years ago, I almost told them [that I was attracted to minors]. They both asked me, point blank, "Does this mean you like boys?" And by boys, I knew that they didn't mean "men." I'm not sure how old you are, but it was, at one time, the general perception that all gays were also pedophiles. It was a product of their generation.

AW: So when your parents asked you that, you said no?

BRYAN: I said, "That's what some people think," and quickly left the room.

Although many may not consider this "coming out," Bryan did not deny his attractions toward minors, and this allowed him to feel that he wasn't lying and that his parents might be aware of his attractions, without having to take the risks that came with being more open. Gene similarly had suspicions that his parents knew about his attractions to children without him telling them specifically, which let him feel that he didn't need to say the words out loud.

Some of my participants were a bit more specific in coming out to others, but still allowed for some ambiguity. For instance, Robin told me: "I probably have like half a dozen…friends who kind of know that I'm attracted to younger guys. And there's like a sort of like jokiness about that, but it's not like an actual dialogue. We don't have like a heartfelt confessional space about that." Robin told me that he was attracted to "twinks" (younger-looking, effeminate, adult gay men), which is normalized within gay culture. Robin was able to be upfront about his attractions to "younger guys" with his friends without being specific about his preferential attractions toward minor males. Similarly, Bryan told me about coming out to a friend who "didn't seem to take [him] seriously." I asked if Bryan's friend thought he was joking, and he responded, "perhaps he did, yes. Or perhaps he simply thought what I really meant was young, legal men. I'm not really sure." Bryan and Robin were somewhat ambiguous in coming out to these friends, which allowed them to feel seen without exposing them to the risk of feeling judged.

Like Bryan and Robin, Phillip came out ambiguously—in his case, to his sister. He had tried to kill himself in response to his attractions to a 13-year-old girl in his neighborhood. He explained his suicide attempt to his sister and brought up his attractions, telling her that "there was a girl I was really interested in and, you know, she wasn't interested in me. And, you know, it wouldn't have, I mean, it's impossible anyway. And, I mean, I just don't want to live anymore." He explained to me: "I don't know that my sister, first of all, even knows the extent of my feelings. I don't think she does know. I just told her that.... But I did tell her so my sister is at least aware that I was interested in someone who was younger." Phillip felt he had come out to his sister in a way but had still obscured many of the details about his interest in the girl to her, and she didn't know that he was attracted to younger girls in general. After recounting this story, Phillip started crying. "I'm being extremely honest with you and I hope you understand that," he told me. "This is something.... It's just not something easy for me to do. I'm being honest with you and I haven't with anyone before." Even though he felt he had come out to his sister, he still had not felt that he had been fully honest with her.

Although the degree to which my participants were open about their attractions to minors varied, many came out to others in no uncertain terms. This introduced the risks participants identified earlier in the chapter but also opened the door for accessing support. Below I explore the outcomes my participants experienced based on coming out to others.

Consequences for Coming Out

The participants of this study were frequently interested in coming out, at least in part, because they were looking for acceptance and support. However, many remained closeted from those closest to them because of fears of being rejected or judged, causing pain to others, or due to safety concerns. I now explore the consequences coming out had on my participants' lives. In this section I specifically focus on participants' experiences with coming out to friends and family—their experiences with coming out to other MAPs are explored in Chapter 3, and their experiences with coming out to therapists are explored in Chapter 5.

Accessing support. Despite the fears MAPs have about coming out, their lived experiences show that there can be positive consequences of telling others about their attractions. My participants' narratives reveal multiple ways of being supported by friends and family upon coming out. This could be in simple ways, such as affirming that they were still loved and trusted, to the more complex, such as showing a change in viewpoint about MAPs or helping them in moments of desperation. As shown in

Chapter 1, upon realizing they were minor-attracted, my participants often believed they were somehow monstrous, or morally corrupt, simply because of their attractions to children. Some of the stories of support that meant the most to my participants were ones that simply involved their loved ones refuting those fears. Hugo told me about coming out to his father, who was a member of the Church of Jesus Christ of Latter-day Saints:

> I was just like, "Hey dad" and he was like, "How are you?" and I'm like, "I'm good. I have a lot of anxiety." He's like, "Why?" I'm like, "Well, please sit down for a bit."...So he sat down and I was like, "Well I'm kind of messed up. I'm not on drugs or anything like that, and you know that's not where I am, but I just feel like I'm attracted to little boys." And I just told him that and he was like, "Oh okay. Well what's your age of attraction, is it before puberty?" And I'm like, "yeah."...We just talked a little bit and I never felt any judgment, I never felt, like, anything like that. I just felt love, basically. And like he just told me that, you know, it's okay. I told him I felt like a bad person inside and he goes, well you know you don't act on it or anything like that. And that makes you a good person because honestly it makes you honorable, you know, because you don't act upon it. And like, I don't know, it went really well and like, it was like it happened and then we like didn't talk about it for the rest of the day, kind of went on about our day, but I know I could always come to him about it if I'm having an issue.

Hugo's dad's words meant a lot to him, because he not only affirmed that he still loved Hugo, but he also let Hugo know that he still thought he was a good person due to his commitment not to let his attractions to minors dictate how he would act.

Gene had a similar experience with a family member. He came out to his aunt when he was still in high school, at a time when he was "emotionally vulnerable and...just coming apart." He was crying upstairs in his room, his family downstairs. His aunt came up and put her arm around him.

> She said, "What's going on? Whatever it is, tell me." I was in an emotionally vulnerable state and I just, it just came out. You know? I had to say [it]. Maybe I just didn't give a shit anymore, you know, I was just like, "I'm gonna, I'm gonna tell them. And I don't care if they reject me, then they reject me, I'm just gonna tell 'em."...You know, somebody that you like and somebody who's holding you and telling you it's okay and you're emotionally vulnerable. Even if you didn't mean to tell them, all of a sudden it's just coming out and, whoops you just told them,

basically…she was…supportive and being real sweet. And she said, y'know, "It's okay, and you don't have to ever think—Don't you ever think you can't look me in the eye. You don't have to feel bad about this."…because I told her [that] I'm not ever going to be a child molester. This is just something I have to deal with.

Gene's aunt and Hugo's dad let each of them know that their attractions alone did not dictate whether they were a good or bad person—that their actions alone did that. Gene and Hugo understood that their attractions did not mean that they would commit a crime against a child, which itself was validating to them.

My participants felt supported by people in their lives when they demonstrated that they still trusted them after they had come out. This was especially true when they were trusted to be around children. My participants who felt intrinsically that they would never be at risk of committing an offense against a child nonetheless were often worried that others would have that concern. Desmond described feeling supported by an aunt who showed that she trusted him around children. He said:

[My aunt] lived in the UK…and I think I just emailed her to say hi. From there she asked how I was doing and we mailed back and forth a bit.…I eventually told her that I thought I was gay and she was sympathetic and helpful…then I started moving in the direction of paedophiles and what she thought about them. And eventually I told her that I was one. She was really helpful and understanding.…At the same time, I started getting involved in her grandson's—my second cousin—life because his dad, my cousin, didn't really seem too interested in him and I wanted to try and help him if I could. She knew I was involved, but I gave her my word that I only wanted to help and would never hurt him and she trusted me. [Her trust was important to me], since it was her grandson.…I wanted to prove to her that I was a "good" paedophile who wouldn't harm anyone.…I genuinely cared about him and wanted to help. He was a little bit like the son I'll never have.

Desmond had only fatherly feelings toward his cousin, but he understood that many people would think it risky for him to be around any children at all, no matter his feelings toward a given child. The fact that his aunt trusted him around her grandson therefore meant a great deal to him.

Gene's brother demonstrated trust toward him in a similar manner. Gene told me:

My brother who's a year and a half younger than me, um, he found out [about my attractions to minors].…He was surprisingly, and my sister in law then, they were pretty supportive. They were like, "We still love you. You're still allowed to have a relationship with your nephews." He was kind of like, not that I get a chance to do much anyway, because they live in a different state full-time. But he was like "We're not going to leave you to babysit. No offense, just because I don't know if it'd be really appropriate. But, you know...you're always welcome, it's always okay for you to be around them. You know, your nephews love you and everything." So, that's kinda how, that was how that one went.

Gene's brother and sister-in-law let him know that the revelation of his attractions to minors did not change their love for him. When he first talked to them about his attractions, Gene specifically said that he would understand if they didn't want him to have a relationship with their sons until they had grown up, and his brother rejected that right away, saying "I know you wouldn't hurt them." The fact that his brother and sister-in-law no longer felt comfortable with Gene babysitting, however, suggests that they did *not* know Gene wouldn't hurt them. Although they did not feel that he should be alone with their children, Gene still felt supported by them because they affirmed that they loved him, and they trusted him to be around their sons in the presence of other adults.

Mitchell was not interested in coming out to his family, but had sought support from religious institutions. He was grateful to find what he was looking for from the pastor of a church he went to. As he recalled:

> I was attending a church where the pastor was pretty unconventional and sort of, it was clear that he would be more accepting and less judgmental than the average pastor or average person in general. An M-A-P friend of mine who visited me and went to church with me also suggested that this guy is probably safe to come out to, so I did....I told him I was attracted to teenage boys. And, um, he didn't show any kind of, like, shock or fear or anything like that or judgment. He told me later, like a couple weeks later, that he was a little surprised because it was something new to him, but pretty soon after that, it was clear that he was very supportive and accepting. He told me one time that I'm probably much more careful about my behavior with kids than the average person would be because I have to be so careful about it. And so he trusted me interacting with kids in the church, but I was never in a situation where I was, like, in private with them anyway, but it was like he didn't have this sense that I should be kept away from kids or anything like that.

While Mitchell was hoping for acceptance from his pastor, he wasn't necessarily expecting it: that he didn't show judgment or fear was noteworthy to him. Like Desmond and Gene, Mitchell was especially grateful that his pastor trusted him to be around children, and he felt accepted because of that trust.

In addition to finding support through trust, my participants indicated feeling supported when the people they came out to changed certain behaviors as a result. By coming out to his friends, Lee told me that they began to recognize that comments they had previously made about pedophiles were problematic.

> They were a little bit taken aback [when I told them], but I think it's more because of them than because of me. 'Cause I have these friends that...I don't know how things are nowadays, but you don't hear it so much anymore, but back then people just joke about pedophiles and, uh, they joke and talk about things on TV and how all pedophiles should be killed and this and that. And a couple of them, after I told them, they were like, "Oh. Oh my God, I am so sorry. Everything I said, I didn't really mean it." And instantly regretted saying these things to my face and it completely changed their opinion of the whole thing. That was something that was really interesting to see.

The comments Lee's friends had made to him were not uncommon in today's society, due to the link many people make between pedophiles and child molesters, and the gravity we (rightly) place on child sexual abuse. So it was strikingly meaningful to Lee that his friends realized their assumptions were incorrect once he had come out, and he was happy to see that they changed their viewpoints. West's sister also changed her behavior after he came out to her, although this behavior was of a different sort: she had previously been trying to set him up on dates, which had continuously left him in awkward situations.[7] His sister had read an article that was sympathetic toward MAPs before West came out to her. "She knew where I was coming from," he said, and she accepted him.

Robin's partner not only made him feel accepted but also helped to normalize his feelings. Robin recounted:

> About two years into my relationship with my partner...I just felt like I was really coming to a point where I was dealing with a lot of this stuff in my private therapy and a lot of stuff in my regular, daily life. And it was important for me to tell him in a real way, because we were talking about moving in together and I was like, this is...I need to share all of me. It was very much like coming out for the first time, which was like, my heart raced. I felt...I had fantasies, like imagined fantasies that he would like reject me, that he would leave me, that he would not want to talk with me...None of which were based in any sort of reality, because I knew him well enough to know that he would've at least been neutral, if not supportive. And I basically—I mean, I over an ongoing conversation for over an hour and a half, I basically said, "Look I'm attracted...I think you know I'm attracted to

younger guys. Um, but like I'm attracted to teenagers and like pubescent boys and even like sometimes younger guys. I really want you to know this. It's important for me that you know me, and that like I want to know what you think." And he was extremely supportive. He's incredibly supportive, actually. I mean, he seemed to have few, if any, of the hang-ups that I have about it. He was just like, "Well of course like you're attracted to younger guys, and a lot of people are and like, it's not unusual and it's not an issue for me and like, we'll deal with it." You know. So that was really sweet.

Robin was the only person in my study who had this particular experience—of coming out to someone who immediately normalized their attractions. Although Robin was intensely grateful to his partner for having this reaction, ironically his support had created a problem for Robin by the time of our interview. Robin described their relationship as potentially coming to a close, and his partner had been so supportive that Robin was afraid to be with someone new. The prospect of beginning a relationship with a new person and coming out to them was daunting, because Robin's partner had set such a high bar. He thought it was unlikely to be met by anyone else.

My participants sometimes came out to others as a very last resort. Jeremy, whose story is detailed at the beginning of this chapter, was one of them: he came out to his parents only after he had made the decision to end his life. Coming out allowed him to come to terms with his attractions and to access the support he needed to cut off ties from a therapist who had been subjecting him to aversion therapy. Gene also had an experience of reaching out in a time of need. When Gene was 19, he felt that he could no longer manage his attractions. He felt that he was "on the verge of suicide" and decided to come out to his friend, who was studying in college to become a therapist. "I was just, like, bawling to him on the phone," Gene recalled, "and I just told him everything." His friend was nonjudgmental and put him in touch with a therapist who provided help.

While participants' narratives about receiving supportive reactions from others were sometimes overwhelmingly positive, as in most of the previous anecdotes, many told me about friends and family who reacted with varying degrees of discomfort, and respondents nonetheless identified these reactions as supportive as well. Often participants told me that these individuals initially made them feel accepted, but that they got the impression that they didn't want to discuss their attractions afterward. Charlotte, for example, told me about coming out to a friend she had known since kindergarten:

CHARLOTTE: I told my best friend. I spent a lot of time...sort of giving these hints—sort of, like, making jokes....So, yeah, I would give hints to prepare her and then I wrote her a note and she read it and she was like...I think she said something like, "I kind of guessed that."

AW: Wow. Did you feel supported by [her]?

CHARLOTTE: Oh, yeah. Yeah, definite—well...I, I certainly didn't feel judged. But I also feel a lot like...it's not something she really wants to talk about. I, that might just be my anxieties, but it's hard to tell and I don't want to just keep asking, you know? I don't want to keep saying, "Hey, by the way, does my sexuality make you uncomfortable?"

Charlotte wasn't sure whether her friend didn't want to talk about it or if she was projecting that onto her, but either way she sensed that her friend was uncomfortable.

This lack of discussion about attractions after participants' initial disclosures was a common theme in interviews. For instance, Dominick recalled telling several friends of his over the internet so that he "wouldn't have to see them face to face." In each of those cases he said that his friends were comforting, but that after their first conversation about it, they never talked about it again. Similarly, Vincent came out to a friend while both of them were drunk and high. He recalled "sobbing and babbling, and [I] really just told him the whole story. I think we were just like on the couch talking about this for like several hours." Vincent described his friend as "uncomfortable, but...he did care and wanted to help and wanted to be there and, like, he wasn't, you know, gonna just run out of the room." When the topic did not come up again, Vincent had an "uneasy feeling," wondering where their friendship stood. He was unsure whether his friend remembered his confession and felt they had to "retalk about it" six months later. Unlike the experiences of other participants, however, Vincent found that after that six-month period of avoiding the subject, his friend demonstrated openness in discussing the subject regularly.

While some of my participants felt uncomfortable over talking to the supportive people they had come out to about their attractions after initially telling them, others encountered more negative reactions at the start and yet still described these reactions as supportive. Kevin told his wife about his attractions to minors before they had even become engaged. When I asked about her reaction, he described it as "very understanding." I asked him to describe how the conversation went.

KEVIN: Out of the blue I pretty much just said, "I got this thing I need to talk to you about." Um, at that point I still had a lot of guilt over it. I don't really live with any guilt at the moment. I've sort of accepted who I am. But back then I had a lot of guilt and it was wearing me down. That was the main reason I told her and I just said, "I'm just really struggling with something." And yeah, we discussed it, and ever since then she's really helped me come to terms with it.

AW: Mm. What was her reaction initially?

KEVIN: Uh, a little bit of shock. I think the first response was, "Have you ever abused anybody?" So, I think we needed to able to clarify those things. I was very surprised, I've never told anybody else and the manner in which she reacted I respect. I wish everybody could be like that.

Given that Kevin is exclusively attracted to minors, the shock experienced by his then-girlfriend can't be too surprising. Nonetheless, it surprised me to hear Kevin describe her reaction as "understanding" (and a reaction he respected) when the first thing she asked him was whether he had molested a child.

While at first this was difficult for me to understand, it was not the only narrative like this that I encountered during my interviews. Lee described the first time he came out to someone:

When I realized my attraction, I went into this really bad depressive phase for about more than six months. I couldn't do anything. I was thinking about suicide the whole time. And there was this one friend who stuck with me throughout the whole thing. So, he was wondering what was wrong with me and I started telling him things and then…I never really told him exactly what it was but he guessed. And he asked me and I said, "Yeah, that's it." And he was like, "Oh, okay then, no problem." "You're not really hurting anybody. It's not really worse than a regular person that, say, that wants to rape women." So, he was very kind. He was very understanding. And I couldn't really understand how he was so understanding because in my mind he was freaking out. And I make everything that I could just to make up for it. Like, I can't, I can't, just focus this whole burden on him. So over time…he would talk about it several times, but it's not a very comfortable topic for him. He just understood and tried to help whenever he could, but he never really knew what to do. And that was basically…we never really discussed it afterwards.

Lee's friend compared him to someone with an interest in raping women—an inherently violent fantasy. Importantly, Lee did not fantasize about violent sexual encounters, but rather had fantasies of consensual relationships with children, which he knew were not possible. Despite this comparison, Lee still found his friend's reaction to be supportive, and he referred to his friend as both "kind" and "understanding." Surely, Lee's bar for supportive reactions was low by any metric. As with other participants, his friend only discussed it with him a handful of times before Lee got the feeling that it was too uncomfortable for his friend to talk about.

Oliver's parents similarly made assumptions about him when he came out to them. He told them: "'I've known since I was around the age of 13 that I was a pedophile.' And I used that word—if I had my time back, I might not have used that particular word 'cause it has . . . such a negative connotation." He regretted this his word choice, because his father's reaction was to say, "But Oliver, being a pedophile is illegal." His father had misunderstood, thinking that Oliver was disclosing offending against a child, and he had to backtrack and explain that while he was attracted to children, he had never acted on these attractions. Oliver described his parents as being "understanding but not quite comfortable" with his disclosure, asking him not to tell other members of his extended family for fear of being ostracized. He explained that he had to keep it a secret from those family members, "to protect the other people that I cared about"—in other words, to protect his parents from the stigma of being associated with a pedophile.

I had trouble placing some this in a section about accessing support, because these reactions didn't feel supportive to me. Upon coming out, Lee's friend compared him to people with urges to rape. Oliver's father used language that implied he thought Oliver had committed a crime. Nonetheless, my participants experienced these reactions as supportive. This raises questions for me. Why did my participants identify these reactions as positive? Perhaps because they were not judged outright; only their potential behavior was judged. Or perhaps because they were expecting to be rejected, or even physically harmed, so anything other than that felt like support.

Facing rejection. While many of my participants felt supported by the people they came out to, about one-third of those who had come out to someone else described feeling rejected by them. Rejection took multiple forms, from feeling judged by a friend or loved one to being turned away by family, or asked to leave by educational programs. These rejections had consequences in the lives of participants that ranged from discontinued friendships to being reported to the police. The first person Charlotte told about her sexuality was a friend in high school. As she recalled:

I told someone almost out of desperation. It wasn't someone I was super close to....We had been friends for a while and he was opening up to me about, about things—about his gender identity and stuff. He knew that I was educated on that subject, being kind of queer and gay and all that stuff. So, I said like, "Okay, he's opening up to me. This is my chance to open up to someone." And so I did. And he took it... okay? I think he was very weirded out and not sure how to express that to me. He automatically assumed that I was looking at illegal pornography and told me to be careful with that. Saying something about "my brother's a cop" and to be careful. I was like, "Uh-huh, I'm not doing that, dude." And like, the next day at school he was acting kind of awkward. He made a joke about how he was judging me, and that was devastating. Even though he was joking, that was horrifying.

Charlotte had taken her friend's disclosures about his gender identity to indicate that he would be an understanding person to disclose her sexuality to. Unfortunately, his first reaction was suspicion that she was engaging in illegal behavior, which she was not. Nonetheless, Charlotte told me that they remained friends for a while afterward, although years later they had a falling out, and were no longer friends.

William also experienced rejection by a friend as a result of his disclosure. He recalled: "We were pretty close, and I felt like she would understand. I told her over [text chat] because I didn't feel comfortable with telling her face to face. At first she was okay with it but then she was all like, 'Oh well actually you can't be a pedophile because pedophiles are bad people and you're not a bad person!' and then a little later she decided she couldn't deal with being friends with me anymore." William's friend had conceptualized pedophiles as "bad people" and therefore had difficulty reconciling this conceptualization with her understanding that William was a self-identified pedophile. Complicating his disclosure was that his friend was a survivor of sexual abuse, which he had not known at the time when he came out to her. Not long after William's disclosure, she ended their friendship, which left him feeling lonely as he had few other friendships at the time.

William was not the only person who experienced a loss as a result of coming out. Brooke came out to her girlfriend a year into their relationship, after her girlfriend divulged having a sexual response to holding her own niece, who was a young child. Brooke took this to mean that her girlfriend was also minor-attracted. She recalled:

I thought, oh, maybe I finally don't have to hide this anymore from my significant other. And we started talking about it, and it turned into her forgetting that she'd ever mentioned anything, and immediately researching, and trying to find ways for how to "fix" me, and panicking, and freaking out. The fact that at that time we lived on the same block as a high school and an elementary school was crazy for her, because she couldn't handle the fact that there is no way I would simply grab a random stranger and force myself on them.... She couldn't handle [it]. In fact, she was determined to [do] research. She found a couple of articles that she thought kind of talked about minor-attracted people, and when I say wanted to fix me, [she] was looking for the cures for this, saying well here's this chemical castration.

Soon after Brooke came out to her girlfriend, their relationship ended. Brooke said that although they had other problems as well, her girlfriend's adverse reaction to her coming out was a significant factor in their breakup. After the breakup, Brooke's ex outed her to her friends, which left her "without any significant support system."

Oliver faced consequences of a different sort when his friend of more than seven years found out about his sexuality. They lived together, and she overheard him discussing him "keeping something private from my parents" on the phone, when he was in a separate room. Eventually she confronted him over it, and he opened up to her about his attractions to minors, explaining that he had never acted on them. He said:

She seemed fine with it, very understanding and supportive. I was happy that I could perhaps go and discuss this every now and then, but then two days later when she came home in the early morning or whenever it was, she told me she in fact wasn't comfortable with this. And it was her house and I was staying there as her roommate and she wanted me to move out and seek, sort of, professional help to sort of change this about myself. And if I didn't do that, she didn't want to see me anymore again as a friend....I was shocked, I was sad, there was a bit of arguing. But...I didn't want to get too confrontational with her about it because she was almost...giving me the impression she would contact authorities about this. She didn't say that, but I remember thinking she was very... her attitude was very, "Oh my god, don't even debate this with me, get out immediately." She did tell me that she had discussed it with her therapist, it was a social worker... according to her, this social worker therapist that she was seeing recommended that she ask me to leave as soon as possible. I didn't want to rock the boat too much and get anyone's negative attention outside of me and her involved with this, and I chose to sort of—I argued a bit at first, but then I chose to leave her house and move back in with my parents...that was well over around five years ago now. I haven't seen her since.

Oliver's friend did not suspect that he had committed an offense, nor that he would. Despite this, she had, on the advice of a social worker, told him to move out and indicated that he should try to change his sexuality through therapy (despite the fact that sexual orientation change efforts have been shown to be ineffective—see Chapter 5). Oliver lost his good friend and his housing as a result of his disclosure.

Felix and Quentin each experienced strong negative reactions from family. When he was in college, Felix became emboldened and energized by an enlightening experience in a sociology class in which the professor spoke compassionately about minor-attracted individuals. In response, Felix went home and came out to his mother. "Let me tell you," he recalled, "she was absolutely livid. God, she started yelling, crying, saying all these outlandish things, trying to blame random people for it, et cetera. I told her, no, it's not a phase, it's who I am." Although it took some time, Felix described his mother as ultimately being accepting of who he was. "Most of my friends and family know about me. My dad and I don't talk because his new wife doesn't want me to be around.... My mom has grown to accept me for who I am. My brother and I talk amiably, but I can tell he's put off by it."

Quentin described damaging outcomes of his disclosures. He had lost his wife to cancer when his sons were eight and ten years old, raising them on his own. When his sons were 18 and 20, Quentin decided to come out to them, after hearing positive experiences from others who had come out to family on online forums. He described feeling that "[with] everything that has happened within our family prior to that time, one would have thought that there would have been sufficient trust ... but you never know how late teenagers are going to react." Quentin reported that his sons "reacted violently," outing him to their friend network, which resulted in public confrontations, after which he said he feared for his life. Quentin's response was to burn all of his belongings and live out of a tent, until finally moving out of the country sometime later. At the time of the interview, Quentin had not seen his sons in six years.

Isaac detailed an experience that had significant, negative consequences for his future. He had been enrolled in a master's degree program for mental health counseling. He explained:

> I came out to a small group of students, maybe 10 or 12 students in each group. And we had an instructor and he told us to share something that we were really dealing with. And I said, "If I share mine everyone will reject me." One of the female students said, "I'm upset at that, we would not reject you." So I went ahead and told them, and they

took it well at first, then they promptly distanced themselves from me, ignored me. And the teacher, the instructor, broke the confidentiality that we were assured of, and told the administration. And they...told me I had to leave the residency....So they sent me home. That's where I was probably most devastated. I was very stressed and anxious. I would shake without any cause for it.

Isaac took legal action against the school because their handbook stipulated that they did not discriminate on the basis of sexual orientation. In the process, he was outed to the judge, attorneys, and others involved in the case. Despite his efforts, he lost the case.

Isaac and Quentin were not the only participants in my study who were outed to others upon disclosing their attractions. After coming out to others, Gene and Elias were outed as well. In each of their cases, they were outed as a result of coming out online. Gene said:

I was outed on the internet a few years ago, by some vigilantes from, um, Perverted Justice. They're the same people that did the [show] "To Catch a Predator," but they have, like, a little side project where they would get on the internet, y'know, which is like, where people were talking about being pedophiles. And I just made the mistake of giving away too much personal information and they connected the dots, who I was and then outed me on my MySpace. So much more people found out that way. So, I'm pretty much about, I would say, to all the people I know right now, I'm, like, 70% out of the closet.

Not only was Gene outed to most of the people in his personal life, but law enforcement also became involved. His computer was confiscated and searched for illegal child pornography, which Gene did not possess. He did not face arrest but ended up working with law enforcement to end a now-defunct website for pedophiles. The bigger consequence, from Gene's point of view, was that most of his family and friends found out about his sexuality, which he would not have otherwise chosen for himself.

Elias was also reported to the police after coming out online. In his case he came out via a personal ad. He told me that he had isolated himself because of his attractions to minors, but that the isolation was too much for him. He explained: "The ad was saying I'm a law-abiding paedophile looking to make adult friends who accept me." His experience with the police was very different from Gene's. "Someone reported [the] ad I'd made to the police," he recalled, "and they found my address and came to my door, so they know [about my attractions to minors], too. Fortunately [the police] were looking out for my safety...they said they were required to investigate, but they understood that I had no illegal intentions. They said if they could find my IP address, so could others, so I should be more careful." Elias was grateful that the police had been looking out for him. As a Canadian, he expressed relief that he did not live in the United States, where he believed police would not have been as understanding. Although Elias was distressed by the responses he encountered from coming out online, he continued to do so.

DOUBLE LIVES, MANY DECISIONS

The MAPs in my study faced a difficult choice when deciding whether to come out to the people in their lives. On the one hand, they often wanted their friends and family to understand them fully, and they hoped for acceptance and perhaps support. In order to receive these benefits, however, they often had to take what they felt was a big risk. Sometimes the risk was too great. Although much of my sample had come out to someone in their personal lives, few were out to many. Participants often did not tell their family members or close friends, due to fears of judgment, rejection, suspicion, or even due to a perception that it would hurt their loved ones too much to know. Those who did come out to others illustrated the risks and benefits for those for whom coming out was theoretical. Indications among my sample of the risks of coming out were founded for many of my participants. These risks ranged from the less harmful, such as comments or jokes about being judged, to rejection that had large consequences for their lives: some faced break-ups, losses of living situations, and forced outings to friends, family, and even law enforcement.

Although participants ran the risk of negative reactions, some encountered reactions that demonstrated acceptance, love, and trust. Even among my participants' friends and family who were previously unfamiliar with the idea of non-offending MAPs, some understood right away that their attractions did not indicate illegal behavior. Often, my participants told others about their attractions in times of emotional distress. When encountering accepting reactions, they felt supported, which helped them cope. But among those who lacked support, those who were rejected by others or who could not come out to others at all, other methods of coping were needed. The next chapter delves deeper into the coping strategies my participants used to deal with their attractions.

3. "Enduring a Rainstorm"
MAPs' Strategies for Coping with Their Attractions

Harper began our interview with apprehension. She said of our conversation: "I feel like this may be the bravest thing I've done." Within the first few minutes of us talking to each other, she explained: "I've never verbalized any of this out loud before. Like ever. Ever in my life. I've not even ever said it out loud to *myself*.... I started to suspect it when I was fifteen or sixteen, and I was very vigorously and enthusiastically in denial about it. I still am to some extent, I...I've begun admitting it to myself in maybe the last four or so months....I think there was a period of time when I really thought I would outgrow it, and, uh, I never really did." Harper, 24 years old by the time of our interview, had spent a long time in what she deemed denial about her attractions toward minors. She was primarily attracted to girls ages 8 to 14, but she also had some attractions toward adult women. She was in a committed relationship with a woman her age as well, which helped her not to focus on her attractions to younger girls.

Nonetheless, Harper's attractions to minors seriously affected her day-to-day life. She was a seminary student, deeply invested in her commitment to God. She was also deeply disturbed by her attractions. She explained that she did not feel she was a danger to children in any way and had never felt at risk of acting inappropriately, but she felt "a tremendous amount of angst about the attractions themselves." She clarified: "I'm not at risk for offending, and I...I haven't, I don't feel that I've engaged in any actions that are morally anywhere near the line, let alone over it. But I... I do feel like there's a line for thoughts, too, and I've probably crossed that one several times over." She referred to her attractions as "detrimental to my human experience," feeling that not only is sexual behavior with children morally reprehensible but her thoughts themselves were also wrong. Harper said she felt God had made a mistake with her, which as a seminary student was distressing.

Her attractions to minors were so upsetting to her that the only way she could think of dealing with them was through self-harm. She explained:

> When I was in denial about it, and in the moments when it was most obvious to me and it seemed like there was nothing I could do about it, and I had to keep trying to ignore it and hoping it would go away. Again, I felt very unable to cope with those emotions. And I didn't always handle them in the best ways....I'm a cutter....And, um, uh, [pause] around the time that I was beginning to realize where my attractions actually lie, so, late high school, was not a good time period for my skin. I had the kind of scars you could see from an airplane....[I got treatment] for the self-harm, but it wasn't really helpful, because I couldn't talk about that piece of *why* I was self-harming.

Although Harper wished she could have been truthful about her attractions to minors when she was seeking help for her self-harming behaviors, she told me this was not an option. Partly this was because she was in seminary, and she did not believe others in the church would understand. In fact, she did not feel anyone in her personal life, including friends or family, would be nonjudgmental toward her if she came out to them about her attractions, so she kept them entirely to herself.

And then one day, about four months before our interview, Harper read an article on a popular liberal news site written by a self-described pedophile. He had mentioned VirPed in the article, and Harper found herself on the website. She introduced herself in writing as someone who "might be a pedophile," and although she was not very active on the forums in terms of posting content herself, she found the experience of joining the VirPed community to be life-altering. "Hearing people talk about it as a part of their lives is certainly something I never experienced before," she said. "Talking about solutions to issues they might pose rather than thinking about the attraction as the issue itself, which I'm kind of on the fence about that, um, even cracking jokes about it sometimes. Everyone's favorite joke on the forum seems to be 'What kind of shoes do pedophiles wear? White Vans.' Even just people cracking bad jokes. It's refreshing."

On VirPed, Harper found a place where MAPs could feel less alone, less judged, and more understood. She found a place where people recognized that she could not change who she was attracted to and where others were struggling as well. She found a place where people could let their guards down enough to make bad jokes—those that people who are not attracted to minors may find distasteful or offensive, but that allowed her and others to find shared humor about stereotypes (even if they retain the link between pedophilia and predatory behavior). In other words, this was a place where MAPs didn't have to feel anxiety about their attractions all the time. Although Harper did not agree with everything said on the website, VirPed meant so much to her that she told me that her first piece of advice to someone else struggling with attractions to minors would be to find community. I asked her to tell me more, and she expounded:

> I'm gonna try not to preach a sermon here....I do think that the, the root of who we are as human seeks connectedness and seeks community, and whether you want to say that comes from God or you want to frame it in different language, I think that that's our most important need, is to be in relationship and in community with one another. And I think that when people are cut off from that, that is dangerous to them, dangerous to the people cutting them off. It's...it's not what we're made for. We're not made to exist in isolation. And at the foundation of my theology is the need for humans to be a part of a greater body. And to be connected to something greater than themselves. And I think that part of why this transition to not being in denial has been a little bit easier than one would think is because of the VirPed community, because if I tried to be—I don't know—if I had decided to be honest with myself before I had joined that community, I think it would've been a lot harder.

I asked Harper what she thought would have happened if she had not found VirPed, and she told me: "I probably would've started cutting myself again. Probably would've been, uh, kind of an emotional wreck. I might have been so desperate for any sort of community that I would've felt the need to tell someone and ended up telling the wrong person. Uh, I don't know. I think it could've had all kinds of consequences." Harper had stopped cutting herself about a year before our interview, but in being more honest with herself about her attractions, she had been at risk of self-harming again. Finding community kept her safe from self-harming, safe from disclosing her attractions to someone she may not have been able to fully trust with the information, and even gave her connection in a spiritual sense. Her need to be connected to a part of something greater than herself was fulfilled through joining the VirPed community and connecting with other like-minded MAPs.

· · ·

Throughout our interview, Harper talked to me about how she coped with her attractions to minors. Her coping strategies took a variety of forms, including ones that she did not even recognize as a coping method (such as denial) and those that she identified as unhealthy (such as self-harm). Other coping strategies Harper used took the form of seeking information and engagement with community, which she perceived as helpful to her wellbeing. Chapter 2 explored MAPs' experiences with making difficult decisions about coming out about their attractions or staying closeted, as well as some of the consequences faced when disclosing their attractions to loved ones. This chapter takes a deeper look at the day-to-day and ongoing stigma faced by MAPs as well as other challenges faced by these individuals. This chapter also discusses strategies developed by MAPs to cope with these struggles.

A wide literature has been dedicated to stressors experienced by various stigmatized groups, such as individuals with mental illness, individuals with physical disabilities, people with criminal records, drug users, LGBT populations, economically disadvantaged groups, and groups stigmatized based on their race or ethnicity. Sociologist Erving Goffman[1] initiated the study of stigma, its consequences, and the responses of stigmatized individuals. Goffman described individuals whose stigmatized traits are readily apparent as *discredited,* while calling individuals whose stigmatized traits are concealable *discreditable.* People whose sexualities are non-normative, such as MAPs, fall under the discreditable category. Prior research has more often focused on discredited groups,[2] due to their inability to escape the stigma associated with them. However, discreditable people cannot escape the stressors associated with their stigmatized traits due to their ability to conceal them alone—in fact, the act of concealing stigmatized traits and choosing who to disclose them to can introduce stress in and of itself.[3]

That MAPs are a stigmatized group is undeniable. Psychologist Sarah Janke and her colleagues have found that large percentages of the general population believe individuals who are attracted to minors, even those who have never committed an offense, should be incarcerated and would be "better off dead."[4] The researchers found that people feel more fear and anger toward pedophiles than other groups frequently thought of as objectionable, such as individuals who abuse alcohol, people with antisocial tendencies, and sexual sadists. Prior research conducted with MAPs themselves has shown that MAPs are acutely aware of the stigma against them.[5] Some survey research has shown that MAPs' experiences with stigmatization correlate with lower psychological wellbeing.[6]

Decreases in wellbeing are a common occurrence for other groups that experience stigma-related stress. Among groups with discreditable stigma, such as members of LGBT communities and individuals with mental illness, researchers have found that their stigma results in lowered self-esteem,[7] depression and suicidality,[8] and even cognitive difficulties.[9] However, the effects of stigma-related stress can be mitigated by the coping mechanisms of the stigmatized individual. While reactions to stress can include both voluntary and involuntary responses,[10] coping specifically refers to "conscious volitional efforts to regulate emotion, cognition, behavior, physiology, and the environment in response to stressful events or circumstances."[11] Research has indicated a difference between coping strategies that engage with the stressor and those that disengage from it, suggesting opposing outcomes for each. Although researchers have shown that MAPs face stigma from others, their lived experiences in dealing with this stigma and other difficult aspects of their attractions have yet to be explored. Stigma research has shown that some coping mechanisms result in better outcomes than others, but what coping skills are MAPs employing? The remainder of this chapter focuses on stressors faced by MAPs as well as the coping mechanisms they use to deal with them.

STRESSORS FACED BY MAPS

MAPs face multiple stressors connected to their attractions to minors. In interviews, my participants discussed these stressors and their effects on their lives. Common stressors discussed included social rejection (either personal rejection or rejection toward MAPs in general) and internalized stigma as well as loneliness and grief over an inability to ever have a fulfilling romantic or sexual relationship. While some of these stressors were covered in more depth in Chapters 1 and 2, I briefly describe them here as well to more effectively illustrate the unique difficulties MAPs cope with on a daily basis.

Societal rejection. In Chapter 2, I discussed MAPs' experiences with coming out to others, including in some cases facing rejection from those they disclosed their attractions to. Although many MAPs were able to access support after coming out, about one-third of my participants who had come out to others faced some form of rejection. Rejection from friends and family took the forms of harsh words said in anger, breakups by romantic partners, and even being cast out of homes and families. Rejection for my participants extended further than these often one-off occasions, though: in addition to these interpersonal experiences, the individuals in my study noted often hearing negative messages about minor-attracted individuals in society more broadly. Those messages were constant, whether or not my participants actively discussed or looked up information about MAPs.

Some participants were actively engaged in discussing attractions to minors with others or had a particular interest in looking up research or popular opinions about MAPs. Generally this occurred online. Participants who engaged in behaviors such as reading comments on articles or videos about or by MAPs described hearing negative messages ranging from multiple times a week to multiple times a day. Participants who were open about their sexuality online, in platforms such as Twitter or Tumblr, commonly reported experiencing harassment as a result. Charlotte, who wrote frequently about life as a MAP on her Tumblr page,[12] told me that she needed a "strong stomach" to read the comments, stating: "I'm so used to all of the arguments and all of the, like, death threats, even…we all get a lot of 'kill yourself.' You get used to that phrase." Those who read comments about MAPs in general also faced negative messaging about MAPs, although it was not directed specifically about them. "[When you come out]," West said, "your only image of pedophiles are people in the news, and the comments are like, 'he should be raped in prison,' and, 'he should be put to death,' so not a lot of support there. I always tell people never to read internet comments." Those in my study often regarded reading these types of comments, whether directed toward them or about MAPs in general, as distressing.

Some MAPs followed advice like West's against reading online comments faithfully. Brooke, for instance, used an internet browser add-on to block comments from websites like YouTube, for the specific purpose of escaping negative messages. Nonetheless, even those among my participants who avoided comments sections in articles and videos about MAPs saw negative portrayals of this population with relative regularity. Multiple participants described hearing hateful messages about MAPs on Facebook or other social media websites from friends who were unaware of their attractions. Kevin and Gene referenced a particular meme posted by their Facebook friends, picturing an electric chair or other methods of execution as "the cure for pedophilia." Participants also detailed stigmatization in the form of fictional media representations of MAPs. Zach reported:

> ZACH: I hear negative messages almost constantly. Every time a fictional novel needs a villain. In fact, that's even listed as a common TV trope on the website [TVTropes.org]!…If you want a villain, and you want your viewers to hate him, make

> him a pedophile. Sure way...You know, how often do you
> see pedophiles or hebephiles who are good guys, or at least
> neutral?
>
> AW: I'm not sure I ever have.
>
> ZACH: That's my point!...But if I asked you how many you've
> seen portrayed as villains—you know, I don't think we have
> enough days in the week to mention.

Zach was actively involved in multiple television and movie fandoms and was enthusiastic about monster movies in particular. He noted that not only were pedophiles frequently used as villainous characters in media, but that it was their pedophilia itself, rather than any other aspect of the characters, that demonized them. It disturbed Zach that he could not find any positive representations of people like him in the media.

Aiden raised a similar point about representations of pedophiles in fictional media coverage. "I still see it [in] TV or movies or wherever," Aiden said, "and pedophiles are, like, the one class of people that it's okay to just totally bash on and hate...you can just hate them and nobody disapproves." In the words of Tyler: "I'm on most people's lists of the most hated groups in the world. It's, like, 'ISIS. Me.'" Of course, Tyler did not mean himself exclusively, but he felt that the group he was a part of was especially hated, and this hatred was agreed upon by most of his nation. Mason echoed this sentiment: "I know that the world hates me, and I feel that heavily. So, I don't, I don't know what to do about it."

In addition to comments encountered online and portrayals in popular media, study participants described hearing coworkers, friends, and family members making sweeping generalizations about "pedophiles" as a dangerous population in their day-to-day lives. This often occurred when national or local news scandals broke out about child molestation cases. "When an article comes up in the media about charges laid against a pedophile," Floyd explained, "people are very quick to demonize with extraordinary disgust and hate." Of course, he was talking about articles about people who have committed sexual offenses against children, which are not necessarily talking about pedophiles. Although his comment conflates the two, this is reflective of the discourse Floyd has encountered—when news stories are released about child sexual abuse, conversations typically focus on pedophiles.

Lee described an incident that crystalizes Floyd's comment: "I was working and there was this news of this one child molester that was arrested. There were people around me that were like, 'Oh my God, that's horrible. [Pedophiles] should be tortured and killed,' and all of these terrible things. And it was really really hard for me to get that. Like, working around people that you know and trust and they're saying all these things about people like you. And how do you reconcile that? That person being your friend and being your colleague? That person would probably really, really hate you if they knew." Lee, who self-described as an exclusive pedophile, had depression, anxiety, and suicidal thoughts, which worsened when he heard comments from his coworkers about pedophilia. Hearing people he worked with and considered friends talking about pedophiles deserving to be tortured and killed strongly affected him, sometimes making him feel physically ill.

Internalized stigma. While my participants frequently discussed friends, family, and broader society rejecting them and MAPs in general, many made it clear in interviews that they had similar thoughts about MAPs themselves. Psychologist Patrick Corrigan and colleagues[13] describe internalized stigma, or self-stigma, as "a multilevel process that begins with awareness of public stigma. Self-stigma begins when the person internalizes the stigma and applies it to people [who share their stigmatized trait] in general (stereotype agreement) or to him or herself (self–concurrence)." Study participants showed evidence of following this type of process through their narratives. Gene explicitly described this process of becoming aware of public stigma toward MAPs and later applying it to himself. He told me:

> I remember being 13 and just kinda sitting there, looking at these pictures [of boys] in [the] Sears Catalog, and I suddenly saw them as attractive. And I was just sitting there on my bedroom floor thinking, "Am I…am I gay? Like, I can't believe I have…I don't want to be gay." Especially in 1988. There was a lot more stigma attached to that then there is now.…Probably within a few months, I starting realizing I'm not gay. That's not what this is. This is something—worse. This is not— you know, I didn't even have any reference, because I knew that there were people who molested children [Sigh] but I never had even heard the word "pedophile" at that time. I just thought people who molested children were weird, evil perverts who hung out in alleys and snatched children in their vans. I didn't really have any concept of what a pedophile was. And, you know, I had that concept of a guy in his van. I thought, "Oh God, is that what I'm becoming? What's wrong?" And I was kind of horrified by it and just bewildered, because I didn't have any real control over it. That's where my mind was going. I didn't really have, you know, anything to compare it to, or reference it against. It was just, I was completely alone with it, you know? And then I kind of learned what a pedophile was.…I went, "Oh God, that's what I am." And then I went on to my teen years with that, thinking for my first 12

years or so, thinking, am I gonna wind up being a child molester? Like, is it, am I doomed to this?...I didn't have any other frame of reference....I did start, by the time I was 15, seeking out, like, any article I could find about that topic, but it was always, it always, always from the, the seedy child molester angle.

Gene spoke of his experiences in becoming aware of stigma and applying it to himself in two different scenarios—first as a potentially gay person and then as a pedophile. He identified gaining awareness of gay people and pedophiles as undesirable populations with which he did not want to associate when he was younger, then later connecting those identities to himself and believing he was dangerous upon making that connection. Like Gene, many of my study participants showed evidence of internalized stigma through either stereotype agreement or self-concurrence in interviews. This frequently occurred when they first realized that they were minor-attracted.

While the majority of participants described stereotype agreement or self-concurrence shortly after recognizing their attractions to minors, many continued to exhibit self-stigma long afterward. In interviews I asked my respondents what feelings came to mind when thinking about their attractions. In addition to a small number of positive emotions, the vast majority of responses included a number of negative emotions, such as "guilt," "frustration," "disgust," and even "fear." Participants felt disgust and frustration over their attractions, because they believed it was morally wrong to have them, yet they were unable to get rid of them. As Phillip noted, "I'm not okay with it. I'm not okay at all with my feelings." Not only did they believe that sexual offending against children was wrong, but they also believed that the attractions they experienced were wrong as well.

Chapter 1 described MAPs' experiences forming identities as minor-attracted. They frequently believed, at least initially, that they were "monsters." Desmond retained this idea over ten years after he had realized he was attracted to minors. He explained to me why he had not told anyone in person about his attractions:

DESMOND: Telling someone that you're a paedophile is probably not a very good idea! Most people would automatically jump to the conclusion that you're a sick monster. In a way, they're right...

AW: You think of yourself in some ways as a sick monster?

DESMOND: To a degree, yeah, I do.

Not only did Desmond describe himself and other MAPs as "monsters," but he also referred to them (and himself) as "sick" and referred to his attractions to minors as his "issues," indicating that he thought of himself as mentally ill due to his attractions. As described in Chapter 1, MAPs' opinions reflect a current debate among researchers and the general public regarding whether attractions to minors can correctly be described as a mental illness. For those MAPs who felt their attractions to minors constituted an illness, this added to their sense of shame.

Loneliness and grief. In addition to stigma, another issue threatening the emotional health of participants was related to their limited or non-existent opportunities for romantic and sexual relationships. This was particularly true for those who were exclusively attracted to minors. Of my participants, 21 reported experiencing intense and persistent feelings of loneliness. Harper empathized with those who were exclusive, aptly summarizing their situation: "If you're exclusively minor-attracted, then no, you're never going to be in a relationship with someone you're attracted to. No, you're never going to experience sexual intimacy with someone you're attracted to. And that really sucks, and I'm sorry."

Respondents noted that their futures appeared much different than they had imagined when they were younger. Multiple participants expressed feeling discouraged by the idea that they would not have the marriages that they had imagined for themselves. One participant, George, felt that his life lacked purpose, because he believed he was supposed to get married to a woman and procreate in order to make a positive contribution to society. Even though he was interested in getting married to a woman, George was primarily attracted to boys ages 10 to 14 (with a secondary attraction to younger-looking adult men). He detailed his frustration with his sexuality, both in terms of his attraction to minors and his same-sex attractions; his attractions precluded him from the future that he wanted to pursue with a wife and children. George had a boyfriend three years his junior at the time of his interview but was fatalistic about the future of his relationship, believing that his boyfriend would age out of the range to which George was attracted. He lamented that being a MAP reduced opportunities in his life. When asked about the missed opportunities to which he was referring, George replied: "Uh, for example, my parents have a great relationship, a great marriage, and I'm quite sure that I will never have something like that. And also, just in general, [I have a] fear of being alone when I'm old, because I probably will not have a partner and especially will not have children, so there's this anxiety that I will be a lone man when I'm old." Although George was not alone in that he was in a romantic relationship, he expected loneliness to be a part of his future and felt saddened by the impending loneliness that he anticipated.

When I asked participants what they would tell another MAP who was struggling with feelings of loneliness, many responded that they had not figured out this answer for themselves yet. Some suggested that exclusive MAPs need simply to focus on other aspects of life. "While sex is obviously a great part of life," Jeremy explained, "there's other parts you can still pour your life energy to and get as much satisfaction." Hugo suggested that people who are exclusively attracted to minors have to "try to find other ways to be happy," but added, "I think sometimes that can be a hard pill to swallow." Overall, the challenges participants encountered in their day-to-day lives were immense. Many indicated significant negative effects on their wellbeing, which they frequently connected to their attractions or to the stressors they faced as a result of them. Robin described the outcome of these stressors on his psyche:

> I don't actually think that I'm doing a particularly resilient job of this in some ways. Like I'm, I think what I know what, in some ways, I should be doing, but it's super frustrating. It kind of feels like a chronic disease. Like, what am I supposed to do? There's no fix…there's just, like, perpetual frustration. Sometimes resilience can be seen like enduring a rainstorm. And the rainstorm [is] the stressors in your life. So, if the stressors about being minor-attracted, and being perpetually in the closet about that all the time, and having to be hypervigilant about what I say, and what I look at, and how I act, and having to be hypervigilant about my own internal thought processes, and like, constantly fearing social opprobrium because of that? Like, it's just raining all the time…and, you know, I can put on galoshes, then I can put up my umbrella, I can wear my slicker, but it's just raining…and it just feels, like, it's hard enough to feel sick. It's hard enough to feel exhausted.

Robin was trying his best to deal with the stressors he faced as a MAP, but he felt the effects of them constantly. He used the metaphors of dealing with a chronic illness and enduring a never-ending rainstorm for handling these stressors—metaphors indicating that there was nothing he could do about the underlying cause of the stress, even if he could deal with the effects individually. He felt exhausted by his efforts. Robin was not alone in this—many participants felt defeated by the weight of the stressors brought on by their attractions to minors. As a result, they sought ways to manage these stressors—some more successfully than others.

COPING STRATEGIES

Between facing social rejection, internalized stigma, loneliness, and grief, along with everyday stressors, MAPs can have a lot to cope with. My research participants' narratives revealed a number of ways that they attempted to cope with these stressors. Their strategies included both those identified by coping researchers as "engagement strategies" (those that engage with the stressor) and "disengagement strategies" (those that attempt to separate themselves from it). Disengagement coping strategies can include withdrawal, secrecy, avoidance, wishful thinking, and denial, while engagement coping strategies can include problem solving and acceptance.[14]

Recent research has evaluated forms of coping with stigma-related stressors. In tests of the effects of various coping styles among groups with discreditable stigma, disengagement coping has been shown to be detrimental to wellbeing.[15] Tests of more specific forms of coping show that engaged coping mechanisms, such as becoming involved with the stigmatized community one is a part of as well as engaging in humor, are considered especially effective. More specific disengagement strategies such as avoidance, withdrawal, and secrecy can be ineffective or actively harmful.[16] Next, I explore a number of disengagement and engagement coping strategies described by my participants as ways that they attempted to deal with the unique stressors that they face as MAPs.

Disengagement Coping Strategies

In stigma research, disengagement coping strategies are, as the name suggests, strategies used in an attempt to disengage with stress resulting from stigma, or in other words, to dissociate from it. Researchers have described disengagement as the "flight" scenario in a "fight or flight" choice—that is, rather than gaining control over the stigma-related stress or adapting to it in some way, these strategies are used in an attempt to avoid thinking about stigma and its resulting stressors entirely. Three common disengagement strategies that frequently came up in participants' narratives included avoidance through denial/wishful thinking, secrecy, and drug use.

Denial/wishful thinking. Many participants explained that they avoided engaging with their attractions to minors (and the resulting stigma) by denying them to themselves. Even after realizing in some way that they were minor-attracted, participants frequently described a period of time in which they avoided thinking about their sexuality at all, or pretended to themselves that they were not attracted to minors. As Harper said, "I was very vigorously and enthusiastically in denial about it." She described herself as continuing to be in denial occasionally, even in the same period of time as she was speaking to me about her attractions to minors.

George also described this attitude in himself. "In the first period after realizing [my attractions]," he said, "I often had the sensation of, uh, this is unreal. This, this cannot be.... It was like my, my initial reaction: Try to not believe that this is what I am." George did not necessarily believe he was attracted to adults, but he described an active attempt not to believe that he was a MAP, even though he still had "the idea" that his attractions were toward minors. He explained that seeing a movie about a pedophile was what took him out of this denial, and left him with an unavoidable realization that he was, indeed, a MAP. He described this period afterward as intensely sad for him, "because all [these] thoughts came to my mind and I knew nobody to talk to." In this way, his period of denial had been a protective strategy, because while he was able "to not believe" that he was a MAP, he did not experience the sadness that overtook him afterward.

While Harper and George described a period of denying that they were attracted to minors at all, Kevin described a slightly different thought process, involving both wishful thinking and later denial. He told me:

> I always assumed it would go away. Even when I was around 11, 12, 13, 14, I assumed this is just a little fetish, I'm just going through it, it will pass. And as I continued to get older, I realized it's not passing, and everything, I realized I just didn't have that attraction to peers my own age, or to older females. By that time, 17, 18, I was pretty sure I knew what I was. And it was difficult, I guess I tried to act as if, and I tried to pretend as if I [had attractions to people in my age group]. I remember being young and looking at pornographic magazines with my friends, which I just had no interest in, it didn't appeal to me. And just trying to pretend I enjoyed that and having physical relationships with girls my own age... but I struggled with it because I wasn't particularly attracted to them.

Kevin's story was representative of many—as he aged, he realized that the ages of those he was attracted to did not age with him. As he recognized that he was attracted to girls who were younger than him, he coped through wishful thinking, hoping that his attractions to these younger girls would go away and be replaced by attractions to people the same age as him. As he realized that this was not the case, he coped through denial, pretending to be attracted to adult women and to find evidence for himself that he was not minor-attracted. He explained that he never grew out of trying to find this evidence: at the time of our interview he was married to a woman, which he connected to his attempts to pretend to himself that he was attracted to adults, although by the time of our interview he had disclosed to his wife that he was a MAP.

Jeremy described a similar mentality to Kevin's. In the first few months after beginning to recognize he had attractions to children, he said: "I think I decided to just try, I guess, carry on with life and I didn't really think too much about it... [and then] I started to realize a little bit, there, that it wasn't normal that other people didn't have these feelings. And so I was certainly quite confused. But I guess I sort of tried to push it away... and carry on with my life at that point.... I guess slowly over time it sort of festers in the back of your mind.... I think you sort of put it away, but everything always comes back eventually." Jeremy's initial coping strategy was to avoid thinking about his attractions to minors at all. Originally he denied to himself that these attractions made him different from other people, but he nonetheless had a nagging awareness of his differences from others that he couldn't completely shake off that he described as festering—eating away at him. Eventually Jeremy had a visit from a young cousin and described feeling aroused as he was interacting with her. He immediately recognized the feeling for what it was. He explained that he "removed [himself] from the situation immediately" and that the interaction "finally triggered [a realization] and I thought back to a lot of the thoughts I'd been having for a few years and I was like, 'How did I miss this?' and I suddenly realized, looking back, I hadn't even been fantasizing about a woman this whole time. I'd been fantasizing about children but somehow never actually noticed." Jeremy's denial was so effective that he was able to keep himself from understanding that he was a MAP for years, despite experiencing consistent attractions to minors during that time.

Based on my participants' narratives, denial and wishful thinking seem to be useful strategies for them, allowing them to function without the stressors of a MAP identity to hit them for a while. These coping styles may have kept my participants from being able to actively engage with the stressors that they would later experience, merely pushing off the time when they would have to confront them.

Secrecy and selective disclosure. Another disengagement coping strategy described in participants' narratives was keeping their attractions to minors a secret from all, or most, others. As I explored in Chapter 2, participants worried that the stigma of being attracted to minors could translate into judgment, suspicion, or even threats to their personal safety if their friends and family knew about their attractions. Others worried that the stigma surrounding MAPs would reduce their loved ones' quality of life if they knew. This led eight of my participants to maintain secrecy from anyone they knew "in real life" (i.e., everyone they had a face-to-face relationship with, as opposed to online). The majority of the MAPs in my study disclosed their attractions to minors selectively to others, telling at least one acquaintance but keeping this secret from either all, or almost all, close friends and family members.

For those who chose to keep their attractions to minors a secret from all, most, or some of the people they knew, this total secrecy or selective disclosure was a deliberate coping strategy to avoid multiple effects of stigma in their lives. Participants' narratives show that keeping their attractions to minors a secret from others allowed them to avoid the risk of feeling stigmatized by friends and family. However, coping research has suggested that keeping stigmatized identities secret from others does not protect those with stigmatized identities from psychological distress, and may in fact actually further distress.[17] My participants' own experiences reflect this: for those who had not come out to family or friends "in real life," the burden of their secret weighed on them. They wondered how their family and friends would react if they were made aware of this secret, and whether they were missing out on support by not telling those close to them.

Drug use. Of my participants, 11 explained that they were coping with their attractions, or had previously coped with them, through drug and/ or alcohol use and abuse. Some regarded drug use as a positive way of managing their emotions. William described using "magic mushrooms" as a therapeutic experience that allowed him to put his attractions to minors "in perspective." Likewise, Shawn related that he was "drinking to kill something within me." He interpreted his drinking as helpful, because it provided him with a distraction. Gene called himself a "basket case" and said that for him drinking was a way to "stay sane." Drugs used by participants included alcohol, marijuana, prescription medications, crystal methamphetamine, heroin, cocaine, and psychedelics.

Participants' reasons for engaging in substance use and abuse mirror those of individuals within the general population. Self-medication (i.e., controlling emotions or reducing emotional pain through the use of substances) is a commonly noted coping mechanism used by people who have various stigmatized identities.[18] Psychologists Amelia Talley and Andrew Littlefield have noted multiple explanations for drug misuse by individuals who have concealable stigmatized identities, including as a form of cognitive escape, a way to induce positive emotional states, to decrease negative self-awareness, or because of an increased desire to fit in with peers.[19] Nonetheless, the risks of drug and alcohol misuse are well known, including decreased cognitive functioning, addiction, risk of injury, and health complications later in life.[20]

Although some of my participants believed that drug use assisted their ability to manage negative emotions, others were ashamed of their habit and had cut back, quit, or were interested in doing so. Charlotte described her previous drug use as problematic: "I had an alcohol abuse problem for a while. I think I probably had a marijuana abuse problem. Um, I think my psychiatrist would describe it that way. But I was definitely using it to cope, coping every single day. And those are the things I have stopped using as a coping mechanism and I only use them socially now." Charlotte was glad that she was no longer using marijuana to cope. Although MAPs such as Charlotte found that using drugs was helpful to them in the moment by helping them not to think about their attractions to minors and the resulting stigma, they often found their use of drugs unhealthy. Not only did my participants often feel shame about their drug use, but it occasionally had harmful consequences. For example, although West started drinking as a way to cope with his attractions, he was now drinking because he felt that he needed to:

AW: Do you connect [your drinking] to your attractions or do you feel like that's like a separate thing?

WEST: I think it started out that way and then it's just sort of taken hold. Like, I don't feel now that I drink because I feel bad about my attractions, because I really don't beat myself up over it. But like, it's just become what I do. Like I've fallen into it and I feel trapped.

West's narrative is common in descriptions of alcoholism; at first, drinking because it is pleasurable or because it has a desired effect of taking one's mind off of something else, but later becoming necessary for daily functioning through physical dependency.

Phillip's drug use became dangerous when he received a prescription from his psychiatrist for Ambien, a sleep medication. One night, when he was drunk, he attempted to use his medication to get high and accidentally overdosed, nearly dying in the process. Still, Phillip continued to drink to excess, identifying alcohol consumption as his only means for support, because he felt unable to talk about his attractions to anyone else. While Phillip perceived alcohol use as a coping strategy and a means to numb the pain, his experience illustrates that substance use did little to improve his situation.

Withdrawal. Withdrawal from society is the final disengagement coping strategy used by my participants. Coping researchers explain that withdrawal from society allows individuals with stigmatized identities to avoid comparisons with nonstigmatized individuals or to avoid situations that will bring about stigmatization. Perhaps due to its extreme nature, social withdrawal was not a common disengagement strategy among my participants, but two of them explained that they rejected society altogether. Elias and Desmond each discussed avoiding people in general. Elias realized he was attracted to young children during middle school. "I gradually realised that people would not take [my attractions to minors] well," Elias explained, "but the stress of it all got to me…this burden broke me." He developed social anxiety and ended up being homeschooled starting that year. "I became more and more reclusive from then on," he said. "I'd never had many friends, but after that it gradually dawned on me that I had to cut myself off from everyone for my own survival…now I have such bad social anxiety and depression that I'm unable to work.… I pretty much avoid getting to know anyone." Elias felt that he needed to avoid other people because if anyone found out about his attractions to minors, he would "probably be killed." His anxiety about his attractions to minors was so intense that he felt it was better for everyone if he avoided face-to-face contact with most other people.

Desmond described similar motivations for withdrawing from society. He called himself "a bit of a hermit," and said, "I am quite shy and introverted and don't have much self-esteem or self-confidence at all, so I feel very nervous and unsure of myself around adults." He wanted to avoid interacting with boys whom he might have attractions to, so he avoided going out in public as much as he could. Unlike Elias, Desmond did leave his house regularly to go to work, but he kept his interactions outside his home as limited as possible.

While Jeremy did not withdraw from all of society, he did withdraw from his own social circles in order to cope. He moved overseas for several months when he was first dealing with his attractions. He explained that he was in a "really, really bad place" emotionally, when he received the opportunity to leave his country on a work trip. "So I took that to get away from life here," Jeremy told me. "It was really bad. I think doing that, being able to get away from everything for a while, really gave me the space to just forget about all that stuff going on and just enjoy life and rest a bit. I think that helped a lot." For Jeremy, this form of withdrawal was positive. He credited being able to leave and have a distraction from his thoughts about his attractions to minors with allowing him to gain some perspective.

Bryan coped with his attractions through withdrawal of a different sort. He talked to me about "retreating" from reality in order to escape his life. He explained:

> I think it may be a specific trait of many (not all) MAPs, but specifically those who have fantasies relating to becoming children again. Their basic coping skills are poor, so they retreat into a fantasy world that is easier to take than the adult world.... [retreating is] constantly in the back of my mind, but it comes to the forefront in times of greater stress. But this typically involves retreating into video games, movies, or other media that some people would consider possibly juvenile, or focusing on such things that were popular at the time that I was younger. This is what I consider "retreating." I'm not referring to an extreme of wearing non-age-appropriate clothing, acting a specific way in public, or something like that. You would say, well, there are adults that do that all the time. The difference, I think (not that I can read minds), is this is an active wish on my part to go back to that. It's not possible. I logically know that. Emotionally is another matter.

Bryan said that his method of withdrawal was through distraction via video games or movies that were popular during his youth in the 1980s, such as through playing Atari games or watching movies like *The NeverEnding Story*. Bryan seemed embarrassed by this coping strategy: he referred to it as a strategy used by MAPs whose "coping skills are poor" and used third-person pronouns to describe this, distancing himself from this strategy even though he was describing a coping skill he actively engaged in. Nonetheless, Bryan felt that it helped him in times of greater stress.

Engagement Coping Strategies

These strategies allow the individual to actively think and work through a given stressor. As opposed to disengagement coping strategies, which research often shows are ineffective or even harmful, research has indicated that many engagement coping strategies can result in positive outcomes for an individual's wellbeing. Next I explore several different engagement coping strategies that commonly emerged throughout my participants' narratives.

Community involvement. Of the 42 participants in this study, 25 of them specifically mentioned seeking out other MAPs who were committed to non-offending. All but two successfully found community via online forums. Websites used to find a community with other MAPs included B4U-ACT and VirPed as well as BoyChat, GirlChat, Visions of Alice, a subreddit called pedofriends (which was shut down in November 2016), and Tumblr (which in 2018 began banning content created by MAPs to support one another), among others. VirPed was by far the most frequently used website among participants. My participants saw speaking to other MAPs as a way to gain peer support. Gaining support from other MAPs was regarded as beneficial in many ways. Tyler reported that he had realized he was attracted to minors ten years prior to discovering VirPed, but when he did find it (about five months prior to the interview), he finally began coming to terms with his attractions. Tyler shared that he had known there were others who were attracted to children, but not individuals who were committed to refraining from acting on these attractions.

This was a common theme in interviews; upon realization of their attractions, individuals felt like the lone "good" MAP among thousands of sex offenders, but finding a community with other MAPs committed to non-offending made them feel more "normal." For most, joining an online community of MAPs was their first exposure to individuals who understood their situations and struggles. For many, it was the first evidence of the existence of other individuals who shared both their attractions and their belief that sexual activity between an adult and a child would be harmful to the child. For Vincent, finding online support meant not only finding a community but also getting in touch with a sense of self-pride:

> Before I found [VirPed], I felt very alone in this. I thought that pedophiles were only, like, middle-aged, creepy men that hurt kids, and I didn't feel like I belonged with any sort of group. Um, but now that I've got involved, it just feels great to be involved in a community. It kind of reaffirmed my identity, almost...and it's a community that I'm proud of, too. Like, a stance that they've taken and you know, the strength that it takes to kind of stand up and talk about this and try to change the way people think. I'm proud to be a part of that.

These communities were also the first platform where many participants felt safe when discussing their attractions. For instance, Dominick told me that before finding B4U-ACT, the information he saw about people who were attracted to minors was fueled by hatred: "I spend a lot of time online, so I've run across a lot of fear-mongering and hatred from all sorts of different people. I keep my attractions to myself, so all the hate has been directed towards other people, but I do still feel it in sweeping generalizations and sentences like 'Pedophiles should kill themselves for the betterment of society.'" Although Dominick had told some of his friends that he was a MAP, he felt uncomfortable talking about the subject with them regularly, but he still wanted to talk about it with someone. Dominick had been on the B4U-ACT website daily for the past six months when we spoke. When he found B4U-ACT's website, it was the first place he could be himself without having to worry about people's responses. "I like being able to connect with other MAPs in a setting [that's] free of hate," he told me, "and where I can say what I feel without fear of getting insulted."

While support from other MAPs was often regarded as integral to the ability to cope with their attractions, participants relied less on online communities over time. For instance, Mitchell described his process, which he believed was shared among MAPs who are coming to terms with their attractions. First, MAPs discover online communities and become actively involved for a period of time; for Mitchell, this period lasted a year or two. Next, MAPs make friends with some of their online peers. As a result, they rely less on the strangers in the forums and more on the friendships that they developed. Nine study participants revealed that they had met with other MAPs in person, sometimes finding others who lived close to them, and other times traveling across their countries, or even internationally, to meet with their peers.

Although finding a community among MAPs was generally regarded as beneficial, some participants underlined certain difficulties in seeking out such support. As a small community with members who have varied life experiences, respondents noted that it was at times difficult to find people who shared their views on key issues. Additionally, a minority of participants reported that the knowledge that there existed other individuals with similar attractions was initially difficult to deal with. Hugo explained that his discovery of VirPed led to depression, because finding a group of others like him compelled him to confront his sexuality. In his own words, this is "when it hit me even harder." Nonetheless, Hugo credited VirPed for his growing self-acceptance, after an initial period to process everything.

Seeking out information. Somewhat related to becoming involved with MAP-specific communities was my participants' strategy of seeking out more information about MAPs in general. Information-seeking has been noted as a common strategy among those attempting to cope with stigma.[21] As discussed previously, prior to becoming aware of their sexuality, most participants had never considered the existence of MAPs who did not act on their attractions. As with the general population, most prior exposure to individuals attracted to minors had been in the form of news stories of child molesters, who were usually referred to (correctly or not) as pedophiles. As West explained, he grew up "without any role models at all," though he clarified, "any decent role models at all." It is therefore unsurprising that participants found it beneficial to find positive representations of individuals like themselves in the media, upon realizing that they were minor-attracted.

Many participants brought up Todd Nickerson, who had written an article for the website *Salon* titled "I'm a pedophile, not a monster." *Salon* has since removed the article after experiencing pushback, although pieces of it are available via a critique from conservative news website *The Blaze*.[22] Nickerson's article was noteworthy due his lack of anonymity (Todd Nickerson is his real name) and its publication on a popular website. Eight of my participants made reference to "Todd" (in a familiar way, using his first name only) and his article during interviews. They admired him for his courage in speaking to the media; those who had met or spoken with Nickerson personally were proud to point this out. One participant, Tyler, shared that reading Nickerson's article was more helpful and made him feel more supported than anything else up until that point (though he had been unaware of forums for non-offending MAPs). Upon reading the article, Tyler identified with the author: "I was like, 'Oh, God. This guy's like me! Aah!'" His exclamation is particularly demonstrative of the rarity of MAPs encountering examples of anyone resembling themselves.

My participants discussed other positive representations of MAPs in the media. Mitchell found role models helpful because it indicated shifting opinions about individuals with attractions to minors. He referred to a Czech film, *Daniel's World*, about a MAP who had not acted on his attractions. In another case, Robin found it helpful to read the works of authors Christopher Isherwood and Allen Ginsberg, who were both known to engage in relationships with much younger men. Robin argued that reading accounts of these individuals gave him a different understanding about people like himself, because "these were men whose intellects I respected, who had, like, a vibrant, rich, complex understanding of the world and their place in it. And who were obviously attracted to younger men and, like, even like wrote about it, or spoke about it." Robin noted that being able to read their accounts was "normalizing" to him. Participants also said that they were able to find examples of others like them in other members of B4U-ACT and VirPed. These individuals also served as role models, albeit of a less publicized variety.

Obtaining support from friends and family. Although the individuals in participants' lives who did not share their attractions could generally not offer the type of understanding received from other MAPs, support from these individuals was nonetheless helpful. Accessing support was a main theme of Chapter 2, and thus I cover it briefly here. Of my 42 study participants, 17 spoke about the importance of getting support from individuals involved in their lives who were aware of their attractions, such as friends, family, and other acquaintances. Receiving support from these individuals made respondents feel more "normal," or at the very least, more accepted. Participants also reported that receiving the trust of others who knew about their attractions was helpful. Mitchell described the process of coming out to his pastor: "He didn't see me differently, that there's something wrong with me and that I'm dangerous and should stay away from kids, as if I'm going to somehow pounce or something. That was very supportive, and the fact that he could just talk to me and I could be open with him about my feelings and thoughts and frustrations, just to have somebody to talk to." Mitchell remarked that his pastor's support meant more to him than the support of other MAPs, because MAPs "know what it's like already" and their support is thus automatic, whereas his pastor's support revealed that he trusted Mitchell as a person.

Participants spoke of the fear of being regarded as unlovable, being disowned, or even being physically harmed by friends and family when coming out to them. It is not surprising that finding support from non-MAP friends and family was an incredible relief. Felix told me he had times when he was full of "depression, anxiety, fear, [and] spiritual desolation." He said that in these moments he had sometimes become suicidal: "I sometimes feel like I'm stuck with this [with my attractions to minors]. There's nothing I can do, and it's never going to go away, so what's the purpose of continuing if all my life is going to be is just being someone who's hated and scorned, and where I can't speak out and change things?" Felix explained that the only thing that has helped him in these moments was support from friends. "If I was absolutely alone," he said, "if I had no one to talk to or describe my life, feelings, experiences, past and present, to identify with—if I'm absolutely utterly desolate of social contact with people [to whom] I can express myself, it's worse." This was also the case for others who received support from family and friends. The support they received helped them confront the stigma to which they felt subjected by others. As Robin put it, it was important to have "the whole me being seen by other people."

Activism. Another common engagement strategy developed by participants to cope with their attractions was to engage in activities that could help others like them. Respondents described engaging in various forms of activism. These included supporting other MAPs by posting in forums, sending messages of support to those in crisis, and volunteering for online forums in various capacities. Six participants acted in official capacities with B4U-ACT and VirPed, as chat or forum moderators or administrators or in other roles. In another case, Isaac was not an official volunteer in any forum but shared with other MAPs a list of therapists in various countries, which had been deemed by many as helpful in seeking out therapy. Participants from VirPed were often referred to Isaac for help. He even spoke with other MAPs on the phone to provide one-on-one peer support. Others expressed the desire to help as well. For instance, Jeremy and Vincent both intended on starting in-person support groups for MAPs. They believed that meeting and talking in person would be helpful not only to them but to others.

For some participants, the mere act of coming out felt like a form of activism in and of itself. For instance, Quentin took pride in coming out to others; in his own words, coming out was an important "way forward with my group to bring about social acceptance of that sexuality." Other participants discussed educating the public, online or in person. Hugo and Tyler both engaged in online discussions with "trolls" who wrote hateful messages about MAPs on Twitter or YouTube. Hugo recalled finding this activity to be cathartic at first but feeling triggered by such conversations later, which led him to stop reading such comments in general. Tyler, however, continued engaging with "trolls," finding that he was able to make connections to those who wrote such messages and potentially change their viewpoints.

Social work research has long noted the usefulness of helping others in similar situations. Psychiatrist Frank Riessman's[23] helper therapy principle theorized that individuals who can help those facing issues related to their own can benefit from this role. Peer supporters in mental health settings often experience increased confidence, benefits to their self-esteem, feelings of empowerment, and a reported increase in ability to cope.[24] In addition, the resilience literature shows that many LGBT individuals identify activism as a strategy for emotional resilience because it leads to an increased feeling of having control over one's circumstances.[25]

Dating adults. Engaging in romantic relationships with adults was another coping strategy employed by many of my participants. Those who were nonexclusive MAPs were more frequently involved in relationships with adults; however, even those who were exclusively attracted to minors were sometimes engaged in relationships with adults in an attempt to deal with loneliness. Those who felt attractions to adults in addition to attractions to minors considered themselves to be privileged for being nonexclusive. Quentin reported that the time he had had with his wife was the happiest of his life. He had felt "normal" when he was perceived to be a heterosexual teleiophile, enjoying a romantic relationship and raising children.

Partners who were aware of participants' sexuality were often a major source of support. In one case, Kevin revealed his attractions to minors to his wife before they were married. Although she was shocked, she was also supportive. He described her as "probably the best thing that has happened to me because she's helped me…come to terms with [my attractions]." Another participant, Victor, got engaged during the course of this study, between his first and second interviews, to a woman who was aware of his attractions to children. He confessed to her about feeling depressed about his attractions, and she linked him to her therapist for mental health care. He credited his fiancée (and her therapist) with his mental wellbeing at the time of his interview. Participants' partners could be instrumental in showing them trust. Charlotte was shown a high degree of support by her boyfriend, who was a pedophile himself and who was a father of children who split their time between their home and the children's mother's. While living with her partner's children made Charlotte nervous, her boyfriend told her he had full trust in her, which helped her to feel trust in herself.

In some cases, dating an adult could be seen as a disengagement strategy as well as an engagement strategy—while relationships with adults could help engage with and solve potential loneliness, they facilitated disengagement with stigma by employing secrecy. Some of my participants, such as Quentin and Harper, felt compelled to hide their attractions from their partners, which they both felt was for the best. Shawn, however, had reservations about keeping his sexuality from his wife, who had a son. Although he was not worried about committing an offense, Shawn worried about feeling awkward when her son reached his age of attraction. In addition, some participants were left by their partners upon coming out to them. Brooke's girlfriend panicked when Brooke told her about her attractions and talked about wanting to "fix" her. When they broke up, she outed Brooke to many of their formerly mutual friends. Klaus's girlfriend reported him to the police when he disclosed his attractions to her. He did not intend to tell any romantic partners in the future.

Multiple participants who were nonexclusive nonetheless felt that they could not pursue relationships with adults. They would feel compelled to lie to their partners about their sexualities and felt that it would be disrespectful to a partner to pretend to be someone else. Zach argued that society applauds MAPs who choose to be in adult relationships despite their attractions to children, regardless of the fact that it can hurt the partner. Relatedly, Klaus felt that it would be "insulting" to be in a relationship with someone to whom he was not fully attracted, adding, "it's like telling her that she's undesirable." Kevin's situation illustrates Klaus's concern: although Kevin's wife provided him with support, he added, "I know it is something she struggles with. She feels inadequate, I guess." Most individuals in this study who dated adults were nonexclusive. For the MAPs in my study who identified as being exclusive, they generally felt that dating an adult would suggest that their entire relationship would be based on lies. Nonetheless, participants often encouraged other MAPs who were exclusive to initiate relationships with adults, if only for the emotional support.

Religious involvement. Perhaps ironically, given strong stances in many religious communities against pedophilia, religion brought great comfort to some individuals. Religion was not a focal point of my interviews, but many of my participants brought it up in relation to stigma and coping. Hugo, who is a Mormon, credited his religion with getting him through his initial realization that he was attracted to boys. Chapter 1 details Hugo's realization of his attraction to minors: he had noticed that he was attracted to a 12-year-old boy in an airport and had a moment of understanding about a previous pattern of attractions. Although upon his initial comprehension of his sexuality, Hugo felt suicidal, his religion played a role: "But then...I'm religious so I felt like God was like, 'It's okay, you can do this. I'll take care of you.'...So I feel like that's the only thing that pulled me through."

Xavier felt similarly comforted by his religious beliefs, maintaining that his attractions were part of God's plan. Although he indicated being interested in getting married and having children, he embraced the idea that if God meant for him to be married, it would happen. Two participants were provided help and guidance through the Christian Pedophile website, which provides religious support to those who struggle with attractions to minors. While seven participants noted feeling comforted by their religious beliefs, or by others within their faith, in contrast, six experienced added shame because of their religion. William traced his feelings of guilt regarding his attractions back to his religious convictions. "There's a bit in the Bible where Jesus says being attracted to someone is as bad as having sex with them," he said, "so for a while I guess I felt like I was as bad as the child molesters I heard about in the news." Similarly, Kevin, who was raised as a Seventh-Day Adventist, recalled believing that his attractions must mean that he was possessed. He finally left his church for unrelated reasons and stated that doing so made him feel dramatically better about his sexuality.

For some participants, feelings about religion were complex. Mitchell described a disconnect between religions' purported belief systems and the behaviors of their members, which resulted in him feeling bitter about his faith. He attended a Unitarian Universalist church and although members espoused a belief in diversity, he believed that he would likely still be rejected if others in his church were aware about his attractions. Strand and Harper also detailed complex relationships between their religion and their sexuality. Strand's belief in Christianity brought him guilt over his attractions to minors, but (somewhat ironically) this guilt made him feel connected to others in his church. Strand explained the following regarding his view of Christians: "Christians have this whole... belief system. They feel very guilty for having any sort of thoughts. And their view is it's all sins so you're going to go to hell. So, how am I any different than you?...So, they already feel incredibly guilty about having the problem themselves with thoughts, so they're willing to support you." Harper also felt guilt that was exacerbated by her religious beliefs, but she noted that her religion brought her a general sense of support throughout her life, even though it did not provide support specifically regarding her attractions. Nonetheless, she felt that her religion had a positive impact on her overall.

Curiously, slightly more participants described their faith as a source of comfort than a source of shame. However, these mixed results seem to mirror research regarding LGBT individuals: while studies have found a connection between nonaffirming religiosity (i.e., participation in a religion that promotes antigay sentiment) and internalized homophobia,[26] studies that do not distinguish between affirming and nonaffirming religions have failed to show such a link.[27] Indeed, research has found that religion can give LGBT individuals a sense of meaning and purpose, despite homophobic teachings.[28] My participants' discussions of religion reflected a similar impact of religion for many MAPs.

Self-acceptance. While the majority of my participants' engagement coping strategies focused on engaging with external factors, by speaking to others about their attractions or looking up information online, a final strategy that emerged in my data was working internally on self-acceptance. Many of my participants described attempting to manage their own self-talk and to value themselves. Josh, Mitchell, and Klaus spoke of their determination not to let others define their self-worth. Rather, they focused on their own opinions of themselves and their belief that they were good people. Some participants spoke about allowing themselves to feel pleasure regarding their attractions as a way of coping. These participants were steadfast in stating that although they did not believe acting on their attractions would be in any way appropriate, they did not find the attractions themselves to be problematic. As a result, they allowed themselves to enjoy these attractions in the same way that teleiophiles might enjoy thinking about individuals to whom they are attracted, without acting upon the attractions. However, these attempts were often impeded by guilt or shame. Robin explained:

> I'm trying to get more in tune with it; just enjoying being attracted to minors. Like, if I see a boy on the street and I'm attracted to him...I'm intentionally allowing myself to appreciate that experience...and enjoy that experience and not immediately shame myself, or stigmatize myself, or judge the experience that I'm having, which is pleasurable... I'm trying to enjoy the pleasure in that. Um, and then of course, like, the sort of apparatus of self-judgment kicks in. Uh, which I'm dismantling, but it reassembles quite quickly....And it can be quite cruel and harsh. Um, so, my self-talk is pretty vicious, and I am trying to keep it in check.

Like Robin, Mitchell expressed that in order to accept himself and achieve some semblance of mental health, he needed to "embrace [his] sexuality" and allow himself to find "beauty" in it. However, also like Robin, Mitchell felt some discomfort with this, particularly in light of societal reactions to the idea of MAPs embracing their sexuality. Mitchell expressed frustration with these reactions, noting: "Self-acceptance, though, is a double-edged sword, because then it has meant embrace of my sexuality, and it has meant that I'm now an enemy of society. [Laughter] Because most of society sees the acceptance of this sexuality as something that's horribly evil and destructive. And that includes the mental health system. They still would say that I have cognitive distortions for accepting my sexuality." Both Mitchell and Robin exemplify a struggle many MAPs face: that of managing competing goals of self-acceptance and societal acceptance. In this case, societal acceptance is predicated on a lack of self-acceptance. While accepting oneself is generally considered to be healthy, accepting oneself when one is attracted to minors is considered to be unacceptable, and both Mitchell and Robin described feeling shame because of this conflict.

Despite these feelings of shame, some participants were able to avoid feeling badly about their attractions. Dominick felt social pressure to tell others that he felt guilty about his sexuality upon coming out. In reality, however, he felt comfortable with his attractions and felt that he was at no risk of offending, clarifying that although he found boys attractive, he had no interest in engaging in sexual activities with them. Similarly, Gene did not express shame regarding his attractions. However, he was also explicit in stating that he did not embrace them, that he was "not proud of it," but that it was "my cross to bear, and I bear it the best way possible, whereas when I was much younger, there was more shame about it. But, y'know, I just learned to accept it, even if I don't like it. I'm accepting." He was troubled when others accused him of embracing his sexuality, to which he would respond: "No. I'm not embracing it. I'm not celebrating it." For most of the MAPs in my study, the very idea of celebrating their sexuality would be unthinkable.

ACCESS TO ENGAGEMENT

As seen throughout this chapter, MAPs struggle with a number of stigma-related stressors, including facing rejection from society and, as a result, facing internalized stigma. They also experience loneliness—especially those who are exclusively attracted to minors, as they will never experience an attraction to someone they could plausibly be in a relationship with. Research has shown that stigma-related stressors can result in a decrease in wellbeing; however, the coping strategies used by a stigmatized individual can mediate the effects of these stressors. Coping strategies used by the MAPs in my study included disengagement coping styles (such as denial and wishful thinking, secrecy and selective disclosure, drug use, and withdrawal) and engagement coping styles (including becoming involved in communities of MAPs, seeking out information about MAPs, seeking support from friends and family, engagement with activism, involvement with religion, dating adults, and working internally toward self-acceptance).

My participants' narratives showed nuance in their uses of these different coping strategies. For example, while participants who kept their attractions to minors a secret from their friends and family often craved potential acceptance and support that they may otherwise have received from them, participants also recognized the inherent risk in coming out to them. While participants sometimes used substances that they recognized were unhealthy, they sometimes did so to alleviate persistent, negative thoughts about themselves brought on by internalized stigma. Furthermore, engagement coping strategies sometimes had negative consequences: coming out to loved ones to ask for support sometimes backfired, leading to rejection; seeking community involvement could be difficult for individuals who did not fit the typical (cisgender, male, hebephile) mold of community members, leaving them feeling less accepted.

My participants may also differ in terms of the ability to access certain coping styles—particularly, to access engagement coping strategies. For instance, those who felt less confident that their loved ones would accept them may not have beeen able to seek support from family and friends. Those who felt more internalized stigma may have felt less inclined to seek out communities of other MAPs—after all, if they believed that MAPs were immoral, why would they want to seek out others? This may leave certain groups of MAPs able only to access disengagement coping strategies. Lack of access to engagement coping skills can be problematic for a number of reasons. Prior research has suggested that engagement coping strategies can effect more positive change than disengagement strategies, which are often associated with harmful outcomes for wellbeing over the long run. Disengagement coping strategies have been linked to increased psychological distress as well as physical health issues such as hypertension.[29] In addition, psychologist Michael Seto[30] has described alcohol use by MAPs as a particular concern for sexual offending against children: drinking lowers inhibitions, and when MAPs who are at risk of committing a sexual offense use alcohol, this can introduce further risk. While none of my participants may have been at risk of offending enough for this to apply to them, it may be of concern for others who lack access to coping strategies that may allow them to engage with the stressors of life as a MAP.

Strategies for coping emotionally with attractions to minors are not the only strategies I have explored in my interviews with MAPs. An as-yet unexplored topic in this book is how MAPs strategize not to commit sexual offenses against minors, given their attractions to them. Some of these strategies, such as reaching out for community support and the support of others, overlapped with their emotional coping strategies. The next chapter explores these strategies among study participants.

4. "It's a Very Strong Boundary for Me"
Resilience to Sexual Offending among MAPs

Xavier realized he was minor-attracted when he was only 14 years old. It was a secret he hid from his family and friends with "disgust [and] a lot of guilt." Despite recognizing his attractions at a relatively young age, Xavier had never spoken out loud about his attractions to children until our interview, which took place when he was 20. He told me that he couldn't tell anyone he knew personally about his attractions because "that would destroy my life." So when his much-younger sister began having playdates with children her age around him, Xavier didn't have anyone in his personal life to talk to about his concerns. He told me with embarrassment about his feelings toward one of his sister's friends. "I know it sounds stupid," he said, "but I kind of fell in love with her. Even though she's so young."

One day those years ago, Xavier found out his sister's friend would be at his grandmother's house, unsupervised, at the same time that he would be there. Feeling like he could not trust himself to behave appropriately around her, Xavier reached out to the only person he felt he *could* trust: "Michel," the founder of a website he had recently discovered called Christian Pedophile. The website's current description reads: "We are Christians who also happen to be pedophiles. We have an unwanted and involuntary attraction to children, but we have decided to obey Christ and not act according to those feelings.... We are God's kids, too, and we know that he loves us."[1] Although Xavier had identified as an atheist for most of his life, the Christian Pedophile website struck a chord with him and gave him a ray of hope. He reached out to Michel through the website, who became a confidant Xavier could talk to about not only his attractions but also about other difficulties he faced, such as drug addiction and suicidal thoughts. When Xavier became concerned about his potential behavior toward his sister's friend, he emailed Michel to say, chillingly, "this girl is coming over tomorrow, and I'm pretty much dead set on doing something to her."

Despite this alarming choice of words, Xavier explained to me: "I never want to hurt a kid. I was looking for any reason at all to not do it." But having few people to talk to, Xavier felt desperate—unconfident that he could rise above the temptation he felt toward committing an offense without receiving some sort of support. Fortunately, Michel was able to give Xavier the reasons for not offending that he was seeking. "He was able to talk me out of it, to tell me that [offending] was not alright." Michel reminded Xavier that acting on his attractions would "ruin" the life of his sister's friend as well as his own. On the day that his sister's friend came over, Xavier recounted: "My stepmom was gone: she was in her bedroom doing something. This little girl was just playing in the living room. And I looked at her, and this feeling came over me: 'You cannot do this.' So I just got up and left." He attributed his ability to leave the situation to the support Michel had given him, and was immensely grateful for it. The support Xavier received "made me realize nothing's worth throwing my future and a kid's future away." Because of help from Michel—another pedophile—a child's wellbeing and bodily autonomy were protected, and so was Xavier's future.

.   .   .

The MAPs in my study had managed to remain resilient to sexual offending against children throughout their lives. Nonetheless, the ability to remain resilient was, for many participants, fraught with struggle. One of the reasons that it's so difficult for the general public to comprehend the existence of MAPs who don't offend is because they have difficulty believing anyone could manage accepting that they will never have a fulfilling sex life or romantic relationships. For non-offending MAPs, especially those who are exclusively attracted to children, this is exactly what they must work at accepting. This would be a challenge for anyone, but combined with a societal consensus that individuals who are attracted to children must either be offenders or likely to offend in the future, it's easy to understand how MAPs would face difficulties in remaining resilient to offending.

Although scholarship and practice within the field of criminology frequently focus on the strategies and turning points of prior offenders who have *desisted* from criminal activity,[2] comparatively little research focuses on the behaviors of individuals who have remained *resilient* to offending.[3] And perhaps this is for good reason. Focusing on the prevention of offending among individuals who have never committed a crime could entail shifting policy and practice objectives from an emphasis on meeting individuals' needs toward an emphasis on surveilling those with criminogenic risk factors, effectively criminalizing non-offending populations.[4] As MAPs are already heavily stigmatized, the process of documenting their strategies for non-offending may read as a call to regard this population with further suspicion. It is therefore important to stress that I focus on resilience to offending among MAPs as a way to illuminate the *strengths* that MAPs possess, and the ways in which they consciously harness these strengths, rather than to suggest a means of protecting the general population from a group of individuals deserving of suspicion.

It has been previously reported that, just as Xavier received help from Michel, MAPs use their relationships with peers who also have attractions to minors as support to help themselves remain resilient to offending. Journalist Luke Malone explained that MAPs may form informal self-help groups online in order to support and encourage each other in efforts to avoid offending.[5] One website that enables MAPs to provide such peer support is the aforementioned Virtuous Pedophiles (also known as VirPed), an online community for self-identified pedophiles who believe that sex with children is wrong and who wish to give and receive support related to their attractions.[6] B4U-ACT, an advocacy organization run out of Baltimore that encourages mental health care providers to understand MAP-related issues and deliver affirming services, also provides online forums where MAPs can offer support and advice to each other.[7]

When I began my research about MAPs, I knew I'd be interviewing people who had remained resilient to offending throughout their lives. At the same time, I had no idea what motivated the people I was speaking with to avoid offending, nor how they managed to do so. Did they use the strategies focused on by other researchers, or use other strategies? Why did they choose to resist offending in the first place? This chapter explores MAPs' reasons for abstaining from offending as well as the strategies they have used to remain resilient to committing offenses.

MOTIVATIONS FOR NOT OFFENDING

I found navigating many of the questions I'd chosen to ask my research participants to be somewhat awkward, but perhaps no other questions were as awkward as the following: "Can you tell me what motivates you to avoid acting on your attractions? Specifically, what motivates you to avoid engaging in sexual behavior with children?" I dreaded the moment in each of my 42 interviews when I asked these questions. It was embarrassing to ask someone why they wouldn't want to do something that I would hope no one would ever want to do. Asking them those questions made me feel like I was suspicious of them, or like I assumed they were immoral. Nonetheless, we haven't known the answers to these questions, because no one has asked them. As the answers could have direct implications for the ability of MAPs to remain resilient to offending, I leaned into the awkwardness and asked the questions.

"The Easiest Motivation on This Planet": Not Wanting to Cause Harm

What I found out about MAPs' motivations for non-offending made me very aware of how much I, too, had internalized about media portrayals of MAPs. Our collective lack of knowledge about this topic is so pronounced that I was wildly off in my assumptions about why the MAPs I spoke with resisted committing offenses. Coming from a background in criminal justice research, I assumed most of my participants would tell me that the reason they didn't act on their attractions was because they didn't want to go to prison. For a minority of the people in my study, this *was* their answer. However, the majority of respondents felt the same way as Xavier: they did not want to harm a child, and they felt acting on their attractions would cause a child a great deal of harm. Nearly three-quarters of my participants believed that acting on their attractions would cause harm to a child, and told me this was their main reason for not doing so. When I asked Mason why he chose not to act on his attractions, he replied: "It's the easiest motivation on this planet. I do not want to hurt anyone. I'm incapable of hurting people, especially a child." Mason identified as a celibate pedophile, and he was emphatic that "anyone who could [commit an act of child sexual abuse] is pure evil." To him, the idea of acting on his attractions was repugnant and unconscionable.

The MAPs in my study anticipated my surprised reaction to their answers to this question. They were aware of the common viewpoint that all individuals who share their attractions are child molesters or are otherwise morally corrupt. They were therefore understandably interested in conveying to me that their moral values were not driven by their sexuality. My participants drew connections between their own moral principles and those of teleiophiles (individuals who are attracted to adults).

To this effect, Mitchell commented: "There are times that I'm definitely…extremely attracted to certain boys, but the idea of actually saying something to him about it, or asking if he's interested, is just certainly bad enough, let alone actually trying to force or pressure somebody. And that, I guess, would be true even if I were attracted to adults. I would certainly not force myself on anybody, so it's essentially the same thing, I think, that prevents people who are attracted to adults from raping." Mitchell was frustrated by the societal perception that MAPs were likely to offend based entirely off of their attractions. Robin similarly explained:

> I don't struggle with urges to act on anything. It's like it's…I mean, the way that I think about it is that, there are adult men who are attracted to adult women, that are alone with adult women, but they don't like fondle, or touch, or inappropriately sexually abuse. I mean certainly that does happen, but like most times, in most people, in most circumstances that's not an issue. And like, I have like self-control and I will and I can have a private sexual fantasy [or] erotic attraction, and that doesn't mean I'm going to have a behavior, so, for me, it's very clear.

Robin's comment echoed Mitchell's. Just as most teleiophiles would not force themselves on another adult just because they may be attracted to one, they explained, MAPs' attractions to minors did not mean that they were likely to commit an offense.

MAPs' own memories of childhood helped them to empathize with children, contributing to their moral viewpoints about acting on their attractions. "I know I can picture myself," Mason explained, "go back in time and be a child for a second, and I know that would be the very last thing I would ever want, to have a man tou-touch me in a sexual manner. And there's no way on this Earth I would ever do that." Mason was so unsettled by the idea of experiencing—or causing—such trauma that just speaking about the possibility caused him to stutter. William similarly understood, from his own experience, what offending would mean to a child. He disclosed during our interview that he had been raped in the past, adding that knowing what it was like for him to go through such trauma, he could never put someone else through similar pain. "My attractions have a massive emotional component to them," William said, "so I want to be a good thing in the lives of any kids I come into contact with." Clearly, for William, sexually touching a child would be the polar opposite of a "good thing" in a child's life.

Like William, other MAPs in my study identified their attractions to children as the source of their empathy: they felt that their strong romantic and emotional attachments to children led to their motivation to resist acting out on their sexual desires. For example, Hugo detailed: "I like boys so much that like I really wouldn't ever want to hurt them....I realize that if someone were to molest them...they would have a lot of shit to go through." While Hugo had sexual attractions to boys, he also had strong emotional attractions to them. In addition, he had faced the death of his mother when he was a child, and he remembered this experience as particularly traumatic. Having experienced his own trauma in childhood, Hugo said, "I wouldn't want to put someone else through that [a traumatic experience]." Similarly, Klaus's motivation stemmed from not wanting to betray the trust of a child. He explained:

> Do you remember the first time in your life when a child looked at you and saw an adult, and not another child? That was really intimidating the first time that happened to me....When you meet a child, when you come [face to face] with a child and you have to have some kind of relationship with that child...they really trust you. They trust you and maybe, also, they love you. Then, at the same time, you have a feeling that the adult that this child is going to become is with you and is asking you, "What are you doing with me?" And I think that experience is what motivates me to not do anything inappropriate.

Klaus, along with many others, recognized that committing an offense against a child would negatively affect that child's entire life, into adulthood. He did not want to be the cause of any harm or suffering to children, nor for children to think badly of him, now or later in life.

"Anti-contact" versus "pro-choice." Despite a general agreement that sexual contact between adults and children would cause harm, my respondents differed in their reasoning behind this thinking. While most participants fantasized about having romantic or sexual relationships with minors, they were adamant that these fantasies were strictly about engaging in *consensual* romantic and/or sexual relationships. None of the MAPs I spoke with expressed a desire to engage in coercive relationships or forceful sexual activity. Many of my participants understood their fantasies of consensual relationships between adults and minors were unrealistic due to ethical considerations regarding child development. These individuals believed societal taboos and laws against sexual contact between adults and minors served the best interests of children, as children lack adequately developed mental faculties to consent. Individuals who agree with this idea often label themselves as *anti-contact*, because of their belief that sexual contact between adults and minors would cause harm in and of itself.

Anti-contact individuals were opposed to the reverse position, which they often referred to as *pro-contact*. When I asked them about this label during interviews, those who were referred to as pro-contact by anti-contact MAPs pushed back against being labeled as such, preferring the term *pro-choice*. Pro-choice individuals believed some minors have the emotional capacity to consent to sex with adults, lacking only the legal capacity to do so as a result of the current social climate. Pro-choice participants provided multiple explanations for their reasoning, often based in academic discourse. They pointed to differences in age-of-consent laws by state and nation, to illustrate that the idea of a definitive age at which an individual can consent is socially constructed. Some also discussed known points in world history when sexual activity between adults and children was tolerated, accepted, or regarded as mutually beneficial.

Four participants (Brooke, Felix, Neil, and Zach) discussed their belief that age-of-consent laws were a form of ageism, a way of denying agency to youth. To Neil, these laws promoted the shaming of minors for their sexuality. "I believe that a better society is possible," he said, "and that in such a society there would be no shame around sex. To believe otherwise would mean to believe that children discovering their sexuality...will always grow up being ashamed." During interviews, pro-choice participants frequently referred to academic works that they interpreted as favorable toward sexual activity between adults and minors. They cited sources by name that they considered to be justifying their position.[8] Other participants argued that they had heard stories from individuals who had experienced positive sexual encounters with adults as youth.

Despite the fact that anti-contact and pro-choice individuals both felt harm would come to minors who engaged in sexual activity with adults, anti-contact participants were highly critical of the pro-choice point of view, arguing this belief was self-serving. William told me that he had taken the pro-choice view when he was an adolescent, but now, years later, he has categorized his view as "rape is bad"—a sarcastic and overly simplistic phrase he used strategically to point out what he saw as nonsense in the pro-choice line of reasoning. Vincent went so far as to say that people who labeled themselves as pro-choice had "a delusion," explaining that they wrongly interpreted children's curiosity about sex as "expressing an interest" in sexual activity with an adult.

Some anti-contact participants, namely George and Harper, took a more moderate view, arguing there *could* be positive romantic or sexual relationships between adults and children, but this possibility was so remote that it was not worth exploring. George put the likelihood of such a positive relationship at "one in a million." Harper explained further:

> I'm anti-contact; I don't think minors can consent to sex....I don't want to invalidate other people's experiences, I'm not going to say every episode of contact between a minor and a nonminor is necessarily harmful to the minor, because we have people saying, you know, "I had a relationship with an adult when I was a minor and I don't feel I was harmed by it."...And if that's your experience, that's cool. So, I'm not gonna say every contact is harmful. But I *am* gonna say that in any situation where contact is possible, the probability of harm is high enough that it negates any possible benefit....And that's why I would never offend, because even with the chance of not causing harm, you're not going to do good, number one. Number two, the chance that you would cause harm is, like, 99%....So, no, I'm anti-contact.

Even in acknowledging the existence of stories of positive relationships that pro-choice participants referred to, Harper recognized that these stories were few and far between. Harper felt most minors could not consent to sexual activity from a developmental standpoint, so the possibility of not causing harm to a minor in such a scenario was so "negligible" that it "should be ignored."

Even pro-choice participants frequently admitted this philosophy served their own interests, and some wondered aloud whether they would adopt this perspective if it were not favorable to them. For instance, Lucas, who frequented "pro-contact" forums online, supported lowering age-of-consent laws, and told me he could "envision a healthy sexual relationship between an adult and child," but like Harper, Lucas felt too many unlikely conditions would have to be met for such a relationship to be possible. He noted that this viewpoint should be "greeted skeptically due to the self-interest involved." He had so many conflicting thoughts about this issue that he divulged he had "been going back and forth in my head a lot."

Despite confusion about the ethics of a pro-choice point of view, Lucas detailed how thinking about children as being able to consent could be dangerous. He told me he felt sexual contact between adults and minors should be legal if the contact were initiated by a child, but added, "I think...I could end up seeing girls' actions as sexual interest in me despite them not being so. My self-interest wants them to be into me." So he, like Vincent, felt if age-of-consent laws were lowered, as many pro-choice MAPs have advocated for, it could be easy for MAPs to misread a situation, believe that a child was trying to initiate sexual activity, and end up harming a child, even if such harm were unintentional.

It's important to reiterate that even my participants who espoused pro-choice views frequently pointed to harm to minors as their primary motivation for not acting on their attractions. While they believed consensual sexual activity between adults and minors was possible, these individuals, like my anti-contact participants, also felt sexual contact between adults and minors would undoubtedly cause harm to minors. While this motivation for not offending was therefore similar between the two groups, their reasoning behind *why* offending would be harmful differed. Pro-choice MAPs argued that society takes away the choice for minors to engage in sexual activity with adults, and the harm caused as a result of hypothetically consensual participation in such activity would be a result of a society that is intolerant of such acts. These participants frequently felt minors could be developmentally able to consent to sexual activity, but that they would not be able to handle the societal consequences that would result.

Bryan explained he was motivated not to act on his attractions because of "the possibility of doing emotional harm to someone I care deeply about…not the relationship, but the ensuing reaction by society to the perception of the relationship." Zach referred to this as "sociogenic harm"—in other words, harm caused by social forces. He felt if he had a "consensual" relationship with a minor that became public, the minor "would be forced into therapy, where they would be told…I didn't really care about them, which would be a lie." He was further concerned that a minor in such a scenario would "receive so much attack and criticism, telling them, 'you're sick.'" In addition, Elias believed consensual relationships between adults and minors were possible but would need to be kept secret. He determined that the stress generated for a child as a result of keeping a hypothetical relationship secret, combined with the risk that the child would later feel ashamed of such a relationship, was too great to consider acting on his attractions. Aiden conceptualized this type of harm in a different way, saying that he believed "loving relationship[s]" were possible between adults and minors, but if they were found out, harm would come to the minor from "the arrest [of the adult] and the aftermath…look at how much it would shatter the family dynamics, you know, like, with the child and his parents and his siblings. Just how much pain it can cause."

Anti-contact participants felt the pro-choice point of view was harmful, and indeed pro-choice logic fails to account for developmental differences between children and adults that make young people unable to consent to sexual activity. Nonetheless, the pro-choice view about "sociogenic harm" has been harnessed by both pro-choice and anti-contact MAPs to convince pro-choice MAPs against committing an offense. Aiden pointed to his own empathy as preventing him from acting on his attractions—despite believing that sexual relationships could be possible between adults and minors, he said, "I feel too much for [boys]" to commit an offense that would have harmful aftermath. He felt that other pro-choice MAPs could be encouraged to tap into their own empathy toward children to keep them from offending as well. Because pro-choice MAPs believe minors may developmentally be able to consent to sex with an adult, the knowledge that minors would be subjected to other types of harm as a result of sexual contact is more convincing to them. However, for many pro-choice participants, because they believed children could potentially consent to sex with an adult, their reasons for not acting on their attractions were mixed between a desire not to harm as well as legal motivations.

"I'm Damn Straight Afraid of the Law!" Fear of Punishment

The second-most highly mentioned motivation against offending raised by participants was related to legal or other social ramifications. The threat of sanctions was a deterrent for more than one-third of my participants, who feared arrest or prison time, and noted that this concern was substantial enough that it prevented them from sexual offending. Isaac reported that although legal consequences were "least on the list" of his motivations against acting on his attractions, they were nonetheless relevant: "I don't want to get into trouble. I don't want to go to jail. I don't want to be looked down on by society." Others indicated that the stigma that would accompany sexual offending was sufficient motivation to refrain from doing so. For example, although Aiden struggled with the morality of acting on his attractions because he was unsure whether minors would be able to consent to sexual activity, he nonetheless said he would feel guilty about offending because of societal pressure.

Despite listing legal and societal issues as motivators against offending, most participants mentioned it secondarily to their motive against harming children. It is therefore conceivable that many of my participants did not need the threat of criminal sanctions to deter them from offending. The only individuals who told me they were *primarily* motivated by legal or social reasons were those who were attracted to older minors whom they believed could emotionally consent to sex. Robin, for example, was motivated not to cause harm to minors. He explained:

I think actually what really motivates me is that…It's important to me that anybody that I have contact with in my life, certainly relational contact, romantic contact, sexual, physical contact, that it's a consensual experience….So that's like a foundational framework for any sex that I have…And I'm incredibly aware of the capital-T Trauma that people have experienced in terms of sexual abuse that they've undergone in their lives.…And that's horrifying and enraging and I have no interest in having anything to do with that whatsoever, so I have a pretty, like, clear, bright line.

Robin was clearly against causing any harm to a minor and therefore was committed to engaging only in consensual sex. At the same time, he held a firm belief that current laws about the age of consent were in some cases unrealistic: "I personally think that, like, most sixteen-year olds are capable of consensual sex.…And I'm aware that age of consent laws are different in different states and in different countries. And if the age of consent were lowered, I would have sex with younger people in my jurisdiction tomorrow, um, or I would seek out sex, because it would be legal.…But I'm not interested in having sex with prepubescent boys, 'cause I really don't think that they can have, can grant sexual consent."

Because Robin felt that older minors were developmentally ready to consent to sex, he did not feel that engaging in a consensual sexual relationship with an older minor would create a harmful situation. Instead, he indicated that when it came to older adolescents, the law was his primary motivation against engaging in sexual activity with them. When asked about his motivations to avoid acting on his attractions, Robin responded: "Well, I'm scared to death I'll go to jail forever and rot in prison. So, there's a deterrent effect.…I have my own moral compass, and then the law is pretty clear. So, I follow the law." Despite the fact that according to his own set of morals, it would be acceptable for him to engage in sexual activity with older adolescents, he indicated that legal limits superseded his own beliefs about age-of-consent laws, therefore effectively preventing him from engaging in sexual activity with minors. The threat of legal sanction was too great. Similarly, Zach, who was primarily attracted to adolescents, said, "I admit! I'm damn straight afraid of the law! Hell, yeah!" He clarified:

First of all, I don't think this is selfish. I think this is common sense. I don't want to go to jail for that reason, okay, because I would be thrown in with, with vicious, I mean, psychopaths and murderers and armed robbers, who don't care a thing about other people, and who will actually think they're morally superior to me! And, and consider me the "lowest of the low," as they call it. Okay? And I don't want to end up in civil commitment the rest of my life. I don't want to end up on a, on a scarlet-letter list [sex offender registry], as I like to call it, which is public shaming, and, and everything. I, I don't want that to happen.

Zach also worried about harm that could come to a minor if he had a sexual relationship with one, but legal issues were evidently a concern for him. The threat of punishment for engaging in sexual activity with a minor therefore kept him from committing an offense. In addition, he saw himself as a moral individual, and the idea of becoming incarcerated and having other inmates look down on him was outrageous to him.

As Zach indicated, participants were aware that punishments for sexually offending against children were especially punitive. Within the United States, punishment for sex offenders, at federal and state levels, can include lifelong sex offender registration and lengthy prison sentences.[9] Civil commitment laws can allow federal or state agencies to determine an offender to be "sexually violent" (with the evidentiary standard being "clear and convincing," a standard less than "beyond a reasonable doubt"), resulting in involuntary, indefinite commitment to a state or federal facility after the offender has served their sentence.[10] Isaac spoke with apprehension about civil commitment laws in his interview, referring to the Minnesota Sex Offender Program: "They say this is not a prison, this is a therapy. But out in Minnesota nobody ever got out of that therapy."[11] MAPs are also aware of opinions of sex offenders in correctional settings. "Prison can be a nightmare," Noah mentioned, "especially for sex offenders."[12] However, as was the case for Zach, Isaac and Noah both felt that their main reason for not offending was out of concern for the welfare of children.

"I Don't Want To Be That Guy": Other Motivations

Participants underlined additional motivations for refraining from acting on their attractions. Religion played a role for some. Isaac told me his religious convictions were a key motivation of his for not offending. Similarly, Xavier said acting on his attractions would be an "act against God." The MAPs in my study also recognized that committing an offense would affect not only their own lives and the lives of a hypothetical victim, but also the lives of those close to them. To that end, study respondents detailed that they did not want to cause harm to their own family members or to the family members of minors. Aiden and others made reference to empathizing with the families of minors, who would themselves experience a great deal of trauma if they committed an offense against a child. In addition, Hugo and Tony said their own families were their main motivation for remaining resilient to offending, because of the shame that offending would bring on their parents.

Finally, MAPs grow up in a society that villainizes sex offenders to an extreme degree. Participants spoke about seeing sex offenders in the news from as long ago as their childhoods, and they did not want be like "those people," whom they often saw as immoral and dangerous. West put it in simple terms: "It's not the sort of person that I am." Gene stated: "It's just, I don't want to be that guy. . . and I told myself, when I was 14, 15 years old, when I was first going through this: I'm not going to let this make me be a child molester. It's just, I'm not. I'm not ever. I'm never gonna be that guy." Erik used the same wording: "I don't want to be that guy"—that is, a sex offender.

As illustrated by these quotes, participants commonly *othered* MAPs who have offended, categorizing themselves as fundamentally different from sex offenders who may share their attractions. This technique of othering offenders has been previously identified by criminologist Cathy Murray as a shared trait among individuals who remain resilient to offending.[13] By making offenders into "that guy," as Gene and Erik explicitly did, they set themselves apart from those who committed such crimes. Despite their strong motivations to refrain from offending, some participants encountered challenges in remaining resilient. The following section explores these challenges as well as strategies developed to counter these hurdles.

STRATEGIES FOR RESILIENCE TO OFFENDING

In interviews I asked participants about the behaviors that they employed to resist committing sexual offenses against minors, which we spoke about at length. Strategies included seeking support from family, friends, other MAPs, or additional acquaintances, interacting with children in positive ways, limiting their interactions with children, and others. Although these strategies may help MAPs not to offend, the consequences of participants' use of these strategies were complex, sometimes resulting in unhealthy outcomes.

"I Made That Choice": Not Feeling at Risk

Before I explore the strategies participants used for remaining resilient to offending, it should be noted that more than three-quarters of my sample did not feel they were at risk of acting on their attractions. To that end, these individuals did not feel they needed to develop strategies to keep themselves from offending. Just as Mitchell indicated that his motivation for refraining from offending was the same as those of individuals attracted to adults, other participants also argued that their impulse control was no different than that of teleiophiles.

When I asked Brooke if there had ever been a specific time when she did something to avoid acting on her attractions, she told me no, adding that there was no need for her to apply any sort of strategy, because she was not at risk of acting out. To illustrate why she found strategies for non-offending unnecessary, Brooke, who is attracted to both minor and adult females, recalled a time when her adult female friend (who is heterosexual) got drunk and made sexual advances toward her. Brooke declined her friend's advances, assuming if they had a sexual encounter, her friend would later regret it. "It was a situation where I might have, or could have, acted on attraction, but didn't," she told me, "because the explicitly stated arrangement was *not* acting on that attraction [a platonic friendship]....It was kind of awkward, but it wasn't any difficulty to not act on that." Brooke knew her friend did not have the capability to consent to sex while she was drunk, and Brooke had no interest in taking advantage of a drunk friend, even though she found her friend attractive. She applied the same reasoning to her choice not to act on her attractions to children—she simply had no interest in taking advantage of someone who could not consent to sex and therefore did not feel at risk.

Aiden also felt he needed no strategies to prevent himself from committing a contact offense against a child. He regarded the idea that he might commit such an offense as ridiculous. "I made that choice," he said. "Like, it's not like I'm going to slip and [accidentally molest] a kid....It's something that I choose not to do and it's a very strong boundary for me....I just feel like I would kill myself before I acted on it, you know?" Charlotte similarly scoffed at the idea that her attractions made her dangerous, telling me, "we don't have these inner demons that are constantly pushing us to rape, or whatever. And it's, it's an anxiety, it's not an actual threat....Our existence doesn't threaten your children."

Because most of my participants did not feel at risk of acting on their attractions, they were often unable to identify strategies that they specifically used to abstain from offending. Instead, these participants frequently framed such strategies in different terms, and said they engaged in certain behaviors because otherwise they would feel uncomfortable. For instance, West and others had a personal policy of not thinking in romantic or sexual terms about minors whom they knew personally—not because they were afraid of offending if they did, but because they thought that would be disrespectful. Other participants framed their strategies in terms of avoiding behaving in ways that could be *construed* as inappropriate. For example, some participants refused to hug any minors—even those whom they were not attracted to—because if people knew they were minor-attracted, hugging any minor might be seen as suspicious. However, even some who felt that they were not at risk said they consciously used behaviors to stop themselves from acting on their attractions. Below, I review the various strategies that participants used to avoid acting on their attractions as well as the consequences of these strategies.

Limiting Interactions with Children

My participants often found that limiting their interactions with children in some way was an effective strategy for not offending, as well as a strategy for avoiding situations that would generally make them or others feel awkward. Of my respondents, 15 explained that they avoided being alone with children, either because they were concerned that they would feel tempted to act out if they were alone with a child or because being alone with a child would make them feel uncomfortable. Others said that they would recommend avoiding interactions with children altogether to MAPs who were feeling at risk of offending.

In their own lives, participants limited their interactions with children in various ways. Several avoided public places where minors in the age range for which they held attractions were likely to go, including malls, parks, public pools, or playgrounds. For some, this meant limiting in-person interactions with people overall; many participants discussed feeling uncomfortable in public places where they regularly needed to go, such as the grocery store. Strand even explained that he avoided services at his church, because he knew children would be present. Desmond indicated that he was reclusive in general, avoiding any location in which he might see a boy:

DESMOND: I try to avoid boys as much as possible precisely because I don't want to end up in that situation [of acting on my attractions]. In general, if I see a boy, I will usually end up checking him out and then I'll mentally berate myself for doing it.

AW: Oh, so you try to even avoid seeing boys? Does that get complicated?

DESMOND: Yeah, hence the hermit lifestyle.

Desmond took his "hermit lifestyle" to an extreme, moving to a remote island and rarely leaving his home, except to go to work. He clarified that avoiding boys was not the only reason for this lifestyle, but that it was a big contributing factor.

Some of my participants even went so far as to change career paths to ensure they would not be tempted to act on their attractions. For instance, as a teenager, Bryan had wanted to be an English teacher, but he decided that teaching boys was a bad idea for him. Although he was uncertain whether he would have committed a sexual offense had he gone into teaching ("I can't tell you for certain that I would've attempted to act," he told me), given that he was unsure whether he would have been able to resist the temptation to commit an offense, Bryan decided teaching was not something he could safely do. Nonetheless, he felt bitter about his decision not to become a teacher. He was unhappy with his current career path and felt that if he could have trusted himself to behave responsibly around children, he would have been an excellent teacher because of his desire to be a good mentor.

Some participants were able to make distinctions between situations in which they would be safe around children and those in which they would not, and therefore limited their interactions based upon the situation. West described his thought process in deciding whether to interact with minors. When he first realized he was minor-attracted, he felt unsure whether he would be safe around children:

WEST: When I was a teenager I was [asked] to babysit a younger boy that I was attracted to, and just to remove myself from a position where I might be even tempted to do something, I had declined that, figuring that it's better not even to go there. I wasn't quite as confident as I am today that I wasn't going to do anything.

AW: So if you were asked the same question today, do you think you would accept?

WEST: Um, probably not. But that's just because of the point I am in my life. I don't have a lot of time for such things. If I did [have the time]...I would probably ask myself how I would feel about it....And sort of try to figure out my motivation for doing it and if I wouldn't care, then, yeah, I'd probably go ahead and do it. If that would make any sort of difference at all to me then I would say that it's probably not the healthiest thing and say no.

In other words, West's litmus test for whether it would be appropriate for him to interact with a minor was to check in with himself about his motivations for doing so. If his motivations were based around a particular interest he had in spending time with specific child, he felt that that would be inappropriate. Otherwise, he trusted himself to be around the child.

Although many participants found that limiting their contact with children was helpful, or even necessary, they often found that this led to awkward situations. Some revealed feeling very self-conscious around children, concerned that looking at them at all may be regarded as "staring." One participant, Raymond, stated when he initially became aware of his attractions, he spent months refusing to look at children at all. This was not a helpful strategy; rather, it led to feelings of sadness and frustration for him and made him stand out in a crowd.

Notably, not all individuals who avoided interactions with children did so because they felt they would be tempted to offend. Some were merely concerned about coming off as "creepy" or being unsure about where a line should be drawn, given their attractions. For example, Lee described being at a family gathering and not knowing whether it was appropriate for him to greet his eight-year-old niece with a hug. For him, avoiding children was not simply about abstaining from offending but also about not being obvious about his attractions. "Think back to high school or childhood when you were in the same room with a crush of yours," he said. "[It's] that kind of awkward. [I] keep some distance because otherwise it's embarrassing."

The MAPs I spoke with exhibited conflicting emotions about the choice to limit their interactions with children. Along with some other participants, Quinten felt resentful about this choice because it precluded him from activities that he felt would be otherwise natural for adults to engage in with children, such as roughhousing with his son's friends or hugging a child. Others felt, perhaps due in part to the strong bonds they felt with children, they would make excellent mentors for them and felt a loss at being unable to fulfill that role due to their attractions. Desmond summarized this succinctly: "I specifically try to avoid boys because of the conflict they cause inside, and it sucks because I really wish I could help boys somehow!" Despite feeling resentful of this (self-) imposed distance with children, participants who chose to limit their interactions with minors generally agreed this was for the best for both children and themselves.

Support from MAPs

Many of my participants reported that seeking support from other MAPs was a helpful strategy in remaining resilient to offending. The MAPs I spoke with generally sought support from other MAPs using the websites B4U-ACT and VirPed as well as a few others, such as Christian Pedophile, BoyChat, GirlChat, Visions of Alice, and subtopics on websites like PsychForums, Reddit, and even Tumblr. Although all of these websites have been used by my participants to connect to other MAPs, most respondents used VirPed and B4U-ACT, which explicitly discourage MAPs from acting on their attractions and are therefore more targeted toward offering support around non-offending than some other websites.

Those participants who used the VirPed and B4U-ACT forums were generally very willing to offer advice about strategies to avoid offending and to remind each other why they should not act on their attractions. Gene stated that the mere fact of belonging to VirPed was helpful to him because it was a community of individuals who supported each other and who believed acting on their attractions was wrong. Relatedly, Hugo had a crush on a teenage boy and was able to talk to other MAPs on VirPed about it. They validated his feelings and agreed that the situation was tough but ultimately reminded him that he could not act on it. "It was still hard, because there's not really a good answer to that where you're all warm and fuzzy or whatever," Hugo said, but he added that it was good to get that type of "tough love" from individuals who understood his situation.

Two participants credited the support they had received from other MAPs with keeping them from offending in situations in which they felt tempted to the point of being uncertain that they would not offend. One of these was Xavier, whose experience I described at the beginning of this chapter. He was convinced not to commit an offense when he reached out for support to the founder of the Christian Pedophile website. Isaac also described a situation in which he was worried about acting on his attractions. He had gone on vacation on a small island where he saw children "running around naked" in public. Isaac immediately went online to seek help from others who would understand: "It was a bit of a challenge for me. The only thing that helped me was VirPed and B4U-ACT; having the moral support. Everybody says, 'You can do it, [Isaac]!'" By this, they meant that he could refrain from offending. Later in our conversation, Isaac relayed to me: "I think that it takes very little to help a...pedophile who's seeking to be virtuous to not offend. It just takes a little bit of encouragement."[14]

Despite the support many participants encountered on these websites, others didn't find sites like VirPed and B4U-ACT to be a welcoming space. Brooke told me that she would "honestly love to find community," but she referred to VirPed as a "sausage fest," noting that as a trans woman, it was hard for her to find a sense of belonging on the website, which was dominated by cisgender men.[15] In addition, MAPs on these websites often found they had less in common with individuals who did not share their attractions toward the same age range or gender. They sometimes felt stigmatized by those who were attracted to older youths as well as hostility toward individuals who were attracted to younger children. West, for example, noted that although he had been active on VirPed for years, he felt for the majority of his time posting on the website that he had to hide his attractions to very-young children from other members. His age of attraction was from about 3 to 13 years old, but for a long time he claimed that he was only attracted to those in the 7- to 13-year-old range. He mentioned that some members of VirPed were "very nonaccepting of that aspect of my sexuality" when he finally admitted to his actual age of attractions.

Tyler illustratively noted that his attractions began at age eight, and he was made extremely uncomfortable by those who were attracted to children who were much younger. "I'm sympathetic to other people who think like I do," he said, "but then when I meet somebody who's [attracted to very young children]...I'm like [gagging noise], my gag reflex is stimulated. Like, 'Oh, that's gross.'" While the irony of being judgmental about those attracted to younger people than he was not lost on Tyler, he nonetheless had a hard time accepting those with a much lower age of attraction than his. These types of divisiveness encountered from others in the MAP community sometimes led my participants to seek support elsewhere.

Support from Others

Almost one-fifth of my participants told me that getting support from others who were not minor-attracted, such as friends and family, helped them abstain from offending. This support was often in the form of simply being nearby if they were in the presence of a child. Cody used the term "accountability agents" for individuals on whom MAPs can rely to remain in their presence if they are going to be around children. He reported that MAPs often divulge their attractions to someone with whom they are close and use them as an accountability agent if they feel tempted to act inappropriately. Several of my participants used this method. Aiden had come out to his parents, which he found helpful when his nephew visited during the holidays. Knowing that his parents were present was valuable to him, because he would not have the opportunity to act on his attractions if he were surrounded by other people. Isaac said that the fact that his wife was aware of his attractions was useful for the same reasons.

Although my participants often came out to the individuals they chose to use as accountability agents, many MAPs do not have the option to come out to others (as explored in the Chapter 2). Nonetheless, some participants were able to ensure that there were other adults present in any room in which they may encounter a child. Hugo, for example, volunteered as a teacher of eight- and nine-year-olds at his church's Sunday school. He was not out to others at his church about his attractions. However, his church had a policy that there had to be two adults in a room at any given time in which a child was present, so Hugo was able to feel confident about his ability to maintain appropriate behavior at all times. He told me about one occasion in which "it was looking like it was just going to be just me and this one boy who was super attractive" in his Sunday school class, which made him apprehensive. Fortunately, moments later several other children and his co-teacher arrived, but Hugo told me that if they had not, he was prepared to ask another adult to be in the room with him: the church's policy of requiring multiple teachers in the room would have allowed him to request such assistance without putting him in danger of outing himself.

In addition to being able to use accountability agents as a physical barrier to prevent offending, the MAPs in my study indicated that having the emotional support of others was just as important. Strand spoke to his pastor and two other individuals at his church for related support, which he identified as helpful to resist offending. Aiden recounted the first person whom he had come out to, who was somewhat of a mother figure for him. He said she convinced him that acting on his attractions would be wrong. He listened to her because she was supportive of him in many other ways. My participants told me that if they offended, it would hurt others in their lives, and sometimes the threat of shame from others was in itself a strategy. Tony was out about his attractions to his mother, whom he identified as a strong source of support for him. If he offended, he told me, "it [would] destroy my relationship with my mother. That's real important to me, right there."

Interacting with Minors

In contrast to the viewpoint that limiting interactions with minors was the best strategy to avoid acting on attractions, some study participants felt being around children actually helped them to refrain from offending. Charlotte noted that MAPs often have romanticized ideas about children that are not realistic. She explained that MAPs' attractions motivate them not to see children as "human beings" but instead as "characters." Being around children helped some participants avoid idealizing their younger counterparts and instead to view them as individuals. While Aiden used to strategically avoid places with children, he regarded that strategy as being more harmful than beneficial:

> It could be having a negative effect for me to do that. It kind of like makes them, puts them on a pedestal, where it makes them this kind of icon. You know, by me avoiding them it gives them this kind of mysterious power....Like, one of the things about having my nephew is I kind of got to know him. You know, once you get to know him, it kind of personalizes them...and you kind of see what boys are really like instead of making them this like iconic, you know, imaginary character of my fantasies, my fantasy ideal. It removes them from the ideal and makes them actual people, it actualizes them.

By restricting contact with children, Aiden felt more able to fantasize about them, which he believed made him forget that they are people who would not *want* to have sexual contact with him. In interacting with his nephew, Aiden was able to see him as a unique individual with his own interests. It also helped Aiden to understand that "you just can't really be equals [with a child] because the level of understanding is so different. Like, the cognitive abilities are so different."

Erik agreed that interacting with children kept him from having unrealistic ideas about them. He volunteered as a youth group leader and said that in his head he felt children were more his equals than adults. This was especially due to his hobbies, which included playing video games and watching movies from his childhood. Erik explained:

> [Children] feel like my peers in a way. They feel like they are the people, um, that I most relate to. And most of all [being a youth leader is] a constant reminder that children are not this idyllic, wonderful creature of fantasy. They can have tantrums. They can be annoying. They can not listen. They can not do what I need them to do during an event or what have you. And it's a constant reminder they're real people...and it's a constant reminder that, this is what you would destroy if I was to act on what I was feeling....So, yeah. It's, it's really just the reminder that these are actual people who grow into adults, and you don't want to ruin, or I don't want to ruin those lives.

Erik found his youth group experience to be invaluable to him because it helped him to see that young people are not his equals, nor are they developmentally ready for sexual experiences. It helped him view children as individuals, which decreased his fantasies about them.

Similarly to Erik's experience, Phillip worked in a professional capacity with fourth and fifth graders. Although he disagreed that interacting with children limited fantasies about them (he was clear that he did have fantasies), he believed his interactions reinforced for him the line between appropriate and inappropriate behavior with children. When I asked Phillip whether he had done anything specific to avoid acting on his attractions, he responded:

> No, because I mean, I've never really felt like—I've never really felt like I had to avoid something....Like I said, I work with kids the age that I'm [attracted to] and the idea of doing something is not okay. So I feel completely comfortable in myself with the way that I deal with things, that I'm okay with it....Maybe some people are not like I am. And I understand that. But for me, actually having contact with kids that age, it reminds me that they are human, they are people and it's not fucking okay. You know, for me, it's a huge reminder....You know, i-i-i- it's not okay to act on my feelings, obviously, but I think that...I just, like, need to keep doing what I'm doing, basically, in order for me to be okay. Maybe if I didn't have interaction with kids, maybe I'd feel differently or have different feelings. I don't know. I mean, like, thankfully I have a daily interaction, and it makes things very fucking silver clear to me, you know.

Increasing contact with children as a way to prevent sexual offending against them may appear counterintuitive to many. Indeed, considering the approach used by some MAPs to limit their interactions with children, strategizing to interact with minors may seem reckless. Even those who engaged in this strategy noted that its appropriateness would vary from person to person. Erik, who justified his own interactions with minors, said that he could understand why some individuals would not want MAPs to work with children. He added that he wouldn't necessarily recommend interacting with children as a strategy to others because if he didn't know them, he couldn't trust them not to offend. Although he knew himself and was confident that he would never abuse a child, Erik did not have that same confidence in others. Erik mentioned that in a poll on VirPed asking whether its members would let a pedophile look after their own children, "most of the responses were no."

There were key differences between those who strategized to reduce exchanges with minors and those who strategically spent time with them. Individuals who avoided children in some way generally expressed feeling uncomfortable around them. Those who spent time with minors commonly did so over an extended period of time (such as Erik's youth group experience or Phillip's work with children). This may have helped them to learn appropriate boundaries, a concept that other participants struggled with (such as Raymond, who did not know whether or in what contexts looking at children was appropriate, or Lee, who struggled with whether hugging his eight-year-old niece at a party would be crossing the line). Importantly, those who strategically interacted with minors also described themselves as more comfortable around children to begin with. It is therefore unlikely that such a strategy would be appropriate for individuals who felt uneasy around children.

Using Child Pornography

Use of child pornography was a complicated topic in my study, as it is both a strategy MAPs may employ to resist committing offenses against children as well as a (potential) offense itself. Of my participants, 12 disclosed past use of child pornography in interviews, although it should be noted at the outset that this did not necessarily mean using pornography that involved actual children. Those who used it reported multifaceted beliefs regarding the ethics and legality involved, which I explore below.

It may be difficult to think of the use of child pornography as a strategy to prevent offending. After all, viewing or possessing child pornography is often a crime in and of itself,[16] and when real children are involved in the production of child pornography, viewing these materials incentivizes child sexual abuse. In addition, it is commonly argued that there is a "slippery slope" between the use of child pornography and person offending—that is, that individuals who view child pornography are likely to later commit contact offenses against children. However, these arguments regarding a link between watching child pornography and committing contact offenses are based on unverified claims. The likelihood of later offending by individuals with child pornography convictions was unstudied prior to research conducted by psychologists Michael Seto and Angela Eke, who found that just 4% of individuals with child pornography offenses committed person offenses during the follow-up period of 2.5 years.[17] Subsequent contact offending was even less likely among those whose offense histories only involved child pornography offenses. A follow-up study using the same sample found that 6% of those who had been convicted of a child pornography offense later engaged in a contact offense when the follow-up period was extended to 5.9 years.[18] Furthermore, of those in the study with no criminal history aside from the child pornography offense, only 1.3% were later convicted of a contact offense.

Prior research has explored child pornography as a potential strategy for MAPs to maintain abstinence from sexual contact with children. In their analysis of case studies of people who view child pornography, criminologist Max Taylor and psychologist Ethel Quayle suggested that these individuals may partly attempt to do so as a form of therapy, "as a way of controlling their interests," "as a form of personal survival," or as "a way of dealing with emotions such as anger that had no other outlet."[19] Similarly, in a critique of the ways in which sex offense prevention is currently conceptualized, sociologist Janis Wolak and colleagues theorized that the use of child pornography could inhibit child sexual abuse as it could "serve as a substitute" for individuals who may be "predisposed" to committing a contact offense.[20] In this way the use of child pornography may be seen as a harm reduction approach, as long as it is *simulated.* Clearly, harm is done to real children abused in pornography, and no ethical policy suggestion could possibly argue for its production or distribution for "therapeutic" value of adults. However, harm may be avoided if the pornography in question is drawn or digital, or uses young-looking adult actors.

To that end, not all of my participants who told me that they had used child pornography were referring to sexual images of real children. Half of those participants who indicated viewing child pornography had viewed photos of clothed or nude children that were not intended to be sexually suggestive (such as stills from mainstream movies or pictures in magazines), or drawn or computer-generated images of children, such as *lolicon* (Japanese-style drawn images of girls, in a suggestive or overtly sexual style, named after the Nabokov novel *Lolita*) and *shotacon* (similarly drawn images of boys). *Lolicon* and *shotacon* exist in a legal gray zone in the United States. In 2002 the US Supreme Court struck down a 1996 law banning virtual child pornography that was distinguishable from actual child pornography, on the basis of protecting free speech.[21] Despite this ruling, federal obscenity laws still ban the production, distribution, and possession of "visual representations...that appear to depict minors engaged in sexually explicit conduct and are deemed obscene,"[22] and the Supreme Court declined to hear the case of a man prosecuted under these obscenity laws in 2005.[23] United States–based study participants alternately referred to such images as legal and illegal, indicating confusion, while others referred to its explicit legality in Japan and explicit illegality in Canada.

Several study participants believed that using child pornography was a strategy that helped them remain resilient to sexual offending. Aiden, who was in recovery for an addiction to pornography and who proudly spoke to me about being five months clean, believed that his prior use of child pornography had aided him in refraining from offending against children. He was exclusively attracted to minors, having no attractions to adults, and felt he had few opportunities for experiencing sexual release in a way that felt satisfying. He argued that viewing child pornography provided him with an outlet to engage in fantasies without involving the children he knew "in real life." Aiden explained:

> I would never have allowed myself to fantasize about a boy in real life, I would never fantasize about them because it feels too close to home. It feels too real, or too risky that I might act on it if I fantasize about it.... I would never fantasize, I would never, like, see a boy at a park and then like fantasize about that boy. Like, never. I've always drawn that line where that wasn't allowed. So instead, I would look at pornography. And pornography, at least, I'll get that fix, so you know, that release. And, and not feel the guilt. The guilt of wrecking someone in real life.

Of course, Aiden's statement devalues the children who were sexually abused in the videos that he watched, who are just as real as the children he might see at a park. At the same time, he felt that viewing child pornography was the lesser of two evils when compared with committing a contact offense against a child.

Aiden felt shame when he viewed child pornography, although he told me his decision to "get clean" was based on social shaming and the potential legal ramifications of viewing such materials, rather than concern for the children who were harmed by them. The distinction in perceived acceptability of unknown children experiencing harm versus causing harm to known or identifiable children illustrates a problematic tension I encountered in these interviews, one that is difficult to talk about even-handedly given the nature of this study. Hearing research participants speak about real children in the pornography they watched as though they were expendable because they did not know them in person left me feeling both upset and disturbed. While their reasoning for using this material is unjustifiable, it may have implications for abuse prevention, which is why I discuss it here. I do not do so lightly.

Floyd, who lived in Japan and had access to legal images of what he described as "child models," used this legal material as a way to keep himself from offending, as he explained during this exchange:

AW: Thinking back, has there ever been a specific time when you did something to avoid acting on your attractions?

FLOYD: Yes, I would wait until I had full solitary privacy and view legal child model material and masturbate to relieve the energy.

AW: Oh, I see. Did you find that helpful?

FLOYD: Yes. I find it useful as a regular means to manage my emotional balance.

AW: Mmhmm. And if another MAP asked you for advice because they were having difficulty avoiding acting on their attractions, what do you think you might tell them to do?

FLOYD: If in Japan, I would tell them to do the same, as there is a large range of material available for legal retail sale. If in another country, I would advise them to find something similar, that was legal and did not harm anyone. But I would caution them to find out very [specifically] what is locally regarded as legal and what is not, in order to protect themselves.

Japan outlawed child pornography (videos or images depicting children's "naked genitals, buttocks, or chest") in 2014, but depictions of *chaku ero*—or "erotically clothed" children—are considered legal throughout the country.[24]

As opposed to Aiden and Floyd's experiences, Klaus used pornography as a strategy to abstain from offending, but rather than getting a release from the material, as Aiden and Floyd alluded to, he empathized with the children involved in the pornography and used it as a reminder that acting on his attractions would be harmful to the children.

KLAUS: I think, um, I think an important reason for why people don't act on it is because they understand the consequences of it. And so, uh, the different survivors of child sexual abuse, they've done a great job in just telling their stories because it brings home to people what comes of it. I think another thing about not acting on your attractions is actually watching stuff on the internet and then just trying to identify with the child you see, and start asking the question, "What if the (pause) what did the abuser do to that child?" Like you might start to pass judgment on their abuser. I think that does a lot to stop somebody from, from, uh, offending sexually against a child.

AW: Oh, I see. What kinds of things on the internet do you mean? What kinds of things would you watch?

KLAUS: The really hard stuff.

   AW: Oh, pornography.

KLAUS: Yeah.... Just the face of the [child]. And you imagine if that child was looking at you with that face. And I think doing that as an exercise, it will make you much less likely to offend.

For Klaus, watching pornography was similar to an aversion tactic: perhaps counterintuitively, it kept him from being interested in offending against a child.

Although those who consumed child pornography (especially when depicting real children) indicated that it had been helpful to them, these participants nonetheless felt conflicted about the morality of these habits. When Klaus watched pornography, he asked himself: "'Do I provide [those who made this] with an incentive to do what they do?' It got to me at some point and I gave up looking at stuff on the internet for that reason." Aiden also expressed contradictory thoughts about the ethics of watching child pornography: "If somebody is watching a molestation video, then [society says] they should go to federal prison for many years. You know, just like not ever actually touching a boy. So I think that it's confusing, but, it seems again, I'm making this argument because I have a personal motive."

Aiden argued that individuals who watch pornography should not be punished for merely watching an immoral act, given that they had not committed the act themselves nor could they intervene on behalf of the child. Nonetheless, Aiden neglected to connect the act of watching child pornography with incentivizing the creation of it, as Klaus had done. Aiden further admitted having a personal motive (his attractions) that influenced him to think that watching child pornography was ethically ambiguous, implying that if he were not attracted to minors he may feel differently.

The distinction between viewing sexual depictions of actual children and viewing other types of images (drawn or digitally rendered images, or nonsuggestive photos of real children) was an additional aspect of ethical importance for my participants. Those who viewed only drawn or nonsuggestive images were less concerned with the morality of their behavior. Charlotte told me of *lolicon*: "I don't personally think it's immoral." Cody even referred to such images as "art." These participants did, however, find the idea of looking at sexual depictions of real children to be unethical. Hugo, for example, told me he had never looked at what he called "full-on child pornography" because of a belief that even viewing such material would result in "hurting people." Lucas referred to viewing such material as "abusive."

Aside from the ethical issues at stake, study participants discussed further adverse consequences to consuming child pornography, both emotionally and legally. For instance, Avery believed that looking at *lolicon* had an effect on his attractions, noting he thought they increased them. Similarly, upon realizing that she was minor-attracted, Charlotte felt she had brought her attractions on herself with her consumption of *lolicon* materials. Later, she concluded that the pornographic material did not cause her attractions, but for a time she described it as a "paranoia." Many participants discussed the legal consequences, worrying that the consumption of child pornography would result in incarceration, even if they only viewed pornography that was considered to be legal. Gene described an incident when federal agents came to his door due to his prior involvement in a now-defunct forum for MAPs visited by several individuals who possessed illegal child pornography. Gene's home computer was searched, and legal drawings of children were found on his hard drive. He was not ultimately charged, but as a result of this incident, he felt that viewing even legal images caused too much risk.

It may seem like laws prohibiting the use of drawn or digitally created child pornography are in the best interests of children. However, regarding the subject of simulated child pornography, in which no children are involved, let alone harmed, it is unsurprising that some of my participants would choose to view this material and that they would describe it as a strategy against offending. MAPs—especially those who are exclusively attracted to minors—have no socially acceptable sexual outlets. It may therefore be impractical for society to expect people who have attractions to minors not to seek out material that is drawn or digitally rendered. However, in jurisdictions where even drawn material is illegal, accessing this kind of material encourages secrecy, discourages help-seeking behavior where needed, and may lead to harm. Legalizing simulated pornography that does not cause harm to children would create a sexual outlet for people with no other nonharmful options, and when having a sexual outlet can prevent the sexual abuse of children, this may be a practical (if uncomfortable) solution.

BEHAVIORAL RESILIENCE, EMOTIONAL RESILIENCE

This chapter has discussed participants' motivations and strategies for remaining resilient to sexual offending against children as well as some of the consequences of these strategies. Participants were most often motivated not to offend against a child due to a strong belief that offending would harm children, and their deep desire to cause no harm. Secondarily, legal and other societal influences contributed to their motivations not to offend. While these motivations for remaining resilient to offending were fairly straightforward, participants' strategies for resilience were varied and complex, including limiting their interactions with minors, or conversely, engaging in pro-social interactions with minors; seeking support from MAPs; seeking support from others; and watching child pornography. Although many participants had specific strategies for non-offending, others did not, and argued that they needed no strategies because they were of no risk to children in the first place.

Although I've used the term "resilience" in this chapter to refer to study participants' shared ability to refrain from sexual offending against minors, this term originated within developmental psychology and social work literatures to refer to individuals' ability to cope emotionally with life stressors. It is therefore somewhat ironic that I use the term in this context, as my participants' strategies for remaining resilient to offending in some ways put them at risk of facing a number of stressors, ranging from the innocuous to the severe. For participants such as Desmond, remaining resilient to offending was accomplished at the expense of an average social life. Those who limited their interactions with children sometimes chose career paths that they found less desirable, or felt they missed out on opportunities to be a positive influence in a child's life.

Participants who sought support from family and friends had to first face the unknown risks of coming out to people who could have had intensely negative reactions (as explored in depth in Chapter 3). Even seeking support from other MAPs was accomplished with some risk, as some participants, such as West and Charlotte, faced invalidating reactions on websites such as VirPed. Despite the risks incurred by my participants in employing their various strategies to avoid offending, they generally felt these risks were worthwhile because the end result was knowing that they would not cause harm to a child.

A final as-yet unexplored avenue that my participants took in seeking not to offend was attempting to find appropriate mental health care. Not only did mental health care offer support in resilience to offending, but such services presented an opportunity to address the emotional issues that participants faced. Despite these opportunities afforded by the mental health care industry, participants were often unable to find the care they sought. The following chapter provides an exploration of MAPs' motivations for, and experiences in, seeking mental health care.

5. "Their Intention Wasn't to Help Me"

Mental Health Problems
and Care-Seeking Experiences

I heard about Quentin weeks before he reached out to me for an interview. Other research participants of mine knew of his story as a cautionary tale, and talked to me ominously about it, lamenting how easily Quentin's story could have been theirs. Early in our interview, I asked Quentin what being a MAP meant to him. He responded: "It means mainly sadness and despair, I think." Quentin had hidden his sexuality from all others as he raised a family with his wife. His two sons were eight and ten years old when his wife died of cancer, and he continued to raise them alone, as a single parent, until they reached adulthood.

Ten years after his wife's death, Quentin could no longer hide the secret of his sexuality from his sons, and he came out to them. They had an intensely negative reaction: as Quentin described, they "didn't want anything more to do with me." They distanced themselves from him and outed him to other people in his life. Devastated and feeling utterly alone, Quentin reached out to his doctor, who recommended a counselor. He took his doctor's advice and told his counselor that he was attracted to minors. His counselor informed him at the start of his second session with her that based on nothing more than his disclosure of his sexuality, which he had never acted upon, she had reported him to the police. "My whole world just disintegrated then," Quentin said, "because then I had absolutely no one to trust, no one to turn to for help."

Quentin has "limited memories" of what came next. He cannot recall leaving his counselor's office, nor the path he took from it. He remembers that "my only focus was my own death, my own demise." The strain from the rejection of his sons and his experience with the mental health provider ignited in him the desire to end his life. The next thing Quentin knew, he was "looking down on top of the cliff down below and just about to jump.... A member of the public was on a footpath and someone saw what I was going to do. And then all hell broke loose, at least one helicopter in the air and police on the ground. And [someone tackled me] and then [I was] carted off in a police car to a mental health hospital." Quentin was treated at the hospital as a result of the suicide attempt, but his experience with mental health care made him distrustful of care providers. He did not seek further services.

Quentin's experiences with mental health care were disastrous, but not inevitable. Mental health care providers can be sources of support for MAPs. Quentin's experiences contrast with Gene's. Like Quentin, Gene had reached a low point in struggling with his attractions to minors when he sought out a therapist, but that is where the similarities in their experiences with mental health care end. Gene first began to recognize that he was a pedophile when he was 14 years old and worried for about two years that he would "wind up being a child molester" and that he was "doomed to this." By the time he was 16, Gene had decided that "probably everybody else on the planet who has this attraction is a child molester and molests kids, but *I'm* not going to be." Nonetheless, his attractions to minors continued to haunt him for years, and by age 19 he described himself as "absolutely suicidal."

One night, when Gene says he was "on the verge of suicide," he called a friend and confessed, through tears, that he was attracted to minors and that he was suicidal. His friend was understanding and helped Gene find a therapist. Originally Gene hoped to "get rid of [his] pedophilia," a goal that he referred to in our interview as "naïve." But at the time his main thought was: "I need to be able to talk to somebody, or I'm going to kill myself. Like, there's no way I can deal with this on my own anymore. There's no way I can survive if I don't just talk about this. And I managed, y'know, and I didn't kill myself. So that was pretty much my only goal: get through this part of my life... alive... and I did." His therapist was unable to help Gene purge his attractions to minors, but he offered support and Gene didn't feel judged in his sessions. Gene continued seeing the therapist for a year and a half. He said: "I'm not sure if I would've made it if it wasn't for him and my sessions with him."

. . .

Previous chapters have explored various challenges faced by MAPs, including hiding their sexuality from their friends and families, facing stigma, and coping with loneliness. Participants in my study have coped with these difficulties to the best of their abilities, often alone or with limited outside support, using a range of strategies. Despite their best efforts to resolve these challenges, many respondents discussed issues that they felt warranted assistance from mental health professionals. Depression, anxiety, and suicidal ideations were common among study participants, as was fear that they would eventually commit an offense against a child. Gene credited his therapist's understanding nature and support with his ability to make it through his late adolescence, but while MAPs such as Gene found support through therapy, Quentin's therapist contributed to his decline in mental health, resulting in a suicide attempt. The rest of this chapter provides an in-depth exploration of help-seeking among MAPs, including theoretical barriers to care, my participants' reasons for seeking out and rejecting mental health care, and MAPs' experiences with providers once they have sought them out.

STRUCTURAL BARRIERS TO CARE

Mental health care providers have a long way to go in terms of providing supportive care to MAPs. Some of this is due to individual differences among providers, but much is due to a lack of structural factors that could promote help-seeking behaviors among MAPs. Such factors include a lack of education for practitioners about MAPs and the type of care that they need, the interaction between that lack of education and mandated reporting requirements for providers, and acceptance among mental health providers for sexual orientation change efforts (SOCE) as a treatment for MAPs.

Absence of Provider Education

As discussed throughout this book, the general population frequently assumes that MAPs are offenders. Even within research and theory, the term "pedophile" is often used interchangeably with "sex offender" or "child molester,"[1] indicating a lack of awareness among even highly educated individuals about the differences between these populations. This extends to mental health treatment providers—without specialized education, providers are not likely to understand that MAP clients are not necessarily sex offenders (and may never commit an offense). Without even this baseline knowledge, providers lack understanding about best practices for working with this population.

As researchers begin to understand more about MAPs, so are they beginning to look further into providers' perceptions of MAPs. Although there is a shortage of research in this area, mental health providers' understanding about MAPs and willingness to work with them has begun to be explored. Social work researchers Jill Levenson and Melissa Grady[2] examined opinions and understandings about MAPs among mental health professionals, finding that many were willing to work with the population and that a 90-minute training could help providers understand MAPs better as a population.[3] Research by psychologist Sarah Jahnke and colleagues[4] showed similar findings; most surveyed providers were willing to work with MAPs, but they often had stigmatizing viewpoints about them that were improved through participation in an educational training program. My colleagues and I have also conducted research exploring understandings regarding MAPs among students in the social services—most of whom were enrolled in an accredited master of social work program.[5] The results showed that these students, all of whom planned to work in direct practice with clients, had received no specific education about work with MAPs. The majority of the sample assumed that the term "pedophile" indicated having committed a sexual offense against a child. Given that these students were preparing to become clinical practitioners, many of whom may have minor-attracted clients in the future (whether or not their clients make such a disclosure to them), it is disconcerting that these students were uneducated about MAP-related issues.

Practitioners' Dual Commitment

Mental health care providers' lack of education about MAPs is complicated by the fact that practitioners have a dual commitment: to their clients and also to society more broadly. Practitioners' responsibility toward their clients includes protecting their wellbeing. To that end, licensing bodies for social workers, psychologists, and other mental health fields have strict confidentiality requirements for care providers, which generally stipulate that providers may not disclose what has been said in sessions with their clients to anyone else. However, there are exceptions to this condition of confidentiality. Because of their commitment to broader society, mental health providers have a "duty to warn" or "duty to protect"—in other words, a state-issued responsibility to report clients to outside individuals and/or agencies—if and when they have reasonable grounds to believe that a client poses an immediate danger to themselves or others.[67] Providers are also subject to mandated reporting guidelines issued by their state, requiring a report to child services if a client has disclosed harming a specific child.[8]

At first consideration it may seem reasonable for providers to make a report to law enforcement if a client discloses attractions to minors: after all, common judgment would suggest that if someone is attracted to minors, that person has some kind of proclivity toward offending. However, upon closer inspection of duty to protect regulations, we find that this is not the case. For example, take the statute of the state where I work and live. Virginia law states:

> A mental health service provider has a duty to take precautions to protect third parties from violent behavior or other serious harm *only* when the client has orally, in writing, or via sign language, communicated to the provider a *specific and immediate threat* to cause serious bodily injury or death *to an identified or readily identifiable person or persons*, if the provider reasonably believes, or should believe according to the standards of his profession, that the client has the intent and ability to carry out that threat *immediately or imminently.* If the third party is a child, in addition to taking precautions to protect the child from the behaviors in the above types of threats, the provider also has a duty to take precautions to protect the child if the client threatens to engage in behaviors that would constitute physical abuse or sexual abuse as defined in § 18.2-67.10. The duty to protect does not attach unless the threat has been communicated to the provider by the threatening client while the provider is engaged in his professional duties.[9]

These limitations on a practitioner's duty to protect are common among state laws—the client must make a specific threat against an identified or identifiable victim and must have the means and intent to carry out the threat imminently.

As I have argued throughout this book, MAPs do not pose a distinctive threat to children based on their attractions to minors alone. And certainly, the disclosure of attractions to minors in general does not equate to identifying a victim and demonstrating a risk of imminent harm to that victim. Therefore, duty-to-warn regulations are not sufficient justification for making a report to the police based exclusively on a client's disclosure of being a MAP. Nonetheless, states and professional bodies often protect therapists who report "in good faith."[10] In other words, even if there is no justifiable reason for a report, a mental health provider may incur no consequences for reporting MAPs based solely on their attractions. Penalties are also frequently more serious for failing to make a report than they are for making an erroneous report. Therefore, upon learning that a client is attracted to minors, mental health care providers may feel immense pressure to report the client to law enforcement.

Providers may especially feel this pressure if they have not been provided with education about the difference between attractions to minors and offending against minors. This may further account for providers' behaviors in turning participants away from care. If counselors feel that they may be liable for a client's actions, but they do not feel comfortable reporting them, refusing to provide services may be seen as a compassionate option. However, providers' responsibilities to their clients themselves should not be downplayed. Practitioners are responsible for understanding both duty-to-warn and mandated reporting guidelines so that they are not overstepping on their professional obligations toward their clients' confidentiality and wellbeing. Providers should also never turn a client away from care without offering a referral to another qualified clinician.

While little research has been completed to examine mental health providers' understandings about how duty-to-warn and mandatory reporting policies relate to practice with MAPs, my colleagues' and my study with social service students[11] did explore this issue. Most students in the sample indicated that if their client disclosed being a pedophile, they would have to report that client to the police. This attitude was not significantly affected by the amount of time students had been in their degree programs, their religion, participation in ethics classes, or whether they had specifically covered mandatory reporting requirements in their courses—it was largely consistent across the board. It is likely that students' opinions about reporting pedophiles to the police stemmed from misunderstanding the term "pedophile" to mean that their client had committed a sexual offense against a child, as most students also indicated such a belief. These results indicate that mental health providers are going into the field without the necessary education to understand that clients who disclose having attractions to minors need not necessarily be reported to the police.

Sexual Orientation Change Efforts

Sexual orientation change efforts (SOCE) are a final prominent barrier likely affecting MAPs' care-seeking. Generally associated with lesbian, gay, and bisexual (LGB) populations, SOCE are more commonly known as "conversion therapy" or "reparative therapy." These efforts are attempts by mental health professionals or members of religious groups to—as their name suggests—change another person's sexual orientation. SOCE have historically been used to supposedly "treat" unwanted attractions (including homosexuality and attractions to minors) through psychological and/or religious therapies.[12]

"Therapy" using SOCE, however, has not been found effective in changing sexual orientation.[13] Rather, SOCE has been found to lead to a range of harmful outcomes among lesbian, gay, and bisexual individuals, including depression, anxiety, suicidality, and decreased sexual functioning.[14] As a result, using SOCE as a means of "treating" homosexuality has been condemned by the American Psychological Association and was additionally condemned by the Obama administration. When these efforts are used on minors, they have been criticized as child abuse.[15] As of the end of 2019, administering SOCE on LGB minors had been made illegal in 19 states throughout the United States.[16]

Despite widespread criticism for SOCE when used on LGB individuals, however, when used on MAPs, SOCE has generally been tolerated by governmental parties and the media. Some of the techniques that continue to be employed include having MAPs inhale ammonia or submit to electric shocks while thinking of sexual fantasies in an attempt to create an aversion to their own attractions.[17] SOCE has not been shown to be any more effective on MAPs than on LGB individuals,[18] but as mental health care providers are ill-educated about MAPs, well-intentioned practitioners may continue to use similar techniques on minor-attracted clients out of a belief that they can be reoriented toward attractions to adults.

Other Barriers

In addition to those barriers to care discussed so far, which are specific to MAPs, MAPs can bump up against obstacles to treatment faced by other populations—particularly those related to individual financial and insurance issues,[19] as well as geographic access.[20] In the United States, not everyone has access to health insurance, and those who do may still owe a substantial amount of money to mental health providers for services. On top of these difficulties, quality therapists can be few and far apart, especially in rural areas. Some individuals may be able to access mental health services over the phone or online, but insurance often does not cover these services.[21]

Practitioners' lack of education about MAPs, combined with their duty to protect, mandated reporting requirements, a general absence of condemnation for SOCE for MAPs, and an inability to access counseling services outside of these MAP-specific concerns creates a climate in which

MAPs may feel unable to seek out care from providers.[22] Nevertheless, many MAPs have an interest in mental health services, whether or not they choose to seek such help. Below I explore MAPs' reasons for desiring mental health care.

MAPS' MOTIVATIONS FOR SEEKING MENTAL HEALTH CARE

Although practitioners have contributed to a variety of barriers to care, interest in care is high among MAPs. Jill Levenson and Melissa Grady found in a survey about international interest in mental health care among MAPs that 75% of 179 participants had sought help regarding their attractions from a counselor, therapist, or social worker.[23] Within this study, 36 of my 42 participants indicated feeling motivated to seek out counseling regarding their attractions to minors. My participants were interested in obtaining professional help for various reasons. While they had coped on their own with their attractions in various ways (see Chapter 3), their varied coping styles had diverging implications for their wellbeing, often leading them to seek external help. Some wanted services for mental health disorders, such as depression and anxiety, which they often felt were linked to their attractions. Others sought help to gain confidence in their ability to refrain from offending or to learn strategies to abstain from acting out. Some participants expressed an interest in ridding themselves of their attractions to children. These motivations are described below.

Mental Health Problems

Among my participants, the most common reason for being interested in professional help was experiencing mental illness. The MAPs in my study reported having a variety of mental health disorders, either at the time of their interview or at some other point since realizing their attractions. Of the study's 42 respondents, 25 (60%) reported struggling with depression, and 15 (36%) reported experiencing anxiety. While this study is not meant to be representative of all MAPs, it is still alarming that these rates are much higher than those found in the general population; in the United States, lifetime prevalence estimates of depression range from about 16% to 21%,[24] and an estimated 28.8% report experiencing an anxiety disorder over the lifetime.[25] Although I can't say whether these mental health issues were caused by my participants' attractions (directly or indirectly), or if they were merely exacerbated by them, all of the participants who expressed having mental health problems stated that they believed these problems were related, in some way, to their attractions. For example, Charlotte theorized about the origins of her depression: "It's difficult to say if my depression is caused by my sexuality, or if my sexuality is just more difficult to deal with because of my depression. And a lot of us [MAPs] are depressed, so that's just the fact of it, is a lot of us have mental illness stuff, and it's probably because we experience so much stress in our teen years. That's when most of us realize that [we're minor-attracted], and just all that cortisol is going to affect your brain development as well."

Although Charlotte felt that her mental health was generally improving, she described her moods as a "roller coaster," explaining that she had some months in which she felt great, and others where she felt depressed and hopeless. Aiden was also unsure that his depression was caused by his attractions. He said: "I just have like so much self-hatred and self-loathing and just like angst [over] all of it. I don't know how much of that is, genetic depression....I have depression amongst the family.... And how much of it is being a pedophile. It's all kind of mixed together for me." Struggling with drug addiction and unemployment, Aiden felt it was impossible to determine which issues fed into his depression the most—he referred to his life as "shit in every direction." But he felt that at the very least, the shame related to pedophilia exacerbated his symptoms of depression.

While Charlotte and Aiden were uncertain whether their attractions were at fault for their depression, Hugo directly connected his experiences with depression to his attractions. "Real depression didn't start until about like almost about a year ago now," he told me, "when I found VirPed [and] I had to confront it finally." Although Hugo began to become aware of his attractions to minors during his adolescence, he put them out of his mind until his twenties. Joining VirPed and reaching out to other MAPs made him begin to acknowledge that he was minor-attracted, and at that time he started to feel depressed. He said that he has generally felt better lately, after getting medication, but that depression still came in waves for him.

Charlotte also described one period of heightened depression that connected directly to her attractions: "[Thinking] of a time where I was particularly affected by an event, I think I'd have to point back to when intrusive arousal was going on with, uh, with my partner's kids. I don't know, there was just this fear that it was going to go on forever. And I mean, it was just like, I don't want to say that I was bed-ridden because of that event, but it certainly heightened my depression and anxiety." Charlotte was disturbed by her attractions to her adult romantic partner's four-year-old daughter, who stayed with them on weekends. She was concerned that her attractions would amplify as his daughter got older, as she felt most attracted to girls around the ages of 10 and 11. She did not feel any impulses to commit an offense against her partner's daughter, and she discussed her attractions openly with her partner, who was supportive and confident that she would never harm his child. Nonetheless, being attracted to her partner's daughter made Charlotte so anxious that she considered suicide. She and her partner eventually broke up, in part because she felt she needed to focus on her mental health.

Charlotte was not the only participant to experience thoughts of suicide. Of the 42 participants in my study, 18 (43%) told me they were either previously or presently suicidal or that they had suicidal ideations. Again, this rate was much higher than trends in the general population. Psychologist Matthew Nock and colleagues reported that 9.2% of the adult population across 17 countries had had suicidal ideations at some point in their lifetime.[26] Respondents often explained that feelings of hopelessness and anxiety regarding their attractions and stigma led to suicidal thoughts. Lee described having suicidal ideations shortly after realizing that he was attracted to minors:

> I think when I first realized my attractions...I think it was the worst depression that I've ever had in my life. I never wanted to die so badly in my life....And I couldn't really do anything. I was still working, still going to school no problem. But I still couldn't really handle myself. I was feeling sick all the time. I couldn't really focus. I felt really empty inside....Really horrible feeling. Every little thing would get to me and every comment...about pedophilia in general.

Lee recalled an incident at work in which he had complimented a photo of a young-looking coworker. His colleagues had teased him, asking him, "what, are you a pedophile or something?" The teasing set him off, and he remembered crying when he got home after work. He sought out a therapist shortly thereafter to help him cope with the stigma and feelings of anxiety and alienation.

Gene had been helped by a therapist when he was an adolescent, but had not been to therapy in about 20 years. He told me: "I still deal with a lot of depression on a suicidal level on a day-to-day basis." Gene related grimly how he was coping with his suicidal thoughts. "Emotionally, I'm, I'm, a little bit of a wreck. Y'know, I'm not exactly what you'd call a happy person. I haven't killed myself [laughs] I haven't killed myself yet, so that's good…in terms of dealing with pedophilia and dealing with it from an emotional standpoint, I kinda do what I need to do to keep myself sane too. That involves sometimes, probably too much alcohol." Gene felt he was doing his best to survive but that he was not "emotionally healthy." He expressed shame regarding his use of alcohol to cope with his emotions, and added, "I'm a basket case. I'm definitely a basket case." Gene thought about going back to therapy to deal with his suicidal thoughts but did not feel comfortable doing so.

For some of my study participants, suicidal thoughts became overwhelming. Three of my respondents made attempts to end their lives. Another four participants disclosed making serious plans to do so, but they sought help before trying to carry it out. Two participants checked themselves into a hospital to avoid carrying out their plans. Aiden recalled making the decision to die by suicide after he was kicked out of a drug treatment program. He had come out as attracted to minors, and the program asked him to leave because they were worried about liability issues—there was a daycare in the same building. He said:

> So, I tried to kill myself. I'm in an area where it snows a lot in the winter, so I guess I waited until my roommate went to sleep that night, and I got drunk and then I went outside into a snow storm just in shorts and a t-shirt and I got lost in a swamp. [Laughter]…[I lived] in the hills, you know, in a rural area and, during a snow storm I tried to freeze to death.…It was pretty serious.…I mean, it wasn't like a cry for help.…It was pretty intentional. But, after I got kind of lost and I was falling down in the snow and swamp and I got scared and I went tracing my steps back out. After about an hour, hour and half, so I was already blue, I mean, I was already getting pretty…Because, you know, I was drunk, which was the intentional part, like, in essence, [freezing is] so much faster. So. If I really wanted to do it I probably would have, should have, poured a bottle of water over my head before I went out.

Aiden decided to seek help and requested to be hospitalized for psychiatric care the next day. But incongruously, the hospital refused to admit him due to the fact that he was no longer considered to be in crisis. Although he eventually made it to therapy, several months passed before he met with a service provider.

My participants discussed a number of other mental health conditions for which they sought care. Three of my participants had been diagnosed with autism (although two of the three expressed skepticism regarding this diagnosis), two individuals had been diagnosed with bipolar disorder, one participant had been in counseling for self-harming behaviors, and one individual was diagnosed with schizophrenia. These disorders may have largely been unrelated to their attractions, although in some cases their attractions to minors could have exacerbated the effects caused by these disorders.

Desire to Avoid Acting on Attractions

Another prominent reason provided by my study participants for seeking mental health care was a need for support in remaining resilient to offending. Participants had cultivated a number of strategies against offending without the help of mental health providers (as explored in Chapter 4), sometimes alone and sometimes seeking the support of family, friends, or even other MAPs. Although these strategies were often considered useful, participants had a number of concerns surrounding resilience to offending that they believed could be addressed with professional counseling. These included impulses to watch child pornography and fears that they may commit contact offenses against children. Some of my respondents were merely looking for validation that they were capable of remaining resilient to offending and wanted to hear from a professional that they did not pose a threat to others.

As detailed in Chapter 4, some of the individuals in my study viewed child pornography to cope with loneliness, for sexual release, or as a strategy to abstain from committing a person offense. Despite this strategy, many of those who viewed child pornography had dual feelings about it, expressing guilt or confusion about the ethics of the act—particularly those who watched pornography involving actual children (as opposed to drawn/electronically rendered images). Those who used illegal pornography also worried about the potential legal ramifications. Often, study participants who had used child pornography in the past had sought help to stop using it, and some needed assistance beyond what was provided by other MAPs online.

Raymond was clearly uncomfortable discussing his use of pornography, which he did covertly, referring to child pornography during our interview only through the euphemistic term "images." He told me he had been "addicted" to viewing them. "It didn't feel okay," he specified, "but I longed so much for it and that strong desire still comes back to me.... It was the only satisfaction for my attraction." Raymond said that he wanted to "be a good person," but that quitting on his own had been a struggle. Aiden also referred to his interest in child pornography as an "addiction" and sought treatment for it. Before treatment, he said he had viewed watching child pornography as a "kind of a necessary vice." Aiden had previously seen child pornography as his "only sexual outlet," which, before seeking treatment, he felt able to rationalize away. Before therapy, Aiden had "rationalized it as you know, it's better that I have pornography than I act on my desires, than that I hurt somebody." Despite the legal and ethical motivations to stop using child pornography, the fact that it was perceived by some of my participants, including Aiden, as their only recourse for sexual release made it difficult for them to stop on their own. Their difficulty in ceasing to use pornography on their own motivated them to seek out help from mental health care providers.[27]

While the majority of my participants were adamant that they were not in danger of committing a sex offense against a child, a minority of them did discuss the motivation to seek therapeutic assistance to help them abstain from committing contact offenses. Neil told me that he thought about seeing a doctor for help when he was about 14 years old, when he first started looking for answers about his attractions to minors online. "I thought," he said, "'Maybe I should go to a doctor because I'm like a ticking time bomb and I'm a bad person.'...I felt like a bad person because I thought, I have to tell everyone because I'm like a ticking time bomb. And [you must think] that it's just ridiculous but yeah, I kept so much internalized all these prejudices that come, that I was really confused." Neil had seen someone who self-described as a pedophile on an online forum inquiring about doctors who might perform castrations. At first, the idea scared him, but he explained that he then wondered if he was supposed to seek some kind of medical care himself regarding his attractions. He explained, as did many of my participants, that he had seen so many examples of people with his attractions committing crimes against children that when he first started recognizing that he was minor-attracted, he assumed he would eventually commit a crime himself unless he sought some kind of treatment.

While my participants tended to gain more confidence in their ability not to commit an offense over time, some individuals were interested in seeking treatment for help with non-offending long after first realizing they were minor-attracted. Isaac, for instance, told me: "The problem [was] I came to the place where I bought into society's attitude that I would eventually have sex with a little girl. So I just was hopeless for most of those last years. Especially from the time [I sought counseling]. I felt helpless and hopeless and was at greatest risk during those years I'm sure." At that time, Isaac had not told anyone else in his life about his attractions to minors, and he was struggling with impulses to act on them decades after he had first realized he was attracted to minors.

He explained: "I have urges. People don't like that word, but I'm willing to admit that I have an urge that I have to resist to touch them inappropriately." Isaac admitted that he did not know where "the line" between appropriate and inappropriate behavior with children was. "You folks on the other side, you say, 'Oh, well the line is very clear,'" he said. "Well, it's not to me, to most of us." Although Isaac's assertion that this boundary was unclear to "most" MAPs was not corroborated by the majority of my other participants, he had spoken with other MAPs who did not fully understand where the threshold for inappropriate behavior with minors lay, and he evidently struggled with this himself. He had wanted counseling to help him understand appropriate boundaries and for help in calming his "urges" to commit an offense.

Some of my respondents who were interested in therapy for reasons related to resilience to offending merely sought validation from a professional that they did not pose a threat to children. Charlotte, for example, clearly expressed to me that her attractions to children were not impulses. Nonetheless, she was attracted to her partner's young daughter, which she described as distressing. "There wasn't a fear that I was going to hurt them," she noted, "but there was—there was this paranoia and this anxiety that I could just turn into a monster." In other words, although Charlotte did not actually believe she would commit an offense against her partner's daughter, she did not fully trust herself. She became interested in talking to a therapist about this, to reaffirm that her attractions alone did not mean she was dangerous. Participants like Charlotte wanted to speak about their fears to a mental health practitioner, to whom they felt they could be held accountable and who they felt would be a better judge of their ability to remain resilient to offending than themselves.

As discussed in Chapter 1, many study participants had anxieties about becoming a child molester, especially when first realizing that they were attracted to minors. Although not everyone who had this concern connected it with a desire to seek mental health care, those who shared this fear with me frequently said they had wanted to talk to a therapist to "fix" their attractions (discussed in the next section). Seeking mental health care out of a desire to change their attractions or orientation may have partly been motivated by their fear that if they continued to have these attractions, they might one day harm a child.

Desire to Alter Attractions

The final major reason my participants said they were interested in therapy was based on a belief that therapeutic intervention could alter their attractions. Most participants did not, by the time of our interviews, believe that changing their attractions was possible (and some expressed that even if they could, they would not want to); however, many participants had at one point believed that changing their attractions was possible and had been interested in doing so. Five participants who sought out mental health care originally did so because of an interest in changing their attractions. In contrast to individuals who thought of their attractions as a sexual orientation, these participants spoke of wanting to be "fixed" or "cured"—at least at the time that they had desired treatment.

My participants' hopes of being cured of their attractions to minors are not without precedent. As described earlier in this chapter, some mental health providers are willing to provide "treatment" in the form of sexual orientation change efforts (SOCE). Although MAPs looking to alter their attractions may be initially encouraged by mental health professionals who offer to provide SOCE, in the long run, my participants who sought these services realized it was not a feasible solution. Gene, Jeremy, and Isaac all explained with some embarrassment their initial desire to seek therapy to be cured of their attractions to minors:

> ISAAC: At first I thought they could fix me! Change my orientation!…I was doing counseling just to get myself fixed between my marriages while I was single to work on my issues.
>
> GENE: Y'know, going in, I almost didn't really have goals. I mean, I, I guess I kind of had one, which was kind of unrealistic 'cause I was naïve. Which was, like, "I hope I can go to this guy and he can help me get rid of my pedophilia." But, uh, well, obviously that was a reach. [Laughter]
>
> JEREMY: Um, I guess when I first went, um, I wanted to somehow believe that it could somehow be cured or that it could somehow, yeah, move on from this in a way that it wouldn't be an aspect of my life at all.

While all three had sought therapy in an attempt to somehow erase their attractions to children, they looked back on this idea as ignorant and somewhat laughable. Each of these men learned after a time that their attractions to children could not be eliminated and found other ways of coping with them. Gene's therapist was helpful to him in this endeavor, as described earlier in the chapter. Jeremy's and Isaac's experiences in therapy were less beneficial to them—I detail these later in the chapter. Before looking at my participants' experiences in mental health treatment, however, I first describe the reasoning of those who decided not to seek out care.

REJECTING MENTAL HEALTH CARE

Notably, not all of those who believed therapy would be useful to them for any of the reasons explored earlier sought out professional help. 11 participants told me that they would be interested in speaking to a mental health professional about their attractions if circumstances were different—but they decided not to seek one out. Even some participants who were in therapy declined to share with their providers that they were attracted to minors. The main reason that those in my study declined to seek care regarding their attractions was because they felt that mental health providers were untrustworthy. My participants were particularly concerned about providers reporting them to law enforcement or outing them in other ways, often citing MAPs they knew from online forums who had such experiences.

For instance, Cody was in therapy for mental health issues but had not disclosed his attractions to minors to his therapist. He struggled with an interest in child pornography, which he had managed to avoid watching on his own but which tempted him nonetheless. When asked if he had wanted to bring up his attractions to children during his therapy sessions, Cody replied:

> Sure, it has crossed my mind. It might even be beneficial to the therapy in some way. However, I don't take risks without at least an equal return. There [are] so many things that could go wrong. Even though they are not required by law to tell anyone anything about [attractions to children] unless there is someone in immediate danger, it's still a risk. That person will have that knowledge. Actually, I talked to someone about this. A fellow [Finnish person]....He told me the story of how he asked his parents for a therapist....He talked about [his attractions to children] to the therapist and she was very shocked. He talked with her for that session and then she told his parents. Completely illegal, but there was basically nothing he could do at that point. The parents kept it under wraps and got mad at him. I'm not sure he ever got proper help. He's in some sort of boarding school now. You need to make sure you stay safe yourself, because there's no telling what could fuck you over. You simply cannot outsource a part of your safety and reliably stay safe...I hope this brings a bit of light into what creates stress [for] people like us. This is a completely everyday thing. Out of the blue. One day you fuck something very little up [by telling some-

one else about your attractions]. It'll bite you in the ass after eight months.

Although Cody admitted that the potential support he could receive from his therapist regarding his attractions to minors could have been very beneficial to him, he felt that coming out to anyone, even to his therapist, would be much too risky. Finnish law protects client confidentiality, but Cody added: "Laws only help you after something has happened. If you're a pedophile, anyway. After something has happened, it is too late." Although Cody believed that he could seek legal recourse if a therapist broke his confidentiality, he did not feel that this adequately protected him from the possibility of being outed by a therapist. To him, the consequences of potentially being outed made the risk too great to trust in protections the law provided. Many others in my study echoed this point. The participants felt that each disclosure of their sexuality to a new person brought on the possibility of compromised safety or privacy, and therapists were no exception to this rule.

Many other respondents also lived in areas where laws or practitioner licensing board policies should have protected their confidentiality in therapy unless they had committed, or were planning to commit, a sexual offense, as is the case in the United States. But similarly to Cody's viewpoint, their fears of being outed were often not assuaged by confidentiality policies. As Xavier explained to me:

XAVIER: It's not like you can just go to a therapist's office and say, "I have an attraction," and tell them what it is. There are some therapists that might be able to deal with that, but a lot of them have, uh, mandated report laws and they'll report you if you tell them . . .

AW: You think that a therapist would report you just for saying you have an attraction?

XAVIER: Yeah, I think there's a lot of hate towards us. Yeah, and they don't really understand. I know there's a good reason. There's also people [who] don't want to understand. . . . I just feel it's too risky. I haven't done anything illegal, but I don't want to have cops come invading my house because a guy thought I was a bad person.

AW: Yeah. If, if you knew that the therapist wouldn't make that kind of call, would you be interested in talking about it to a therapist?

XAVIER: Yeah, if I knew for sure. One hundred percent.

Xavier was interested in receiving therapy regarding his attractions to minors, but he believed that some therapists might report a MAP just for disclosing their attractions not only because of a lack of understanding about mandated reporting laws but also out of sheer hatred. While this was an extreme view among my participants, others, like Noah, were unaware of whether mandatory reporting laws would mean that a therapist would have to report MAPs who had never committed an offense. "I don't know where I would go for [support about my attractions]," said Noah. "A few years back I saw a psychotherapist for anger problems, and I was afraid to tell her I was a pedophile because I wasn't sure how far my state's mandatory reporting laws go."

Although Noah was unfamiliar with how the law might affect his provider's responsibilities, participants who understood how the laws were supposed to protect them were nonetheless skeptical. Many worried that providers lacked an adequate understanding of mandatory reporting laws. Erik told me: "I started looking into [therapy], and...I began to come across this thing of mandatory reporting. And I was worried that even though, even without having done anything wrong, if a therapist has to report, what if I got, you know, an inexperienced one or a bad one who didn't really understand and might report anyway to cover themselves. And that was a concern, that, I felt it was too big a risk." Erik, Noah, Xavier, and others felt that the potential liability in coming out to a mental health professional was too great when compared to the potential benefits of doing so and decided not to explore therapy any further.

My participants had reasons to mistrust mental health providers beyond being outed or reported to authorities. They were also concerned about being judged. Multiple respondents said that they were worried about the reaction of their mental health provider if they discussed their sexuality in a session. They feared that the professional may grow suspicious or regard them as dangerous, which would be counterproductive to their mental health. Harper had been in therapy for years, and although she discussed her mental health issues more broadly with her therapist on a weekly basis, she was unwilling to disclose her sexuality in therapy. She told me she had not told her therapist about her attractions to minors because she would "fear judgment and stigma, even just from that person." When asked if she would be willing to talk to a therapist about her attractions if she knew that they would not be judgmental, she said: "Oh, yeah, yeah! I mean, if there was a therapist that routinely dealt with minor-attracted people, who knew the difference between being minor-attracted or a pedophile versus being a sex offender, who could hear me say 'I am not in danger of offending,' and *hear* 'I am not in danger of offending,' yeah, absolutely, that would be awesome. I just don't know that that exists."

Harper was in therapy for self-harming behaviors, which she attributed to her anxiety about her attractions to minors. As a result, she believed that her therapy was less effective than it could be if she felt able to freely discuss the underlying reasons for her self-harming. Harper was not the only person in my study to be concerned about facing judgment by a therapist. Floyd explained: "I think it is very intimidating for people to explore the issue with a psychologist, for fear of being reported or judged. I've met some savvy psychologists that I [still] would not feel comfortable disclosing my attractions to...I haven't felt comfortable enough with any psychologist I have met." In addition to believing that any psychologist he may come out to would judge or report him, Floyd worried that they would insert their own objectives into sessions and that the therapist would want to focus on "eliminating" his attractions to minors, which he did not see as an achievable goal.

While Harper's and Floyd's skepticism about the existence of non-judgmental therapists was echoed by many of my participants, others recounted strategies to find therapists who had been previously recognized by MAPs as providers of supportive care. Isaac, for instance, maintained an extensive list of therapists recommended by MAPs worldwide that was used by other MAPs seeking therapy. For those who lived too far from any therapists on the list, telephone counseling was an option. Others searched for providers in their area and made calls or sent emails "asking for a friend" about therapy modalities for someone with attractions to minors. These strategies took some of the risk out of the disclosure process. Mitchell described engaging in all of the above strategies to find a provider he felt comfortable disclosing his attractions to:

> I did seek therapists to try to deal with...poor self-concept...but also deal with stigma and society's negative views of myself. So, I, uh, it took three tries over a long period of time to find a therapist to help with that. The first one I emailed anonymously. And his response was...I just asked him a few questions and one of them was what he thought about my interacting with boys [platonically]. And he responded that it would be like throwing a lit match in a can of gasoline. I said, "Well, that's not the guy for me." [Laughs] And then another MAP recommended to me a psychologist in Baltimore and so I did go to see him. And he didn't seem to understand what I wanted, which

really surprised me because this other MAP recommended him....[He] implied to me that he was thinking that I was somehow out of touch with reality and I needed him to put me back, to help me stop, so I wouldn't, in my deluded state, abuse a child. That's the way it came across to me, which maybe I should've asked him more what he meant by that, but it just hit me wrong and so I said, "Well, I guess I won't see him, either." And I gave up on it for a number of years, then, but eventually, another MAP told me that he had done some therapy by phone with a therapist he found that had worked with another MAP before him. So, so I did do therapy with her by phone.

Finding a therapist took Mitchell years, but with a combination of consulting other MAPs for recommendations, asking questions ahead of starting sessions, and engaging in therapy over the phone, he found a provider with whom he felt comfortable. He recalled speaking with her on a biweekly basis for about nine months. "Her brand of therapy was mainstream," he said of her, and she "treated me like any other client. It was very helpful and humane."

Although participants such as Mitchell were able to find providers through these various methods, mental health care remained inaccessible to some respondents, in large part due to the financial costs. Some did not have insurance, and even when they did, telephone counseling is often not covered by insurance companies. These barriers—including the belief that their privacy would be compromised if they spoke to a mental health provider about their sexuality, the fear of being judged of treated with suspicion, or financial costs—prevented 11 individuals who would otherwise have sought out mental health care from doing so.

EXPERIENCES WITH MENTAL HEALTH CARE

Although many participants were unwilling or unable to find mental health providers to whom they felt comfortable disclosing their attractions, 24 individuals found such providers. Respondents' experiences with therapy varied drastically in each stage of developing therapeutic relationships—from the process of finding appropriate providers and coming out to them, to attempting to meet therapeutic goals. Some participants ran into no problems with this process and were able to find providers who delivered effective, nonjudgmental mental health care. Others, however, experienced misunderstandings, suspicion, or loss of privacy based on disclosure of their attractions from their providers.

Dealing with Providers' Assumptions

Providers' general lack of education about MAPs was evident throughout participants' narratives concerning their experiences with mental health practitioners. A common theme throughout their stories of seeking mental health care was handling inaccurate assumptions made by providers, whether about what attractions to minors entail or appropriate methods for providing treatment. Of my participants, 16 described interactions with mental health practitioners that were in some way related to these inaccurate assumptions. Assumptions made by providers frequently translated into misunderstandings between them and my participants. The MAPs in my study often faced awkward conversations with their providers, and providers did not always understand the nature of the participants' attractions, especially among those who did not come out to their therapists before their initial session.

Charlotte qualified the experience of coming out to her therapist in person as "anxiety-inducing." Charlotte had been struggling with what she referred to as "intrusive arousal" toward her partner's daughter. She described the time when she first tried to discuss this with a therapist:

> I sat down, this was like, the second session.…I just wanted to get it out there, I didn't want to waste time with someone that wasn't going to treat me because of prejudices…So I sat down at the second session and I was like, "Do you still feel comfortable treating me, um, having an attraction to children?" She stared at me for a moment and shakes her head, and she's like, "No, no." And I just got up. I just started to walk out and she was like, "Hang on. Hang on. I can't in good faith treat someone who is—" I forget how she phrased it. But, like, "hurting children"… I was like, "No, no, no, I'm not doing that." And, and she was like, "Oh, well, that is a pretty different thing then."

Charlotte recalled feeling "overwhelming anxiety" in that moment but was able to maintain enough composure to explain to her therapist that she had not hurt anyone, and her therapist was able to listen. Multiple MAPs in my study experienced similar miscommunications, with their therapists immediately assuming that they had committed a sexual offense upon their disclosures of having attractions to minors. In these cases, participants had to explain that they had not. Fortunately, Charlotte was able to explain to her therapist that she had never committed an offense, and they developed a supportive therapeutic relationship. However, not all participants were able to correct their providers' erroneous assumptions about MAPs.

Elias also experienced therapy sessions with a provider who made inaccurate assumptions. He described a doctor who, upon learning that Elias was attracted to minors, became "curious." She indicated to him there could be a biological cause for his attractions to minors, and she ordered MRIs and tests of his hormone levels, looking for abnormalities that she believed could explain his attractions—and, she theorized, could potentially lead to a cure. He recalled: "She got my hopes up." In the end, none of his test results came back as abnormal, and his treatment was discontinued, which left Elias feeling disappointed.

Dominick's experiences in therapy were a mixed bag. He told me his therapist was "completely fine with my attraction, though sometimes she makes statements that make it sound like I should work towards having a 'healthier attraction.'...I'm pretty used to it, so it doesn't bother me too much. She mostly questions me, like, 'And you're perfectly fine with your attractions?' or 'You don't want to change how you feel about young boys?' which I think ultimately come from a place of compassion that's due to a misunderstanding." Dominick was *not* "perfectly fine" with his attractions, but he had privately come to terms with the knowledge that he was unable to change them. Although he initially described his therapist's attitude toward his attractions as "completely fine" with them, the way he described her questions about them indicated that she believed he could, and should, change them. Dominick interpreted his therapist's remarks as well-meaning, but he thought that she lacked an appropriate knowledge base about MAPs' abilities to change who they are attracted to.

Some MAPs in my study had therapists with rigid ideas about the types of services that they should offer to minor-attracted individuals. Several participants who did not seek out SOCE described interactions with providers who nonetheless were focused on attempting to cure them of their attractions to minors. Sometime after he was seen by a doctor who tried to find a biological reason behind his attractions, Elias sought services with a group of providers who ended up "recommending aversion therapy like it was the 1950s....I literally walked out." He recalled feeling that "their intention wasn't to help me, it was to 'fix' me....I did not feel safe with them because their interest was not what was good for me but what was good for them." By that time, Elias was dismayed that his therapist wanted him to engage in SOCE, which was not what he had been seeking. At the time of our interview, Elias was still searching for a mental health provider who might help him cope with the anxiety and depression that he felt was due to a lack of social acceptance.

Like Elias, Hugo had an experience with a therapist that left him feeling deeply disappointed. He had been feeling depressed and suicidal when he began to admit to himself that he was a MAP, and he wanted to find a therapist who would help him work through his intensely negative emotions. He sent out emails to multiple therapists, inquiring on behalf of "a friend" about practitioners who may have experience working with minor-attracted individuals. He was referred to a provider who specialized in working with sex offenders. Hugo remembered:

> He had worked with sex offenders a lot, as a mandatory thing, and I told him I'd never offended. He said that would be fine and like he would be able to help, but essentially what happened is...he tried different things to a mold which I didn't fit in, basically. Like, I felt like he treated me like someone who just hadn't offended *yet*....And it just pissed me off, and in the moment I was just very like, "Uh huh, sure." But after I went home and after I analyzed it and thought about it, it just made me mad and it really effed me up. Like, it really undid a lot of the progress I had made.

Hugo's therapist initially had him complete a risk analysis questionnaire, which categorized him as presenting a moderate risk of offending, based solely on his fantasies about children. He recalled his therapist stating, "Oh, we'll totally fix you," meaning he would cure Hugo of his attractions to minors, which Hugo did not believe. He decided to look for another therapist who was more focused on helping Hugo accept society's attitudes toward MAPs. Hugo felt that his therapeutic work with this second professional was helpful, and that his mental health was much improved as a result.

While respondents like Hugo and Elias were offered a type of care that differed from what they initially expected, others were turned away by providers entirely. Six of my participants had consulted with providers who were unwilling to work with them upon disclosure of their attractions. In some of these cases, the professionals provided recommendations for alternate mental health care providers, but others did not. Isaac, for instance, was worried that he was going to commit a sexual offense. He decided to come out to a counselor he had been in sessions with for a while to obtain help and guidance: "I was single in the late '90s, and I struggled...with being attracted to children. I was at greater risk of acting out on it. I went to a counselor, I was seeing a counselor, and I, when I came out to her, she immediately abandoned me without a referral.... Like, I, then I felt hopeless that I was even at more risk of acting out. Just grace of God that I didn't." Isaac lamented the lack of professional support available when he needed it the most, at a time when he felt he was at risk of offending. He felt compassion for his counselor and guessed that when he came out to her, she felt traumatized in some way, but at the same time he believed his counselor's behavior put him, and potentially any children he knew at the time, more at risk. Isaac eventually grew confident that he would not become a sex offender, first on his own and later with the help of other MAPs on VirPed and B4U-ACT, and he dedicated himself to helping others in this process.

Jeremy, whose experiences I discussed in Chapter 2, also engaged in therapy with a provider who discontinued care based on his sexuality. Jeremy decided to seek services for depression when he was enrolled in a master's program in education and came out to a counselor at his university. Concerned that Jeremy posed a threat, his counselor coerced him into leaving the program, threatening to expose Jeremy to the school if he refused. His counselor felt unqualified to provide him with necessary care and provided no assistance in finding someone who could. "Well, they themselves just told me to go find another [counselor]," he recalled, "they themselves didn't want to deal with it. . . . They said, 'you've got to talk to some other one, and if they can turn around and say that you're cured or whatever, then, yeah, I'll be happy to let you go back to teaching.'" Subsequently, Jeremy dropped out of the program. Lying to his family and friends about why he dropped out of the program intensified his anxieties.

Taking the advice of his previous counselor, Jeremy found a new provider. He believed that this therapist would understand issues related to attractions to minors because he had experience working with sex offenders. Similarly to Elias's experience, Jeremy explained that the therapist employed SOCE. His therapist "had me write down thoughts [about children] I had in my head and then as I read it and got aroused by it use [ammonia inhalants] to try and give [my] body a shock." Jeremy recalled his therapist referring to him as a "ticking time bomb" (an expression employed by many therapists, according to various participants). The therapist advised Jeremy to avoid children altogether, believing that if he "let his guard down," he would be in danger of offending. During the course of his therapy sessions, Jeremy became suicidal. He finally confessed his suicidal thoughts and his attractions to his parents, who convinced him to discontinue therapy, since it seemed to cause more harm than good. At the time of his interview, Jeremy was no longer involved in therapy. He preferred to engage with other MAPs on VirPed instead. He felt that the support of others who could understand what he was going through was more beneficial than therapy with a professional. Jeremy thought often about starting an in-person peer support group for MAPs.

While Jeremy's first provider threatened to out him to others, Quentin's actually did when she reported him to the police. Quentin had also decided not to seek another therapist, preferring peer support with other MAPs instead. Although the experiences of Jeremy and Quentin were extreme among my participants, many MAPs in my study had heard about them or had heard of other stories like theirs. It shows a strong commitment to their own health and safety, and in some cases, the safety of others, that so many of my participants were willing to risk negative experiences by reaching out to providers, knowing stories such as theirs. However, given the experiences of MAPs like Jeremy and Quentin, it is reasonable that even those with a strong commitment to their own health may make the decision not to seek out care, out of the concern that providers could worsen their mental health.

"Start Where the Client Is"

Despite the fact that 16 of my study participants described negative experiences in therapy resulting from inaccurate assumptions made by their providers, 15 of them were able to find a provider who helped them in some way. A noticeable pattern among those who expressed that they received help from a mental health professional was that their providers listened to them and worked on the goals that participants had for themselves, rather than inserting their own. In other words, to borrow a common phrase used in the field of social work, these providers "start[ed] where the client is." Social worker Jeanne C. Marsh[28] noted that this phrase indicates providers should take direction from their clients regarding "client concerns, perspectives, and definitions of the problem" that have brought a client in for services. This is not only because it provides focus for therapeutic work, but because this helps the client to feel understood and helps achieve buy-in from clients in finding solutions to their problems.

Descriptions of positive therapeutic care varied, but the qualities in therapists with whom participants noted having good experiences shared similarities. These therapists were either informed about issues related to MAPs, or became informed about them after their clients disclosed their attractions to them. These therapists also (again, either before or shortly after disclosure) understood that MAPs are not interchangeable with sex offenders. Relatedly, these therapists did not show suspicion toward their clients and even showed trust in them. In addition, they validated their clients' concerns: often this meant that the therapist would focus less on their client's attractions themselves and more on issues that they had surrounding their attractions (such as dealing with stigma or fears of offending).

Participants who felt helped by mental health treatment services commonly commented on their providers' lack of judgment regarding their attractions. Victor's therapist shared this nonjudgmental attitude and thus helped Victor to become less judgmental toward his own attractions. His therapist encouraged Victor to use less stigmatizing language to denote his attractions, to minimize the guilt he had: "My therapist...has helped me to know the roots of it and how to start...referring to my attractions. So, for example, I was really filled with fear about it, and we discovered I used the term 'temptation' whenever I mentioned an attraction....So that made it had a really negative connotation for me, feeling at risk just because I saw how beautiful or handsome a specific boy is....He suggested I should use the word 'admiration,' or 'overadmiration.'" In addition to not feeling judged by his provider for his attractions, Victor found that his therapist helped him with his specific goals, which included gaining confidence in his ability to refrain from offending. Reframing his attractions as "admiration" rather than a "temptation" helped him not to worry that he would one day commit a sexual offense. When I asked Victor how he would characterize his current mental health, he said: "Improving. I'm learning my patterns with my therapist. I used to worry too much about everything, causing me lots of stress, now I'm stopping that unhealthy behaviour."

Importantly, there was overlap between those who had a poor experience with a therapist and those who said their provider had helped them—providers who made an assumption about my participants' actions based on disclosures of their attractions to minors were sometimes able to remedy the situation. Even though Charlotte's therapist initially believed her disclosure about her attractions meant that she had harmed a child, after further discussion they were able to move on from her therapist's misunderstanding. Eventually her therapist helped Charlotte to accept that her attraction to children existed and "allow it to be without judgment. And to just roll through it. And that's what I did, and honestly, it helps a lot." Her therapist also helped Charlotte to trust herself—by recognizing that she was in control over her own actions and that her attractions did not mean that she was a bad person or that she was going to harm a child. Charlotte still struggled with depression, but throughout our conversation she was consistent in her descriptions about her attractions as "an anxiety, [but] not an actual threat."

Lee also had mixed experiences with his therapist. He explained:

> One of the first things he [the therapist] taught was try to not really change myself, but try to expand my attractions a little bit. Try to get myself attracted to older people, try to make things easier. But it didn't really quite work that way. [He wanted me to] try to be around [people] that are not really that much older but trying to—putting myself out there more. Try to meet more people. Try to be around women more. Just try to develop some emotional connection that maybe would help…it didn't quite work. It was more stressful to try than not to.

Lee noted that he had not been interested in trying to expand his attractions to adults, because he had tried this approach previously on his own, and it had not worked for him. However, Lee was able to communicate with his therapist that his approach was not working, and his therapist listened and shifted gears. Lee said that his therapist "changed [his approach] to making me feel more comfortable with myself. More like reaffirming." Once this shift occurred, therapy started to work for Lee. His therapist even introduced him to VirPed, through which Lee was able to feel a sense of community and support. "I think therapy has helped quite a bit," Lee told me, "[because] I don't feel as guilty or ashamed of it anymore. I feel more comfortable being who I am.… It's still difficult but I'm more at peace with myself."

While good therapists generally exhibited traits of "starting where the client is," this pattern was complicated by therapists who did not offer SOCE to clients who were looking for it. Gene, for instance, had originally sought out therapy to get rid of his attractions to minors. It became clear to him early on, however, that his therapist did not believe that altering his sexuality was a viable option. Although his therapist could not help Gene with his goal of changing his sexuality, Gene had other goals underneath his unattainable one: specifically, of being able to survive. Gene's therapist listened to his concerns about his sexuality and offered support. "He was an amazing guy," Gene recalled. "He was really, really understanding, really nonjudgmental. I told him everything. He listened." Gene remembered feeling that he needed someone to talk to go on living, and although his therapist could not "cure" him of his attractions, he gave him an outlet. Gene ultimately credited his therapist with keeping him alive at this time when he was so vulnerable.

Shawn's case further complicates the patterns shown in participants' narratives about their experiences with providers. He sought out alternative therapy and consulted with a hypnotherapist to cure him of his attractions to minors. Because Shawn was attracted to adults as well as minors before his hypnotherapy sessions, his therapist attempted to help him focus on his attractions to adults.

SHAWN: I was hoping he could fix me somehow, that maybe he could flip a switch in me or something. Unfortunately, there is no such thing....As I understood, all he could do was numb it, numb the craving. And I do recall a lot of the hypnotherapy was around embracing the idea of a loving relationship, a, specifically a sexually-based relationship with [an adult] female. That's what the therapy, the hypnosis really revolved around. I do know that.

AW: Okay. And do you feel like it was successful?

SHAWN: Um, [my fiancée and I] do plan on getting married, and I do have a baby, so I guess to some degree it was. I don't know, I guess it could be far more successful...At my age now, my sexual appetite, my sexual drive is very low....Um, but the definitiveness by which the defined age group, the gender, the, the fire of my sexuality is still there. It's the same thing. It hasn't changed, it's just my drive is much less than it used to be.

Shawn admitted that the effects of the therapy were not what he originally anticipated, which was to be "turned straight or gay"—in other words, to exclusively be attracted to adults. The therapy did not have this effect, however. Although Shawn did experience a decrease in his sex drive as a whole, he attributed this to his age rather than to the therapy. While he had always been romantically attracted to women, and mildly sexually attracted to them, the idea of a relationship with an adult had seemed inaccessible to him prior to his hypnotherapy. He felt that this therapy helped him to accept the idea of a relationship with an adult woman. So, although he did not feel that he was "cured," Shawn credited therapy with helping him feel more comfortable about being in a relationship with an adult and with feeling more "in control" of his attractions to minors.

Some participants experienced difficulties with therapy, even when they found it to be helpful. Often therapy that promotes positive growth can create new struggles for clients as they wrestle with inner conflict. This was especially true for Aiden, whose experiences in therapy had pushed feelings of guilt and self-loathing to the surface of his mind. Aiden sought therapeutic intervention for his addiction to child pornography in the form of individual therapy, sex addiction group therapy, and a separate 12-step program for sex addicts. Although he attended all three therapeutic modalities regularly, he experienced some difficulties in the group therapies. He felt that he did not fit in with the other members, all of whom were teleiophiles. Aiden expressed feeling bitter toward other group members, noting: "I'll never have an acceptable outlet. Like, they all have partners. They all have wives. If they stop using pornography, they still get to have sex with their wives. You know what I mean? They have an outlet. Like where with me, this is like the only outlet I have. Like, I mean, there is like masturbation without pornography but, not having a partner or the idea of ever having one."

Aiden felt conflicted over his group therapy with pornography addicts who were teleiophiles because they could legally and ethically engage in sexual relationships that fulfilled them, which was not an option for him. He wished he could be in a group therapy setting specifically designed for pedophiles, where he could process his feelings of shame with people who could better understand him, but he felt that could never exist because of the risk of advertising about a group of pedophiles. "That's just asking for, like, a Molotov cocktail to be thrown into the room through the window or something like that," he said. Despite wishing for group therapy with others who had more similar experiences to his own, Aiden found the therapy effective. He credited his experiences in therapy with his ability to stop consuming child pornography, which was a positive direction for his life, as well as very clearly positive in terms of protecting children. He valued the encouragement he received in his support network.

Mitchell had also had positive experiences with a therapist but still felt conflicted about mental health treatment in general. He said his therapist helped him "address my negative feelings of myself, these cognitive distortions, negative messages I was telling myself about myself. And so that was helpful." Even though he felt helped by his therapist, Mitchell felt let down by the field of mental health care overall:

> What society and the mental health field generally tells me is that my sense of intimacy and desire for intimacy and romantic love is predatory and monstrous. And, uh, so that's worse than just saying I can't [have intimacy or romance]. That's saying that there's just this part of me that's monstrous or satanic or something like that. So that's another issue that needs to be dealt with by the mental health profession, I think, because I think that's unjust. I think it's extremely mentally or emotionally destructive. The mental health professionals are not supposed to be destroying the mental health of their clients.

Although Mitchell had no interest in harming a child and understood that engaging in a relationship with one would be harmful, he wanted his provider to acknowledge his humanity and desire to be loved. Mitchell explained that upon realizing one is a MAP, "you have to mourn this death of a part of you, the romantic intimacy part." Even though Mitchell had found a therapist who helped him with his self-esteem, he struggled with a lack of validation surrounding this loss that to him was very profound. Although his provider helped Mitchell with his self-esteem, in a sense therapy was unable to help him in his struggle for dignity. Experiences such as Mitchell's may reflect just how complex the needs of MAPs can be when they seek care.

HELP WANTED

As this book has shown, MAPs endure massive discord throughout their lives—from facing their own sexuality to dealing with assumption of predatory behavior from family, friends, and even sometimes themselves as well as (especially for those who are exclusively attracted to minors) dealing with a reality of never having a fulfilling romantic or sexual relationship. My study participants were confronted with stressors on a daily basis, including stigma by the public and the media, being subjected to online death threats, the constant fear that friends and family may abandon them if they knew about their sexuality, and feeling perturbed by their own attractions. Given this, a high prevalence rate of mental illness among my participants is hardly surprising. MAPs have a strong need for highly qualified mental health care providers with specialized education and training—many participants were eager to seek professional help. However, among my participants, finding a provider came with many obstacles. Some barriers to care were similar to those affecting the general population, such as financial costs and geographic accessibility of known providers; but most obstacles were specific to MAPs, such as fear that providers may turn them away, treat them with suspicion, or report them to legal authorities. These fears, as evidenced by the experiences of many participants in this study, were not unfounded.

Those who had therapists who were well-educated about MAPs, affirming, and not suspicious reported having positive experiences with mental health care professionals. Conversely, those whose therapists had their own agenda—including expressing the belief that participants were dangerous based exclusively on their attractions; trying to "cure" or "fix" participants without being asked to do so; and refusing to provide services—were unlikely to have benefited from their sessions with the providers, and indeed often suffered negative consequences. Individuals who were able to establish a trusting relationship with a professional, however, often reported positive outcomes, both in terms of their mental health and their confidence in remaining resilient to offending.

As someone who has conducted research with MAPs, and as someone who lives in a society that mistrusts MAPs, I have to admit that I understand the appeal for the idea of a "cure" for attractions to minors. In my version of an ideal world, a cure would be available to those MAPs who want it, or who are unable to keep themselves from committing offenses against children without one. So if SOCE worked to turn MAPs into teleiophiles, I would advocate for it in my writing. The problem is that these efforts have never been shown to be effective. In the real world, SOCE has been shown to do more harm than good for those who have been exposed to this type of "treatment."

Like the appeal of SOCE for MAPs, providers' liberal use of reporting MAP clients to law enforcement is similarly understandable. If a mental health care provider has not been given proper education about MAPs, it is expected that they might misunderstand a non-offending MAP for a sex offender. This just underscores the intense need for provider education about MAPs. Even with proper education, the decisions made by mental health providers about ethical care with their clients are often difficult, and ultimately they have to exercise their own judgment. If their client indicates to them that they are an actual danger to a child, and they fall within professional guidelines for making a report, it is within that child's (and society's) best interests for a report to be made. However, if a MAP client comes to their therapist because of a fear of offending, instead of making a report right away, these fears can be explored: Do they struggle with actual impulses to commit offenses? What triggers those impulses? Can they avoid them? How have they strategized to avoid them so far? Are they actually planning to commit an offense? If they don't have impulses to offend, are their fears based in a lack of knowledge about the existence of non-offending MAPs?

If a therapist cannot provide services to someone because of their own prejudices, they should not be providing that client with services (although a referral to a qualified alternative provider should always be made, in these cases). If a client is actively seeking sexual orientation change efforts, their therapist needs to know that it will not work and needs to discuss with them instead why they want it and what actual options they have for evidence-based therapeutic services. I'm not saying this is easy. But it is vital for mental health providers to have proper education about these issues so they can make informed decisions about how to best provide care to their clients.

6.   "You Are Not a Monster"

Toward a Shift in Attitudes Concerning MAPs

"You have the power to say 'no' and get help if someone has hurt or touched you." This is how an animated girl named Maya introduces a video series developed for fourth through sixth graders called "The Protect Yourself Rules."[1] Its complementary series for kindergarten through third graders features an animated boy named Lenny, who teaches the lesson: "No one should ever touch you on a part of your body that's covered by your bathing suit. If someone tries to, shout 'Stop!' or, 'Don't touch me!' loudly and clearly." Each of these videos features drawings and animated sequences of children with bruises, experiencing forms of "unsafe touch," looking scared, isolated, and confused, while teaching a series of lessons about saying no, learning about safe and unsafe forms of touch, and the value of talking to trusted adults. Wonder Media, which produced the video series, has noted that the videos have been viewed more than 100 million times on YouTube and that teachers in 15,000 cities globally have shared their materials with their students. As of this writing, the Boy Scouts of America had recently adopted the video series, mandating it as part of their Cub Scouts curriculum.[2]

"The Protect Yourself Rules" video series is just one of many different forms of media designed to teach children how to protect themselves from abuse. As of 2019, 20 states within the United States have required public schools to teach children about child sexual abuse, and another nine states allow or encourage this form of education.[3] As a result, educators at multiple grade levels have to decide how to teach this content to children. Puppet shows,[4] lesson plans, plays, and videos from multiple media companies have been developed to teach children similar lessons about recognizing safe versus unsafe touch, saying no, and telling adults when they have experienced abuse.

The goal of media such as "The Protect Yourself Rules"—preventing sexual abuse against children—is undoubtedly important. However, I invite you to examine this type of programming with me. We live in a society in which we teach young children about saying "no" to adults as a policy for preventing abuse. This type of programming puts the responsibility of preventing sexual abuse on potential child victims themselves, rather than on potential offenders. Additionally, because this type of programming often places emphasis on telling adults when abuse has occurred, it may be more effective at helping to catch adults who have already committed sexual abuse than on preventing the abuse in the first place. We have allowed our "sexual abuse prevention" strategies to place the burden of prevention on potential victims and to focus on intervention after the fact, rather than before it happens. To truly prevent abuse, we need to shift our focus.

STIGMA AGAINST MAPS: AN INEFFECTIVE STRATEGY FOR ABUSE PREVENTION

Despite their flaws, it is easy to see why media such as "The Protect Yourself Rules" are necessary in our present society. While we could concentrate prevention efforts on helping adults who feel they are in danger of committing an offense, we have instead made such efforts nearly impossible. Consider Isaac, who sought mental health care when he felt he was at "risk of acting out"—in other words, when he was in danger of committing a sexual offense against a child. Rather than providing the care he was seeking, or at least referring him to someone who could provide competent care, his counselor stopped providing him services altogether, without referring Isaac to another provider. Or consider Quentin, whose therapist contacted the police despite no indication from Quentin that he was going to commit an offense—his story reached other MAPs, who added this to their list of reasons not to seek professional help.

Fortunately, MAPs' strategies for refraining from sexual offending do not begin and end with mental health providers. At the same time, though, many other strategies MAPs have mentioned to me are hindered by stigma as well. While I was conducting interviews, many participants told me that they connected with other MAPs via MAP-related websites such as VirPed and B4U-ACT. Other participants said they sought support from other non-offending MAPs over broader social media sites such as Reddit, Tumblr, Twitter, and Psychforums. Psychforums, a website where people who have been diagnosed with or believe they have various mental health conditions can talk to each other for advice and support, shut down their forums for people with paraphilias,[5] which some MAPs identify with.

Psychforums was not the only website to close its doors to MAPs. While I was conducting my interviews, the subreddit specifically made for non-offending MAPs was shut down by Reddit.[6] After interviews ended, Tumblr also systematically removed all posts containing content that supported MAPs (including my own—I had set up a Tumblr account to learn more about MAPs on the website), citing that these accounts violated Tumblr's policies against posting "inappropriate content involving or depicting minors." And in October 2020, many months after I had finished the initial manuscript for this book, Twitter changed its child sexual exploitation policy to explicitly ban "promoting or normalizing sexual attraction to minors as a form of identity or sexual orientation."[7] With this change, many MAPs' Twitter accounts have been suspended, and I have to wonder whether discussion of my book itself will be banned on the social media site. These websites cited violations of their policies as a reason for shutting down accounts and forums belonging to MAPs and those who wish to provide support for MAPs.[8] Notably, individual accounts encouraging MAPs (including MAPs who are under 18) to kill themselves remain on Tumblr, and Reddit's CEO has defended its lack of enforcement against hate speech on its platform.[9] Clearly, these websites pick and choose which groups they will allow to violate their terms, and which they will not.[10] MAPs do not make the cut.

Of course, MAPs can connect with each other via websites specifically created for them, such as VirPed and B4U-ACT, but these websites are restrictive in terms of the ages of people they allow (they both restrict their communities to ages 18+),[11] and not everyone feels comfortable on them (the majority of members are cisgender white men, which some participants such as Brooke noted made them feel unwelcome). In addition, the more expansive focus of websites such as Twitter, Tumblr, and Reddit means that MAPs who are struggling with their identity, who may not know of the existence of specialized websites such as VirPed and B4U-ACT, could have accessed community, support, and education on the former, where they may not have access to the latter.

Obtaining support from family and friends is yet another integral strategy among MAPs to remain resilient to offending. And yet, stigma toward MAPs has complicated this strategy perhaps further than others. My study participants were all too aware of their family and friends' opinions of people with attractions to minors: they had generally held negative opinions toward MAPs themselves until realizing that they shared these attractions. Many participants continued holding these negative opinions afterward: some clearly held them as we spoke in interviews. How, then, could they share with family or friends—the people whose opinion of themselves they cared about most—that they had these attractions? How could anyone attracted to minors ask for help of someone who has shared a photo on Facebook of an electric chair overlaid with the words "the cure for pedophilia"?

Not that everyone in my study felt they needed help not to offend. Far from it—the majority of participants felt confident that they were not at risk of committing an offense against a minor. As discussed in Chapter 4, study participants frequently explained that the reason they were highly motivated not to offend was based on personal moral values against harming children, and they understood that sexual activity between adults and minors would result in harm to the minor. (Of course, not everyone I interviewed shared this understanding identically, but they refrained for a host of other reasons.) And as a small sample of 42 individuals, who understood I was only seeking to interview people who had never committed a sexual offense against a minor, there is certain to be a particular "type" of MAP who would self-select to speak to me for my research. Perhaps those in my study were less impulsive than those who might be more at risk of offending. Perhaps they were better educated and had a better understanding of child development. There are many questions my book cannot answer. But even some of my participants who felt they were not at risk of committing an offense told me that they were not entirely sure where the line was between appropriate and inappropriate behavior with children, given that their attractions to minors existed alongside culturally approved ways of physically interacting with children. And they often had no one to bring these questions to when they were unsure about that line.

And so, here we are, in an age where we tell each other that MAPs are evil and destined to harm children. In an age where we keep MAPs afraid of coming out to family and friends, even if they need help to keep from committing an offense. In an age where we keep MAPs from supporting each other online, where we keep MAPs from asking for help from mental health professionals, where we ask children to protect *themselves* from sexual abuse. To move beyond these problems, we have one clear path to take: remove the stigma of attraction to minors and place it solely on the behavior of sexual offending against children.

WELLBEING AMONG MAPS: ANOTHER IMPORTANT FOCUS

While preventing sexual offending against children is of course a vital goal, it is not the only story that emerges when considering the potential effects of reducing stigma against MAPs. Increasing wellbeing among MAPs is an objective that is significant in and of itself. My research participants spoke about many obstacles toward their own wellness, as I've covered throughout this book. As discussed in Chapter 5, whether related to their attractions toward minors or not, many participants experienced mental health problems such as depression, anxiety, and suicidal thoughts. Some had made plans to end their lives, and three made attempts to carry them out.

While it is beyond the ability of my research to assess whether study participants had developed mental illness as a direct result of stigma toward their attractions, prior research has shown that the effects of social stigma correlate with an increase in suicidal thoughts among MAPs.[12] My participants demonstrated an intimate awareness of the stigma that they faced by others, describing rejection that they encountered personally from friends, family, and sometimes strangers, as well knowledge of general social negativity toward MAPs. Back when they began to recognize that they were attracted preferentially, and sometimes exclusively, to minors, participants experienced fear—often toward themselves and also over what others would think of them if they knew about their sexuality. As a result, participants frequently stayed closeted from others for long periods of time—some remaining closeted until our interviews. Those who remained closeted coped with their attractions on their own, sometimes in unhealthy ways such as through drug and alcohol abuse.

Just as stigma has kept MAPs from seeking help to resist committing a sexual offense, my participants often explained that they had not sought help for mental health concerns because they were worried about providers' reactions if they told them about their attractions. Participants who did not struggle with impulses to commit an offense but who nonetheless struggled to handle the effects of stigma frequently believed that they could not trust mental health care practitioners, and thus could not fully be honest if they engaged in some form of treatment. Among those who did seek out mental health care, those who encountered providers who continuously made inaccurate assumptions about MAPs often described their mental state as *worsening* as a result of working with these providers.

There are some who would find it harmful for me to talk about MAPs' wellbeing outside of a framework of their risk for sexual offending. We've been so conditioned as a society to see MAPs as offenders, or as people at risk of offending, that worrying about their wellbeing for their wellbeing's sake can seem at best confusing, and at worst offensive. I have encountered the opinion that if you care about MAPs' wellbeing, you must somehow oppose children's safety. The MAPs I spoke to were often frustrated by that opinion. As more than one of my participants pointed out, some children are MAPs. Indeed, many of my participants began figuring out when they were still minors themselves that they were minor-attracted. And perhaps more to the point, in caring about MAPs' wellbeing, we begin to erase a stigma that is currently harming children.

In 2018, I attended a symposium hosted by B4U-ACT titled "Expanding the Focus of Research on Minor-Attracted People." The goals of this symposium were twofold: to provide a venue for sharing current research about MAPs, and to encourage scholars who conduct such research to focus not only on abuse prevention but on wellbeing among MAPs. Attendees noted that when the goal of all research regarding MAPs is to prevent abuse, this reinforces societal suspicion about MAPs as potential offenders. The takeaway from this research as a whole becomes "you should care about MAPs because they are dangerous." I worry about my book in terms of this argument. Does it bolster the common viewpoint that MAPs are likely offenders? I hope that the answer is no—throughout this book I include interview data indicating that not all MAPs are dangerous, arguing that society must learn that MAPs' attractions to minors do not make them a threat. However, by arguing that a main reason stigma toward MAPs should be reduced is because this has the potential to reduce offending, it seems I am saying that we should care about lowering the stigma faced on MAPs because they *do* pose a threat.

While these statements may appear contradictory, the fact is that we know some MAPs do commit sexual offenses against minors. Sexual offending against a child often results in lasting harm not only to the child but to the child's family and community, so preventing this kind of offending is of vital importance. But MAPs' own strategies to resist committing offenses against minors are blocked—they often lack the security to come out to people who could help them with these strategies, such as friends, family, and providers; their avenues for seeking support from other MAPs are frequently blocked by websites that shut them out—and the reason they are blocked is a lack of understanding that not all MAPs will offend and that MAPs who are committed to non-offending deserve, and often need, support. So it is not my intention to describe MAPs as a danger or a threat. It is instead my intention to indicate that *some* MAPs need help in order not to commit an offense, and our poor provision of resources can exacerbate their need for preventive assistance. It is our responsibility as a society to provide that help. That help must include reducing stigma toward MAPs.

TOWARD REDUCTIONS IN STIGMA AND OFFENDING

And so, the question must be asked: How should we move forward? Are there any practical, concrete steps that can be taken to lessen stigma and offending? While I don't have all the answers, I do offer some suggestions. As Bryan told me in our interview, "What would help law-abiding MAPs to be psychologically healthy, more stable, and reduce the possibility of breaking the law? Acceptance that they aren't, fundamentally, evil people." In order both to decrease offending and increase wellbeing among MAPs, we need a broad societal shift in our understandings about MAPs as well as a specific, targeted effort in increasing providers' education surrounding MAPs and policies surrounding client confidentiality.

Because increasing education among providers may be easier, I start here. First and foremost, providers need to understand mandated reporting and duty-to-warn policies. I begin here because this goes beyond education about MAPs specifically: providers should understand the laws of their jurisdictions in terms of when they must keep their client's information confidential, and when they may break client confidentiality to report a client. In the United States, providers have a legal and ethical requirement to protect client information except in very specific circumstances. One of these circumstances is referred to "duty to warn." Therapists have a duty to warn—in other words, a requirement to report clients to law enforcement—only when their client presents foreseeable and imminent danger to an identified victim. Therapists also have a requirement to report suspected child abuse to child welfare hotlines—this is what is referred to as "mandated reporting."

My own research with students in the social services shows that students who plan to work in direct practice with clients are often not aware of the circumstances under which they are permitted to break a client's confidentiality.[13] Those findings mirrored the experiences of participants in this study—one whose therapist reported him to the police, although he did not express being at risk of offending, and one whose therapist threatened to out him to his school if he did not withdraw. Notably, neither of these participants lived within the United States at the time that their therapists reported them to the police, although the respondents in my study did reference other United States–based MAPs whose therapists had made police reports about them under similar circumstances. Jurisdictions that have not yet legislated the circumstances under which counselors may break client confidentiality should do so.

While practitioners undoubtedly need to understand when they may (and should) report clients in general, the other problem that may be underlying practitioners' erroneous reporting of MAP clients is a general lack of education about MAPs. Outside of the context of sexual offending against minors, MAPs generally are not taught about in classrooms for social workers, psychologists, and other future counseling professionals. Because mental health service providers are brought up in the same society as the rest of us, their opinions about MAPs are likely to mirror the assumption that MAPs are a danger to society. Without educational resources to teach them that MAPs are not necessarily offenders, providers may lack the understanding that MAP clients are not, based on their attractions alone, at imminent risk of committing an offense.

This is not the only education that practitioners need about MAPs. As discussed in Chapter 5, MAPs sometimes encounter practitioners who believe they can cure them of their attractions to minors with sexual orientation change efforts (SOCE). While various professional organizations for counselors throughout the United States and abroad have condemned SOCE when used on LGBT people, that same condemnation does not exist when these efforts are used on MAPs, although such efforts have not been shown to be any more effective on MAPs than they are on LGBT individuals. Professionals working in psychology, social work, and other mental health services professions should be taught in their educational programs that SOCE is ineffective and not to be used in therapy with LGBT people and MAPs alike.

In addition to being taught very basic lessons about practice with MAPs, such as not to engage in SOCE and keeping privileged information confidential, more education is needed to best work with MAPs. The MAPs in my research felt particularly helped by practitioners who were affirming and who understood issues faced by MAPs, such as the stigma they were exposed to and fears of committing an offense. To that end, professional organizations should work with MAPs to develop lists of best practices for effective care. Prevention Project Dunkelfeld (aka Kein Täter werden) in Germany has its own set of practices for work with MAPs who are concerned about offending, and they have given their curriculum to other practitioners who work with MAPs.[14] More recently, multiple organizations in the United States have begun to run psycho-educational programs for MAPs. The Help Wanted Prevention Project,[15] run through Johns Hopkins, and The Global Prevention Project,[16] run out of Utah, are programs that can be accessed internationally (via the internet and phone, respectively). These programs have both been developed in part based on discussion with, and feedback from, MAPs. While this is a start, these are the methods of a few specific organizations rather than being developed by MAPs for a wide range of practitioners, and best practices for work with MAPs who do not feel they are at risk of offending have yet to be developed.

Although the participants of my study generally had limited criminal legal system involvement, a few faced interrogations by police due to reports from others based exclusively on disclosures of their attractions. Three of my participants had their computers confiscated and searched for child pornography by law enforcement before being returned to them; two had been targeted by police due to online admissions of their attractions toward children; and one had been reported to the police by an ex-partner. The criminal legal system implications arising from my research are therefore important. It is vital for the police to understand that individuals who have attractions to children have not necessarily committed a crime. Simple disclosures of attractions to minors must be understood as categorically different from evidence that MAPs have committed or plan to commit an actual crime.

The MAPs in this study were generally well-networked with other MAPs, and talked to each other candidly about issues that they faced. This put them in a position to learn about any offending behaviors that others may have committed. Ideally, these individuals would feel empowered to reach out to someone about offending among other MAPs. However, my participants described feeling afraid of law enforcement because of a general societal understanding about attractions toward minors, reducing their likelihood of contacting the police in the event that they hear about a crime. The MAPs in this study also expressed concerns about their physical safety when discussing coming out to friends and family. But again, because of apprehensions that they would be targeted due to their sexuality, they also feared police involvement in their lives. Having no one to turn to in the event of a physical conflict when coming out to family members makes the process of coming out riskier, and potentially less likely. Therefore, my recommendations for the criminal legal system are similar to my recommendations regarding the mental health care system: education is needed for professionals working within the criminal legal system to better understand the experiences of MAPs.

Practitioners within mental health care and the criminal legal system are not the only people who need to be educated about MAPs. To reduce stigma toward MAPs, we need to see a broad social shift in attitudes toward attractions to minors. Such a shift could happen if led by the media: study participants remarked upon the lack of any positively portrayed characters in media who were minor-attracted. Although it may be considered a big ask to see positive examples of MAPs in the media, young MAPs who are beginning to recognize that they are attracted to minors should not have to wonder if they are destined to commit a crime—seeing representation of individuals with similar attractions who live positive lives could go a long way toward letting MAPs know that such lives are possible.

Besides allowing MAPs to see positive representations of themselves, showing positively portrayed MAP characters in the media would help to educate the general public about MAPs who do not offend. Not only might this curtail the number of social media posts encouraging violence against MAPs, but it could also encourage more people to publicly express support for MAPs, encouraging MAPs to come out and seek support from allied friends and family. This support could help MAPs struggling with stigma and could also help MAPs who feel at risk of offending.

IN CLOSING

As I close my book, I want to consider the most important findings from my research. In each interview I asked participants what they would say to a MAP who was just beginning to realize they were attracted to minors. Far and away, the most common response was "You are not a monster." As I heard this over and over, I imagined the people I was speaking to needing to hear these words when they first realized that they were minor-attracted, knowing that they often did not hear them until much later, and possibly *still* had not. The MAPs in my study understood that those who were beginning to identify their attractions would be concerned that they would turn into offenders. They understood this because they had so often felt that concern themselves, based on social stigma and society's ever-present narrative of the MAP as an offender. It has been my goal with this book to make clear the distinction between MAPs and sexual offenders, and to reaffirm that attractions are not equivalent to action.

Sexual offending against children can rightly be considered a monstrous act, yet this is not a fate that must befall MAPs. While the MAPs I spoke to in the course of my research often had experienced many struggles, many were able to find happiness, understanding, and the dignity they had been searching for. They found this dignity through the ability to be seen by others and to have their wellbeing recognized as important, through the knowledge that there were other people out there like them, and through validation that they were not destined to become monsters just because of their attractions. It is my hope that books will be written in the future that can focus on these MAPs—stories that do not focus excessively on MAPs' struggles and instead on their successes. These successes exist, and they deserve to be heard.

Participant Characteristics

Pseudonym	Location	Gender	Gender modality
Aiden	United States	Male	Cisgender
Avery	North America	Male	Cisgender
Brooke	United States	Female	Transgender
Bryan	United States	Male	Cisgender
Charlotte	United States	Female	Cisgender
Cody	Finland	Male	Cisgender
Desmond	Africa	Male	Cisgender
Dominick	North America	Male	Transgender
Elias	Canada	Male	Cisgender
Erik	UK	Male	Cisgender
Felix	North America	Male	Cisgender
Floyd	Japan	Male	Cisgender
Gene	United States	Male	Cisgender
George	Europe	Male	Cisgender
Harper	United States	Female	Cisgender
Hugo	United States	Male	Cisgender
Isaac	United States	Male	Cisgender
Jeremy	New Zealand	Male	Cisgender

Age	Age of preferential attractions	Exclusively attracted to minors?	Gender of attractions
39	9-13	Yes	Male
23	6–12	Yes	Female
35	All ages	No	Female
Early 40s	10–16, adult	No	Male
20	Prepubescent, pubescent	No	Female children, male and female adults
26	6–35	No	Female
35	8–13	No*	Male
19	6–15	No**	Male
28	1–adulthood	No	Female
Late 20s	5–12	Yes	Male, female
Late 30s	All ages	No	Male and female children, female adults
36	8–12	No	Female
40	7–12	Yes	Male, female
24	10–15	No*	Male
24	8–14	No	Female
24	7–14	Yes	Male children, female adults
64	6–12	No	Female
29	Preteen	Yes	Female

Pseudonym	Location	Gender	Gender modality
Josh	United States	Male	Cisgender
Kevin	Australia	Male	Cisgender
Klaus	Denmark	Male	Cisgender
Lee	North America	Male	Cisgender
Lucas	North America	Male	Cisgender
Mason	United States	Male	Cisgender
Mitchell	United States	Male	Cisgender
Neil	Germany	Male	Cisgender
Noah	Unknown	Male	Cisgender
Oliver	Canada	Male	Cisgender
Philip	United States	Male	Cisgender
Quentin	Central Europe	Male	Cisgender
Raymond	United States	Male	Cisgender
Robin	United States	Male	Cisgender
Shawn	United States	Male	Cisgender
Strand	United States	Male	Cisgender
Tony	United States	Male	Cisgender
Tyler	United States	Male	Cisgender
Victor	Colombia	Male	Cisgender
Vincent	United States	Male	Cisgender
West	Canada	Male	Cisgender
William	UK	Agender	Agender
Xavier	United States	Male	Cisgender
Zach	United States	Male	Cisgender

* Among adult attractions, only attracted to young-looking adults
** Among adult attractions, only nonsexual attractions to adults

Age	Age of preferential attractions	Exclusively attracted to minors?	Gender of attractions
Early 60s	3–39	No	Female
25	7–13	Yes	Female
33	Prepubescent	No	Female
28	8–12	Yes	Female
21	4–9	No	Female children, male and female adults
Early 40s	5–12	Yes	Male
50	12–14	Yes	Male
21	12–19	No*	Male
36	Prepubescent	Yes	Male
32	8–14	Yes	Female
35	9–13	No	Female
64	8–13	Yes	Male, female
21	5–13	Yes	Male, female
35	8–18	No*	All
40	11–17	No	Male children, female adults
33	All ages	No	Male, female
43	3–18	No*	Female
32	8–18	No	Female
24	7–12	No**	Male children, female adults
25	9–12	No*	Male
23	3–13	Yes	Male
21	8–13	No	Male, masculine nonbinary
20	2–17	No	Male and female children, female adults
47	11–15	No*	Female

Research Methods for a Difficult Subject

In my social media life, I'm what might be considered a "shitposter." I love a good meme, I like to talk about the politics of the day on my accounts, and I'll get involved in a Facebook argument at the drop of a hat when I notice someone being Wrong On The Internet.[1] I especially get active in posting when current events have to do with criminology and criminal justice, the fields I was trained in. But while I impulse-post about just about any topic imaginable related to my expertise, I'm extremely cautious about my posts discussing MAPs. Usually when I write on social media about attractions to minors, it's to use what I've learned from my research to caution my circle of friends that when they post [insert latest news article talking about "pedophiles" but meaning "child molesters" here], they should be aware that using these terms synonymously can be harmful, for all the reasons this book has discussed. As you might imagine, these are not my most popular posts. While some friends express gratitude for learning this information, others tell me that they feel triggered[2] by my posts about minor-attracted individuals, even when those conversations have nothing to do with sexual offending.

I suppose I shouldn't be surprised to get this reaction, as it's followed me since before I started my research. On my first day of class in my doctoral program in criminal justice, we students were asked to go around the room and state our names and research interests. Having waited for this moment for months, I had my answer ready and was excited to share with my fellow students. My topic was different; innovative; challenging. Surely the class would be impressed! The professor asked several follow-up questions to each student to get to know them better, and my anticipation increased as time went by. When she finally came to me, I shared my name, and said: "I want to engage in research with individuals who are attracted to minors, but who have never committed a sexual offense."

Her response: "Yuck. Next?"

This was my first conversation about my research interests that I had ever had with a criminal justice researcher, and my first encounter with the extent of the assumptions that those in the field of criminal justice have toward minor-attracted persons. Not only have I encountered criminologists who think this topic is "yucky" or even "dangerous," but many I've spoken with cannot seem to understand the topic in the first place. On another occasion within my doctoral program, an instructor asked about my research, and when I explained, he responded, "Oh, sex offenders." When I reiterated that no, the people I have interviewed are attracted to minors but have *not* committed an offense," he replied, "Right, sex offenders."

These responses to my research interests were my first indicators of the challenges I would encounter in researching the difficult subject of attractions to minors. My colleagues who work on research and write about individuals who are attracted to minors, as well as those who provide therapy to such individuals, are not strangers to the courtesy stigma associated with scholarship and practice regarding MAPs: they frequently receive hate mail, including death threats and accusations that they are attempting to "normalize" sexual offending against children. (Quite to the contrary, as I have stated throughout this book, there is ample reason to believe that efforts designed to increase societal understandings about MAPs can *decrease* offending against children.) During talks about my research, I have watched people take out their phones to fact-check my statements about pedophilia indicating something different than sex offending. Attendees of talks I have given have questioned the validity of my research, wondering aloud in Q&A sessions afterward if perhaps my participants were simply making everything up.

Certainly, my research was on a difficult subject. Courtesy stigma aside, the subject of my research brought up challenges for its development, recruitment, and reception. It is therefore vital to discuss the methods that I used in my attempt to produce reliable, valid, and ethical research. In this appendix I present the details of my research methods, for those who may wonder how I accessed a stigmatized population and for those who may wonder about my efforts to obtain authentic data.

DATA COLLECTION AND ANALYSIS

Data for my study were collected and analyzed using a qualitative approach. I conducted in-depth, semi-structured interviews with my participants, and explored the resulting data using inductive methods of analysis. I chose these methods in part because the population of MAPs who have refrained from committing sexual offenses is so understudied that relatively little is understood about them. Quantitative survey methods rely on researchers to create answer categories for participants to select from, requiring a substantial amount of information to be understood about a population before appropriately engaging in this kind of method. Qualitative methods are better suited for understudied populations—in interviews, participants can share a depth of information that cannot be captured on a survey, and their answers are their own, rather than predetermined by a researcher.[3] Therefore, using qualitative methods was essential for understanding aspects about this population that were not focused on in prior research—such as the wide variety of identity labels used by MAPs, their processes for deciding whether to come out to others, their coping methods, and their strategies to avoid offending, among other topics addressed in this study.

Sample and Recruitment

I recruited a purposive sample of 42 respondents for this study, using an advertisement distributed primarily to two online groups of MAPs: B4U-ACT and VirPed (introduced in the introduction and described in-depth in Chapters 3 and 4). My sample was composed of individuals who were 18 years of age or older, identified as having preferential attractions to children, and had never committed a crime involving sexual contact with a minor.

I prepared my recruitment strategy with the help of Luke Malone, a journalist who generated mainstream interest about minor-attracted individuals with his April 2014 piece in *This American Life*[4] as well as his follow-up article on *Medium*.[5] I contacted Luke through Twitter after hearing his piece on *This American Life,* and he graciously met with me and made recommendations to me regarding participant recruitment. He suggested that I get in contact with the founders of VirPed and offered to make introductions for me over email. In the fall of 2014, I was introduced by Luke to Nick Devin and Ethan Edwards (pseudonyms), the leaders of VirPed. I also contacted Richard Kramer (also a pseudonym), the education director of B4U-ACT.

Richard agreed to speak with me over a Skype audio call. He was optimistic and encouraging about my research topic, which at the time I had limited to the experiences of MAPs who had sought mental health services. Over the following year, he offered information about his own life as a MAP, provided advice to me about recruiting B4U-ACT participants, extended invitations to conferences and workshops, shared relevant research regarding my topic, participated in my pilot study, critiqued my initial interview protocol with B4U-ACT participants in mind, and advertised the study on the B4U-ACT website. Nick and Ethan at VirPed were similarly encouraging about the study and offered valuable advice regarding participant recruitment.

Within the first few days of 2016, after the pilot study (explained in more detail later in this appendix) was completed and the final study was agreed on by my mentors and my institution's Human Research Protection Program (HRPP), I began participant recruitment. The study's first participant was well-known on the VirPed forums. He agreed to participate with the understanding that he would evaluate the study before recommending it to others within VirPed. We used Google Hangouts, a text-based online chat program, to conduct the interview. Our interaction was clumsy: both of my pilot study interviews had been conducted orally, and this participant noted that I came off as awkward over text-based messaging. The participant also had concerns about confidentiality, worrying that my responsibility as a researcher to report participants if they disclosed committing a child abuse offense could put VirPed members at risk.[6] As such, he decided not to recommend my study to others on the VirPed forum. Despite this setback, B4U-ACT posted a link to a recruitment on their website, and emails from potential participants started coming in. Within the first week of interviews, an individual who was a member of both B4U-ACT and VirPed posted the study to the VirPed forums on his own, and I began to receive emails from members of that forum as well.

In my recruitment flyer, I asked interested potential participants to contact me either over email or by phone, and all but two of them initiated contact over email. In order to keep my participants anonymous, the recruitment flyer made it clear that those who contacted me should do so without revealing their true names, and any email addresses with which they contacted me should not reflect their identities. Some individuals created new email addresses just for participation in the study.

During the course of my research, a couple of my participants told me that some individuals on the VirPed forums had speculated that I was a cop, or that I was working with the police. Prospective interviewees therefore did some detective work to find out if I was "legit" or not, searching through my profiles on university websites, my LinkedIn account, and my other social media accounts. Interestingly, one perceived indicator of my legitimacy as a researcher (aside from my online presence) was the fact that participation in the study did not entail any monetary incentive. I had originally decided not to offer a financial incentive for participation partly due to a lack of funds, but also largely out of concern for my participants' privacy. While senior researchers were concerned that not offering an incentive would deter some potential participants from engaging in the study, the MAPs in my study specified during interviews that financial incentives were generally thought to be evidence of a "honeypot"—a deception strategy seeking to make participants easily identifiable (paying these participants would have involved some link to their bank accounts, addresses, or other personal information). In this case, not offering an incentive may have increased my number of participants, although that may seem counterintuitive.

I began interviewing participants in January 2016. Recruitment was steady throughout the first four months of the study, tapered off, and dropped and came to a halt in August 2016. I conducted one additional interview in 2017, after meeting an interested potential participant at a B4U-ACT workshop early that year. Before each interview I screened potential participants for eligibility requirements—age, attraction to minors, and non-offending status—over email or phone (depending on the participant's original method of contacting me). I also used email and phone exchanges to ensure that my potential respondents had not initiated contact using their real names, to inform them about the procedures surrounding interviews, for scheduling purposes, and to allow them to choose their preferred platform for the interviews. Participants were originally offered the possibility of engaging in interviews over the phone, Skype (video, audio, or text-based chat), or Google Hangouts, depending on their comfort level. Some respondents were concerned about confidentiality using the options that had been proposed, and suggested other platforms such as TorChat (which uses The Onion Router, concealing user location), Chatzy (an online, private chat service), and CryptoCat (an open-source, encrypted chat service). While I ended up using Chatzy and CryptoCat for interviews, I did not use TorChat (largely due to a failure on my part to understand how to set it up).

At least three individuals who originally indicated interest in participating in the study ultimately declined to do so, due to unavailability or concerns that engaging in interviews would go against their own therapeutic goals. Some individuals ceased to respond to emails without actively declining to participate. Most individuals who emailed me about participating, however, went on to complete an interview. The majority of my study's participants (26 in total) chose to communicate for at least part of their interviews over audio platforms (either over the phone or Skype). Two additional respondents spoke to me over Skype with video, and one participant requested an in-person interview. The other 13 participants preferred to conduct their interviews exclusively over text-based chat platforms.

Interviews

I conducted semi-structured interviews with all of the study respondents. I chose this interview structure because it enables participants to provide in-depth information, and because this type of interview is considered the best for allowing participants to share their own perspectives, rather than providing the types of answers that might be expected by the researcher.[7] I asked participants a series of screening questions to confirm their eligibility before beginning each interview. Eligibility requirements included that participants had to be at least 18 years old and be preferentially attracted to minors. I also set as a requirement that potential participants had not committed a sexual offense against a minor.

Because MAPs who have not committed sexual offenses are a largely understudied population, there existed few examples of previous interview instruments on this subject that I could use as a guide. The phrasing of various questions in my interview protocols was therefore a big concern for me—I worried that my questions could unintentionally be offensive, or might not be understood by the MAPs in my study. Consequently I conducted a pilot study in the spring of 2015 to seek advice from MAPs about the topics covered in interviews, the wording of my questions, and the flow of the interview guide. I asked Richard Kramer to be a participant—by this point, I had met him in person at one of the B4U-ACT's workshops—and he readily agreed to participate. He also sent an email to B4U-ACT participants asking for other volunteers, and one individual responded immediately. The pilot study was limited to these two participants because I worried that having too many participants involved in a pilot study could limit the number of individuals who would be interested in participating in the full study. I was not sure how large the potential pool of individuals interested in participating might be, and those who participated in a pilot study may have been uninterested in engaging in a later interview.

Comments from both pilot study participants were essential to the development of my final interview guide. Prior to the pilot study, my interview instrument included questions about seeking mental health care for purposes of remaining resilient to offending. Pilot study participants advised me to include questions about mental health care-seeking behaviors for other reasons as well. Participants in the pilot study further highlighted the rich information that would emerge by adding in these questions. They also recommended that I reexamine an assumption I had clearly made in writing the original interview guide, that attractions to minors are exclusively sexual. These participants also helped me to better understand the dynamics of online forums for MAPs (such as the ways MAPs with attractions to young children are able to access support on those sites), and questions relevant to this topic were added to the interview guide. Finally, the pilot participants requested clarifications for certain interview questions, which provided additional insight into how best to reorder and reword various questions to maximize the coherence and clarity of the interview. The pilot study participants undoubtedly improved the study by enhancing its clarity, assumptions, goals, and ways to best communicate with misunderstood people.

Subsequent to the pilot study, HRPP review, and extensive conversations with various mentors, my interview guide was finalized. It asked my study's 42 participants questions about identity formation, including questions about their history in figuring out their attractions for themselves and coming out to others. I then asked them about their experiences in facing stigma, including questions regarding the effects of their exposure to negative messages about minor-attracted individuals, and how they coped with hearing these messages. Finally, I asked about their strategies toward and motivations for remaining resilient to sexual offending, as well as more specific questions about seeking mental health services for emotional resilience and resilience to offending. The protocols ended with six basic demographic questions.

Interviews were intended to be conversational in nature. I asked questions in different sequences depending on the direction of the discussion with each participant, and sometimes I skipped them entirely when a participant answered questions before being asked. My personal experience with coming out as queer, and the associated stigma, helped me in developing follow-up questions that were directly relevant to the experiences of participants. Indeed, multiple study participants actively identified as lesbian, gay, bisexual, transgender, pansexual, and/or queer. However, while disclosing my sexuality during interviews increased rapport and eased discussions with some participants, others indicated feeling abandoned by queer communities due to the mainstreaming of LGBT interests, and thus I only selectively shared this information with my participants.

All interviews were conducted one-on-one, and most were conducted when participants were out of the house, or during times when the family or roommates of participants were out. In at least two cases, the family members were aware of the individual's attractions toward minors, and participants felt comfortable conducting the interview with the family members in the home (though in a separate area). Field notes and transcripts were stored on flash drives and kept in a locked cabinet.

In total, interview time added up to 5,243 minutes. Interview times for each participant lasted between 30 minutes and 5.5 hours, but most were between 1.5 and 2 hours. Interviews that took place over text-based chat took longer than others, and those that ran over two hours (and occasionally others as well) were often conducted in segments over multiple days. A total of 51 interview segments were conducted. Audio, video, and in-person interviews were audio-recorded with consent and were then transcribed.[8] I explained to my participants that their interviews would be transcribed by an outside source but gave them the option of having me transcribe them myself instead; only two of my participants indicated that they would prefer this. I transcribed one additional interview for financial reasons. Transcripts were verbatim, and included pauses, false starts, nonlexical vocables (e.g., "um," "uh," "er"), laughter, and other sounds that might not be considered essential to the narratives of participants but that nonetheless added context to participant narratives.

Field notes were also integral to my work. After each of my interviews, I wrote down notes about the interviews beyond what would have been evident from the transcripts. Details from my field notes included factual descriptions of the settings I was in or what I saw during the interviews (especially in the few cases in which I met with a participant in person or over video call), my impressions of my participants and the interviews themselves, parts of the interviews that especially stood out to me, questions that the interviews brought up for me, and suggestions for myself about what I might want to bring up in subsequent interviews based on what I had heard just then. I also recorded for myself notes about how I felt during the interviews, including emotions that came up for me based on what my participants said, or notes about if I had felt distracted during my interviews based factors external to the interviews themselves. These field notes allowed me to process the interviews as they happened, develop questions for subsequent interviews, and contextualize my transcripts for later write-ups.

Method of Analysis

After the interviews were transcribed, I analyzed the resulting data using an inductive approach by open-coding for common themes, which allows themes to emerge from the data.[9] Because I had conducted all of the interviews, transcribed three of them, and cleaned all of the transcriptions using audio files, some of the major themes of the interviews became clear before coding began. Interviews were transcribed and open-coded on an ongoing basis, which took place while I collected data. I used Dedoose, a software program designed for mixed methods data analysis, to code the data. I began with open-coding, allowing for the identification of gaps in the data, and generated ideas about how to gather additional information that could help flesh out key concepts. I then conducted further interviews with the goal of generating this new information in mind.

In some cases, when I had interviewed participants multiple times, I asked them in a subsequent section of an interview for clarification about the new information I was looking for; more often, new participants were asked about emerging concepts as they were developed. The last question of the interview protocol inquired about whether there was any topic I had failed to ask that the interviewee considered important to the research. In some cases, I included the highlighted items in subsequent interviews. After completing the interviews and open-coding, I conducted focused coding, using the most frequently occurring and important codes from the open coding process to synthesize greater amounts of data. I then drew up memos, or details about ideas and the start of analytic construction,[10] reflecting my thoughts about the concepts, before beginning to write full drafts of my findings.

THE QUESTION OF ACCURACY

This book refers to participants alternately as having refrained from sexual contact with minors; as non-offenders; as individuals who have abstained from sexual activity with minors since adulthood; and other formulations. This is specifically meant to be understood that participants in this study, based on their own verification, have not committed a *contact* (i.e., *person*) offense against a minor. However, due in part to the anonymous nature of my study, I was unable to verify that my participants had, indeed, never committed an offense—if I had had access to my participants' names, for instance, I could have potentially looked up legal records to verify a lack of a criminal record. However, I told my potential participants about the requirements for participation in the initial recruitment flyer, and I screened for offending status in preinterview communications. While no one explicitly told me they had committed an offense, two of my potential respondents decided not to participate after we discussed the eligibility requirements over email. They could have declined for other reasons than having committed an offense; I am unable to determine their reasoning.

While I did not verify my participants' accounts by looking up personal information, I did engage in triangulation by gathering other sources. Triangulation is significant in qualitative methods due to its ability to increase credibility in findings: this strategy decreases "the risk of chance associations and of systematic biases due to a specific method,"[11] and adds to the richness of the data. To triangulate findings, I gathered and analyzed materials from both the B4U-ACT and VirPed websites, including mission statements, educational resources, cited research, and forum discussions. As sociologist Glenn Bowen[12] has noted, document analysis can significantly add to the ability to authenticate and substantiate data acquired in a study. I have also attended four workshops hosted by B4U-ACT to better understand issues faced by MAPs. These methods of triangulation helped to provide an additional check to verify that the experiences and opinions of study participants were present among other MAPs as well. Themes surrounding identity formation, stigma, and coping that were explored at B4U-ACT conferences and on both the VirPed and B4U-ACT websites did, indeed, reflect the data I obtained during interviews.

Constructing a false narrative surrounding their lack of offending would have been risky to participants since being a MAP already carries stigma, and considering that there were no direct benefits to respondents for their participation in the research, it is therefore unlikely that they would have taken the risk of participating if they had committed a contact offense. In addition, as shown in Chapters 3–5, participants disclosed a number of socially unacceptable details about themselves, which provides supporting evidence that they endeavored to represent themselves accurately.

Despite all of this, it is indeed likely that some of my participants provided some inaccurate information in their narratives, just as it is likely that some participants in any research study have provided some inaccurate information. Participants' memory, research incentives, and social desirability can all affect the accuracy of information collected through participant responses[13]—the same way they can affect the accuracy of information conveyed in conversations within everyday life. Importantly, all of the participants in my study had established identities for themselves as non-offenders, making their narratives relevant to other non-offending MAPs who share similar identities. To those who question the truthfulness of my research participants, I ask: For how many other research studies have they cast doubt upon participants? Is this doubt about research methods, or about a fundamental mistrust of MAPs? I propose that the questions we may ask ourselves about my participants' degree of honesty says more about us as a society than it does about my participants themselves.

ETHICAL CONSIDERATIONS

In any research study that engages with sensitive material, confidentiality is a major concern and must be given attention. To that end, as previously noted, I asked potential participants to contact me using email addresses that did not reveal any personal information. Some participants devised email addresses with fake names solely for the purpose of this study; often, however, participants already had pseudonyms and email addresses that they used to communicate with each other, or with other researchers or journalists. I requested that participants provide me with a pseudonym that they would like to use in the study. Some participants selected names that they liked; others selected names from their immediate surroundings. One individual provided me the name of an author of a book that was lying around near him, and another gave the name of a company displayed on a truck that he encountered while driving during our phone interview. The latter individual, like many others in this study, participated in the interview in the privacy of his car. Others provided names that were known to individuals in the MAP community, or names that had some kind of connection to their real names. A new pseudonym was chosen for each study participant who had not chosen an entirely new name for the purpose of the interview, to protect their privacy.

The respondents' pseudonyms are the only names that are attached to any of the information that was provided in the context of this study. To safeguard this information, I requested and was granted a waiver of signed informed consent from the City University of New York (CUNY) HRPP. I explained to each of my respondents their rights as a research participant via a consent script, which gave them further information about the study and provided phone numbers of an on-call social worker. The consent script was read orally in the case of oral interviews, and provided over email in the case of text-based interviews. Interviews only proceeded after participants acknowledged that they agreed to the terms of the consent script.

I cautioned my participants that if they disclosed committing past acts of child abuse, any current crime, or intent to commit any future crime, I would have to end the interview and file a police report. A concern among a small number of participants was whether viewing child pornography would be regarded as an act of child abuse; however, mandated reporting guidelines for New York State, from which I conducted all of my interviews, do not consider viewing child pornography an act of child abuse, shielding such acts from mandatory reporting.[14]

At the start of each interview, I provided participants the phone number of an on-call social worker. If they experienced distress during or after the interview and felt that they needed to talk to someone, they could stop the interview at any time and contact her (although this never occurred). During interviews I asked participants about whether they had been on any websites that aimed to connect MAPs with peer support. When respondents indicated being unaware of these different support outlets and expressed interest in seeking support, I provided them with further information about these sources after our interview. Because my participants were likely to experience stigma and a host of mental health concerns, providing potential sources of support was helpful and appreciated by my respondents.

In some cases, I also reached out to my networks to provide other resources for participants. In one case, a participant talked about how the shame he felt about his attractions was affecting multiple aspects of his life, but after our interview he told me that he'd been relieved to finally talk to someone about what he'd been going through. After further communication, he asked me for help finding a therapist. I reached out to other participants who had discussed successfully finding the help of a supportive therapist, and connected that participant with the phone number of a recommended practitioner who provided therapy over the phone as well as advice from other MAPs about questions to ask a potential therapist. I heard back from him later that he had successfully found a therapist close to him whom he was able to come out to as minor-attracted.

SITTING WITH DISCOMFORT

My initial college and graduate school training were in social work, and I've spent years working as a counselor. One of the lessons social workers are taught when they enter the counseling fields is how to "sit with discomfort." In other words, counselors need to know how to be present with their clients as their clients share their experiences of pain, trauma, and other difficult circumstances. It can hurt to see and hear the distress of someone sitting in front of you, or on the other end of a phone call, and feel powerless to end it, but your hurt as a counselor needs to be deprioritized so you can focus on your client's needs. This difficult work requires practice.

Over and over in interviews with my participants, I was grateful for my social work training in sitting with discomfort. Feelings of shame, embarrassment, loneliness, and grief, along with experiences of being harmed by others, flooded the interviews I conducted. My field notes are peppered with descriptions of painful emotions discussed by my participants, or my own sadness as I listened to them. For a number participants, I was the first person they had ever told out loud about their attractions. This created in me a sense of responsibility, not only to write about this topic in a considerate way that took my participants' wellbeing into account, but I also felt responsible to each individual participant. As a result, during interviews, I often toggled between using therapeutic skills and skills I was more used to thinking of as interview-related. Usually these skills overlapped. Active listening, building rapport, and creating an environment in which my participants felt comfortable talking to me are skills associated both with the mental health fields and with interview methods.

Sometimes, however, my social work skills took over where they conflicted with my interview skills. On occasion, the hurt my participants described made it difficult for me to focus on my task as a researcher to keep asking questions, or to delve deeper into a story that clearly upset a participant. There were occasions in which I did not ask for more clarification even when I was not certain of a participant's meaning. In interviews I often let pauses go on for longer than was comfortable. I frequently validated my participants' emotions. Perhaps as a result of these actions, multiple participants told me that they felt their interviews were therapeutic for them.

Vicarious Trauma and Self-care

On the one hand, my social work skills seemed to be paying off for my participants in terms of therapeutic value, and they also seemed to be working for me in terms of building rapport with respondents, gaining more participants via word of mouth, and collecting data. On the other hand, conducting these interviews also had a negative effect on my own mental health. I was asking questions that elicited narratives about stigma, shame, and hopelessness. My participants told me about some of their darkest moments—being assumed to be sex offenders, being outed by others, suicide attempts. In the mental health fields it is common knowledge that regularly hearing about the distress of others can bring on compassion fatigue and vicarious trauma, but I had never heard of these phenomena applied to researchers. Hearing constantly about these experiences brought on feelings for me that were consistent with vicarious trauma and compassion fatigue.

In addition to being open to me about traumatic life experiences, participants were also open with me about some of their prejudices. This became extremely uncomfortable when their prejudices were against my own identities. I initially thought that my identity as a sexual minority might help me build rapport with this group due to shared commonalities, but I quickly found out that that was not universally the case. Some participants had experiences being denied acceptance into LGBTQ groups; others found being gay to be entirely immoral and told me as much. I had participants tell me about the immorality of the "gay lifestyle," that "being gay is a choice," that "TERF is a slur."[15] Even as my participants came out to me in a variety of ways, I kept my statuses as gay, trans, and nonbinary hidden from many of them.

There were times when I felt disturbed by my own research. While it was rare, my respondents occasionally told me about having urges to commit offenses or about having previously watched child pornography. Despite their obvious guilt when telling me about these behaviors, I was profoundly angry at those who disclosed this to me, yet I needed to maintain composure throughout our interviews. I also felt profoundly disturbed when I heard my participants argue against age-of-consent laws, believing that children could realistically consent to sexual activity with adults. In moments such as these, I felt less sympathy toward my participants overall. And yet, these individuals were in the minority. In one illustration of this proportion, at a B4U-ACT workshop that I attended, a MAP derailed a productive conversation about research ethics by arguing against age-of-consent laws, to the unmistakable disdain of the other attendees (all other MAPs included). That attendee was told by the B4U-ACT leadership, which includes MAPs, that his comments were unwelcome, and he was suspended from attending future workshops. Although I felt troubled in certain moments while conducting this research, I needed to keep in mind that occasional moments were not representative of the narratives I was hearing as a whole.

While I sometimes felt uncomfortable over what my participants told me in interviews, I found writing critically about them to be extremely difficult: as MAPs are a deeply stigmatized population, I was aware that I could be adding to stigma by condemning their words. On the whole, I found my participants to be brave for talking to me, considering how our society generally thinks about them. They were generous with their time, talking to me for hours with no compensation. And I empathized with their struggles as people who had attractions that they could not stop and did not want. I did not want to repay their bravery and generosity by censuring them. Simultaneously, however, when my participants occasionally disclosed beliefs and experiences that were deeply problematic, this needed to be discussed—these problems can result in real harm if left unaddressed, and as protecting children is a key goal of my research, leaving them unaddressed is not an option.

As a result of learning about so many traumatic experiences, combined with hearing my participants discuss viewpoints or talk about behaviors that made me uncomfortable, and feeling a great deal of pressure to write about them in the "right" way, I became increasingly stressed as I continued my research. As a social worker, I decided the most effective form of self-care would be to seek out therapy. Fortunately, good therapists were easily accessible to me (thank you, CUNY, for the great health insurance), and my therapist was adept at helping me process the anxieties I felt as I carried out the rest of my research. I continue to recommend therapy to anyone engaged in research about difficult subjects: having support with carrying a heavy mental load can be invaluable. Not only did therapy help me emotionally, but it had the unexpected benefit of helping my research: as I processed my thoughts about my research out loud in therapy, I was also able to more clearly think through many of the concepts in my data.

PAYING IT FORWARD

My participants took a risk simply by talking to me. As I mentioned, some assumed I was collaborating with the police or that I was a police officer myself. Even those participants who understood that I'm a researcher were taking a risk on an unknown—they did not know how I would be using the data that they were providing me; they had no way of knowing whether I would twist or condemn their words. Nonetheless, they decided to open up to a stranger about having an identity that most people would consider monstrous. As a result of the data given to me by my research participants through interviews, my career has benefited—I have been hired since the completion of my research by multiple universities, have been published in multiple scholarly journals, and I currently have a tenure-track faculty position.

I have tried to reciprocate for my participants' engagement with me in interviews by paying it forward in multiple ways, ranging from the simple to the complex. I do my best to educate people about MAPs based on my research—in private conversations, through social media, as I mentioned earlier, and through publications, such as this very book. I also remain active with B4U-ACT, which continues to host workshops for MAPs, practitioners, and researchers. I have served on committees to plan some of these workshops as well and have engaged in meetings with their groups, presenting about my research findings and inviting MAPs and researchers to ask me questions about this research. Many of these ways of paying it forward have also furthered my career—publishing, for example, will help me get closer to securing tenure—though some have no benefit (for example, advocating through the revise-and-resubmit process for using destigmatizing language for MAPs, which could lead to my articles being rejected from journals). I engage regularly with students who are interested in studying MAPs, who will also contribute to the field.

With these efforts I am aiming not only to pay the MAP community back for their help with my data collection, but to move my fields of study forward. Ultimately I hope that these efforts give society a push forward as well. Social work and criminal justice research can have a direct influence on policies and practices in each of these areas, and as researchers push back on harmful and inaccurate ideas about MAPs, more resources can open up to MAPs, and barriers to their care can begin to decrease.

Notes

1. To protect participant confidentiality, all names given here are pseudonyms.

2. Throughout this introduction, and elsewhere in this book, I use the term "pedophile" to refer to individuals who are preferentially attracted to prepubescent children. More and more frequently, scholars are being encouraged to use person-first language (i.e., "person with pedophilia"), the goal of which is to remind the reader of the personhood of those being referred to. While this is an important goal, I have chosen to use the term "pedophile" rather than "person with pedophilia" throughout this book because it is consistent with the identity labels chosen by some of my research participants (more about this in Chapter 1).

3. CNN, 2019.

4. E.g., Jenkins, 1998; Peersman et al., 2012; Pendar, 2007; Rutgaizer et al., 2012.

5. Hall & Hall, 2007.

6. Briere & Runtz, 1989; Cantor & McPhail, 2016; Kingston et al., 2007; Seto, 2018.

7. See Okami & Goldberg, 1992.

8. Blanchard et al., 2001; Kingston et al., 2007; Maletzky & Steinhauser, 2002; Seto & Lalumière, 2001; Seto et al., 2003; Seto et al., 2017; see Seto, 2018, for a review.

9. Cossins (2000), Finkelhor (1984), and Marshall & Barbaree (1990), as well as other scholars, have proposed models that may explain why people may commit sexual offenses against children in the absence of pedophilia, including seeking power, having emotional congruence with children, or experiencing trauma in childhood. See Seto (2018) for more.

10. I refer throughout this book to "official" definitions of categories of attraction that MAPs fall under. However, as a trans individual myself, it's important that I preface this by noting that the sexuality research-

ers who have been responsible for conceptualizing these categories, and whose research is frequently cited (even in this very book), have promoted questionable discourse related to transgender individuals. Ray Blanchard, for instance, has put forward a theory on "autogynephilia" that has contributed to lasting stigma toward transgender communities, and James Cantor resigned from the Society for the Scientific Study of Sexuality after the society condemned the use of anti-transgender rhetoric.

11. American Psychiatric Association, 2013a.

12. Blanchard et al., 2009.

13. Blanchard et al., 2009.

14. Part of the disagreement over use of the term "ephebophile" is because it is not an atypical experience for adults to experience attractions to minors in this age range (see Blanchard et al., 2009).

15. Seto, 2018.

16. Blanchard et al., 2009.

17. B4U-ACT, 2019.

18. Malone, 2014a.

19. Braithwaite, 1989.

20. Importantly, Braithwaite's (1989) arguments about reintegrative shaming indicate that the reintegration aspect is necessary for shame to have its desired effect. Thus, disintegrative/stigmatizing shame, a prominent characteristic of the US criminal legal system, is also likely to be counterproductive (see Mingus & Burchfield, 2012; Robbers, 2009).

21. American Psychiatric Association, 2013a.

22. While pedophilia itself is not considered a mental illness in the DSM-V (American Psychiatric Association, 2013a), the manual differentiates between "pedophilia" and "pedophilic disorder." Pedophilic disorder, which is considered a diagnosable disorder by the American Psychiatric Association, occurs when an individual over the age of 16 is attracted to prepubescent children *and* either acts on these attractions or is significantly distressed by them. In absence of particular distress, or acting on these attractions, the DSM-V originally labeled attractions to prepubescent children as "pedophilic sexual orientation" (American Psychiatric Association, 2013a, p. 698). After the DSM-V was released, however, the American Psychiatric Association received backlash over its use of the phrase "sexual orientation" to describe this population, and they responded by changing this phrasing to "sexual interest" (American Psychiatric Association, 2013b).

23. GLAAD, 2016.

24. Moser, 2016.

25. Seto, 2012; Seto, 2017.

26. Freimond, 2013; Freund & Kuban, 1993; Li, 1991; Marshall, Barbaree, & Eccles, 1991; Seto, 2012; Seto, Lalumière, & Blanchard, 2000; Seto et al., 2003.

27. Goode, 2009; Li, 1991.

28. See Mogul, Ritchie, & Whitlock, 2011.

29. American Psychiatric Association, 2013a.

30. Malón, 2012.

31. Substance Abuse and Mental Health Services Administration, 2015.

32. As of July 2020, 20 states and DC had outlawed sexual orientation change efforts for minors (Movement Advancement Project, 2020).

33. Chenier, 2008; Malón, 2012.

34. Participants in this study, based on their own verification, have not committed a contact (i.e., *person*) offense against a minor. Due in part to the anonymous nature of the study, I was unable to verify using official data that participants had committed no contact offense for which they had been arrested. However, potential participants were told about the requirements for participation before contacting the researcher and were screened for offending status in preinterview communications.

35. It is beyond this study to determine generalizability; this is not a typical goal of qualitative research. However, the lack of diversity in my sample in terms of race and gender struck me as odd as I was conducting my research, and I continuously question it. It is a limitation of my research that I never targeted recruitment at groups who were highly underrepresented in my sample, including women and people of color. Although some may conclude from my sample that men and white people are more likely be MAPs, there are a number of other plausible explanations for the lack of involvement of women and people of color in groups from which I recruited for this study.

36. VirPed refers to its members almost exclusively as "pedophiles," specifying the distinction between pedophiles and individuals who commit sex offenses against children.

37. VirPed forums are heavily moderated. The posts of those who are new to the forums, or who have fewer posts, are read by official moderators before they are published. This control is partly undertaken to prevent vitriolic speech (largely due to the fact that members of the public are welcome to participate on VirPed), but especially to prevent discussions about child sexual abuse and pornography, which are forbidden on the forums. Admissions of past illegal activity not known to police are particularly prohibited. Because the aim of VirPed is to provide a safe space for MAPs to communicate, the moderators make every effort to avoid police surveillance.

38. Multiple participants in my study have speculated that VirPed's vehement stance against sexual contact between adults and minors is responsible for its relative success in attracting forum members as compared to B4U-ACT. Indeed, some VirPed members in the current study have accused B4U-ACT of being "pro-contact," a term I explore in later chapters. Remarkably, other MAPs interviewed in this study, who belonged to neither the B4U-ACT nor VirPed forums, had the reverse view of B4U-ACT

(and VirPed as well), stating that their advocacy for MAPs to follow the law indicated that they were "self-hating."

39. B4U-ACT, 2011.

CHAPTER 1. "AM I A MONSTER?"

1. E.g., Ballard, 1990.

2. Erikson, 1959; Erikson, 1968.

3. Cass, 1979; Coleman, 1982; Minton & MacDonald, 1983; Troiden, 1989.

4. E.g., Rabinovich & Morton, 2016.

5. American Psychiatric Association, 2013a.

6. This would be the British spelling—in Britain, "paedophile" is the accepted use; hence "paedosexual." In the United States, participants commonly use "pedophile," and some MAPs may use "pedosexual." Where my participants used "paedophile" or "paedosexual" in text-based chat, I mirror its use throughout this book.

7. There is indeed a history of the gay community distancing itself from MAPs, although segments of the gay community had previously been aligned with pedophile groups. Chenier (2008, pp. 205–206) noted that in the 1970s, the Pedophile Information Exchange had ties to the Gay Liberation Front. Thorstad (1991, p. 252) documented that "the Stonewall Generation...affirmed the joys of an outlaw sexuality in the face of the outmoded moral norms of the dominant society," including sex between adults and minors. However, Thorstad argued that society became more welcoming of LGBT individuals in the aftermath of the Stonewall riots, which came about at the same time as a national panic about child pornography. This resulted in a gay community that aligned itself more with mainstream values and consequently rejected MAPs.

8. For more about my participants' uses of identity labels along the queer spectrum, see Walker (2019).

9. E.g., Cass, 1979; Coleman, 1982; Minton & MacDonald, 1983; Savin-Williams & Diamond, 2000; Troiden, 1989.

10. The "global north" refers to countries with comparatively greater wealth and political and economic freedom, including the United States, Canada, the majority of European countries, Australia, and New Zealand, among others.

11. Troiden's (1989) model was itself an offshoot of a theoretical model written by Cass (1984).

12. For a review, see Kelly & Lusk (2013).

13. Savin-Williams & Diamond, 2000.

14. Mogul, Ritchie, and Whitlock, 2011.

15. Blanchard et al., 2007; Cantor et al., 2004; Cantor et al., 2005.

16. This line of research has generally been conducted with men who

have committed sex offenses, a population that has not been shown to be generalizable to all MAPs.

17. E.g., American Psychiatric Association, 2013a; Seto, 2012.

18. To clarify, the DSM-V describes "pedophilic disorder" not as attractions to prepubescent children, but as acting on, or experiencing distress regarding, these attractions. Some of my participants argued that this was not unlike the "ego-dystonic homosexuality" (characterized by anxiety toward one's sexual orientation) in the DSM-III (American Psychiatric Association, 1980), or "sexual disorder not otherwise specified" in the DSM-III-R (American Psychiatric Association, 1987), which included "persistent and marked distress about one's sexual orientation."

19. Cass, 1984.

CHAPTER 2. "LEADING A DOUBLE LIFE"

1. Day & Schoenrade, 1997.

2. Chekola, 1994; Cole et al., 1996; Critcher & Ferguson, 2014; Greene, Derlega, & Matthews, 2006; Morris, Waldo, & Rothblum, 2001.

3. Aranda et al., 2009; Carbado, 2001; Couzens, Mahoney, & Wilkinson, 2017.

4. Baiocco et al., 2015; Legate, Ryan, & Weinstein, 2012; McGarrity & Huebner, 2013; Ryan, Legate, & Weinstein, 2015; Schrimshaw et al., 2013.

5. News reports confirm that Bijan Ebrahimi was "beaten to death and set alight" due to false accusations of "being a pedophile" (BBC News, 2018). However, because media often erroneously switches the terms "pedophilia" and "child molestation," it is difficult to tell whether Mr. Ebrahimi was suspected of abusing a child or was merely suspected of being attracted to minors. This distinction would probably have little impact on Elias's concerns, because pedophilia and sex offending are so closely linked in social understandings that to be suspected of pedophilia may also mean being suspected of abusing a minor.

6. It also may be inaccurate to call our interview an "exception," given that it was anonymous and conducted over a secure text chat service.

7. West had an innovative way of shooing off the dates his sister had tried to set him up with. Although his political views are decidedly toward the left, he developed a collection of Donald Trump memorabilia to scare off any potential matches.

CHAPTER 3. "ENDURING A RAINSTORM"

1. Goffman, 1963.

2. For a review, see Chaudoir, Earnshaw, & Andel, 2013.

3. E.g., Greene, Derlega, & Mathews, 2006; Miller & Major, 2000.

4. Jahnke, Imhoff, & Hoyer, 2015.

5. Cash, 2016; Freimond, 2013; Goode, 2009; Grady et al., 2019; Jahnke et al., 2015.

6. Cash, 2016; Jahnke et al., 2015.

7. Beaber, 2008; Frable, Wortman, & Joseph, 1997.

8. Almeida et al., 2009; Irwin et al., 2014; Lewis et al., 2003; Ross et al., 2007; Virupaksha, Muralidhar, & Ramakrishna, 2016.

9. See Pachankis, 2007; Pachankis et al., 2015.

10. See Connor-Smith et al., 2000.

11. Compas et al., 2001, p. 89.

12. Tumblr has since systematically removed users who discuss MAPs and minor attraction.

13. Corrigan, Watson, & Barr, 2006, p. 882.

14. Compas et al., 2001; Connor-Smith et al., 2000; Miller & Kaiser, 2001.

15. Varni et al., 2012; Ilic et al., 2012; Miller & Kaiser, 2001.

16. Ilic et al., 2012; Miller & Kaiser, 2001.

17. In this case, the stigmatized identity was having a mental health disorder (Link et al., 1989; Link, Mirotznik, & Cullen, 1991).

18. E.g., Boyle et al., 2017; Harris & Edlund, 2005; Khantzian, 1997; Russell, Driscoll, & Truong, 2002; Suh et al., 2008; Wardell et al., 2018.

19. Talley & Littlefield, 2014.

20. Brick, 2012.

21. Ilic et al., 2012.

22. Schallhorn, 2015.

23. Riessman, 1965.

24. Solomon, 2004.

25. Russell & Richards, 2003; Singh, Hays, & Watson, 2011.

26. E.g., Barnes & Meyer, 2012.

27. Rowen & Malcolm, 2003.

28. Halkitis et al., 2009.

29. Holohan, Moos, & Schaefer, 1996; Krieger & Sidney, 1996; Major & Schmader, 1998.

30. Seto, 2018.

CHAPTER 4. "IT'S A VERY STRONG BOUNDARY FOR ME"

1. Greenwood, 2018.

2. E.g., Cid & Martí, 2012; Maruna, 2001; Massoglia and Uggen, 2010; Sampson & Laub, 1995.

3. Homel, Lincoln, & Herd, 1999; Murray, 2010.

4. As detailed in Haydon, 2014.

5. Malone, 2014a; Malone, 2014b.

6. Devin & Edwards, 2012.

7. B4U-ACT, 2015.

8. Brooke referred to research by Levine (2002) suggesting that

shielding minors from information about sex could, in some circumstances, cause them harm. Levine's book is an exploration of a societal pattern of limiting youths' access to knowledge about sex in general, from abstinence-only education to media censorship to categorizing sexual behaviors among children as deviance or illness. Mitchell made reference to research conducted by Savin-Williams (1998), which suggested that sexual relationships between adults and older adolescents could be interpreted by those adolescents as beneficial. This finding was based on research with 180 males ages 14 to 25, about first sexual experiences between gay and bisexual males; 25% of Savin-Williams's participants had had first sexual relationships with men more than five years older than they were. Often his participants described these relationships as coming-of-age experiences that helped them to learn how to be gay. However, when the relationship was between an adolescent and an adult more than ten years older than him, the adolescent was less likely to view the relationship as positive.

9. Laws & Ward, 2010; Terry, 2015.

10. Miller, 2010.

11. See Forliti, 2017.

12. See Ricciardelli & Moir, 2013; Trammell & Chenault, 2009.

13. Murray 2010; 2012.

14. Although it is possible that Isaac was referring to "virtuous" in a religious context, VirPed is not a religious organization. They specify on their website: "'Virtuous' to us just means that we can be good people as opposed to monsters" (Devin & Edwards, 2012).

15. Cisgender refers to someone whose gender is the same as the gender they were assigned at birth.

16. In the United States, producing, distributing, purchasing, and receiving visual, sexualized depictions of real children (and computer-generated images indistinguishable from real children) is illegal. Mandatory minimum sentences of at least 15 years are applied to the production of child pornography, and although there are no mandatory minimum penalties for possession, lengthy prison sentences can apply (see United States Department of Justice, 2017). Despite the illegality of possessing child pornography, enforcing child pornography laws presents a challenge to law enforcement (see Wash, Wolak, & Finkelhor, 2013; Wells, Finkelhor, & Wolak, 2007), and its enforcement can therefore vary widely across the United States.

17. Seto & Eke, 2005.

18. Eke, Seto, & Williams, 2011.

19. Taylor & Quayle, 2003, p. 90.

20. Wolak et al., 2008, p. 120.

21. Stout, 2002.

22. United States Department of Justice, 2018.

23. Enforcement of these laws via prosecution and conviction is rare

(see Samenow, 2012) and seems to typically occur when an individual also possesses child pornography depicting sexual images of real children.

24. Varley, 2018.

CHAPTER 5. "THEIR INTENTION WASN'T TO HELP ME"

1. Jenkins, 1998; Peersman et al., 2012; Pendar, 2007; Rutgaizer et al., 2012.

2. Levenson & Grady, 2019a.

3. It is unsurprising that these particular participants were willing to work with MAPs as clients, given that participants had self-selected into a workshop about work with MAPs.

4. Jahnke, Philipp, & Hoyer, 2015.

5. Walker, Butters, & Nichols, forthcoming.

6. Gellerman & Suddath, 2005; Herbert & Young, 2003.

7. States differ in their requirements for whom a mental health practitioner must inform if a client has indicated a likelihood of violence and under what circumstances.

8. Henderson, 2013; Kalichman, 1999.

9. Virginia's Legislative Information System, 2019 (emphasis mine).

10. E.g., National Association of Social Workers: Utah Chapter, n.d.; Small, Lyons, & Guy, 2002.

11. Walker, Butters, & Nichols, forthcoming.

12. GLAAD, 2016.

13. American Psychological Association, 2009; Beckstead, 2012.

14. American Psychological Association, 2009.

15. E.g., Assil, 2014; Hicks, 1999; Schumer, 2014.

16. Law, 2019.

17. Drapeau et al., 2005.

18. Seto, 2012.

19. E.g., Walker et al., 2015.

20. E.g., Cummings et al., 2017.

21. The COVID-19 pandemic has changed some insurance companies' regulations, allowing for more access to services via telephone or video conferencing. As such, it is possible that more MAPs will be able to access services from providers who do not practice near them. As my data were collected before the pandemic began, I was not able to capture its effects on my participants' ability to access services.

22. Grady et al., 2019; Lasher & Stinson, 2016; Levenson & Grady, 2019b; Levenson, Willis, & Vicencio, 2017; and Sibbald, 2019.

23. Levenson & Grady, 2019b.

24. Hasin et al., 2018; Kessler et al., 2005.

25. Kessler et al., 2005.

26. Nock et al., 2009.

27. Within the United States, mental health providers do not have a mandate to report clients who disclose using child pornography. California is the only exception to this—as of 2020, the state was in the middle of legal arguments about the constitutionality of requiring therapists to report clients for admitting to watching or downloading child pornography (Dolan, 2019).

28. Marsh, 2002, p. 341.

CHAPTER 6. "YOU ARE NOT A MONSTER"

1. Barbara Sinatra Children's Center Foundation, 2016.

2. It's worth noting that as of November 2020, the Boy Scouts of America risked bankruptcy after more than 95,000 allegations of sexual abuse have led to hundreds of lawsuits against the organization (Schmidt, 2020).

3. The Enough Abuse Campaign, 2019.

4. Coast Live, 2019.

5. Defined by the DSM-V (American Psychiatric Association, 2013a) as "any intense and persistent sexual interest other than sexual interest in genital stimulation or preparatory fondling with phenotypically normal, physically mature, consenting human partners" (p. 685).

6. A subreddit is an online community within Reddit, with its own user-created message board accessible through the Reddit website.

7. Twitter statement, October, 2020.

8. E.g., Clark-Flory & Andrews, 2016; Tumblr Staff, 2018.

9. Wodinsky, 2018.

10. Although it is unclear exactly what kinds of posts violated the community guidelines of such websites as Reddit and Tumblr, Vocativ has explored the issue regarding the r/Pedofriends subreddit, finding that some "pro-contact" arguments were found in the community. At the same time, Vocativ quoted an alleged moderator from the r/Pedofriends subreddit sharing that the community had "the most vocal opposition to pro-contact...and the most vocal support for non-contact MAPs" (Clark-Flory & Andrews, 2016)—in other words it was a place where pro-contact opinions were allowed by its moderators to be discussed for others to vocally oppose them.

11. As shown throughout this book, MAPs frequently begin to develop identities as MAPs during adolescence—before they turn 18. Nonetheless, neither VirPed nor B4U-ACT allow minors on their forums out of concern that inviting minors could lead to legal issues.

12. Cohen et al., 2019.

13. Walker, Butters, & Nichols, 2021.

14. See Beier et al., 2009.

15. Johns Hopkins, n.d.

16. Global Prevention Project, 2020.

APPENDIX B. RESEARCH METHODS

1. Per the xkcd comic, "Duty Calls," https://xkcd.com/386/.

2. The subject of being "triggered" has come to be ridiculed in popular culture lately, so I feel the need to say a bit more about it here: "being triggered" is a phrase that specifically applies to post-traumatic stress disorder—triggers are thoughts or situations that induce an individual's PTSD symptoms. Whether my friends who discussed feeling triggered by discussions of MAPs were referring to PTSD triggers, or to more colloquial understandings of being triggered (experiencing unpleasant thoughts as a result of a conversation topic), is unclear. Either way, it is understandable that someone could be triggered by discussions about MAPs, as societal connections between MAPs and sexual abuse are linked. While my friends' feelings of being triggered are unsurprising for this reason, unlinking these concepts is an important goal for this book.

3. E.g., Berkwits & Inui, 1998.

4. Malone, 2014a.

5. Malone, 2014b.

6. Potential participants would have been considered ineligible for the study if they had committed an offense, which was both indicated in my recruitment flyers and via individual screening before interviews began. Nonetheless, this participant worried about individuals who may not have understood the study requirements. Despite this participant's fears, I was able to communicate the study requirements with each of my respondents, and I never had to make a report.

7. Becker, 1967; Bogdan & Taylor, 1998; Wright & Bennett, 1990.

8. Transcriptions were made by Rev.com, except for the three that I transcribed myself. I then cleaned all transcripts by listening the audio recordings while following along to the transcripts and making my own edits as needed to ensure accuracy.

9. Charmaz, 2014; Glaser & Strauss, 1967.

10. Charmaz, 2014.

11. Maxwell, 2009, p. 245.

12. Bowen, 2009.

13. E.g., Tourangeau, Smith, & Rasinski, 1997.

14. Child Welfare Information Gateway, 2016; New York State Office of Children and Family Services, 2016; NYC Administration for Children's Services, 2003.

15. TERF, which stands for trans-exclusionary radical feminist, is not a slur: it simply means a feminist who holds anti-transgender beliefs and values.

Bibliography

Almeida, J., Johnson, R. M., Corliss, H. L., Molnar, B. E., & Azrael, D. (2009). Emotional distress among LGBT youth: The influence of perceived discrimination based on sexual orientation. *Journal of Youth and Adolescence, 38*(7), 1001–1014.

American Psychiatric Association. (1980). *Diagnostic and statistical manual of mental disorders* (3rd ed.).

American Psychiatric Association. (1987). *Diagnostic and statistical manual of mental disorders* (3rd ed., revised).

American Psychiatric Association. (2013a). *Diagnostic and statistical manual of mental disorders* (5th ed.).

American Psychiatric Association. (2013b). *News release.* Retrieved March 25, 2015, from http://www.dsm5.org/Documents/13-67-DSM-Correction-103113.pdf

American Psychological Association. (2009). *Resolution on appropriate affirmative responses to sexual orientation distress and change efforts.* http://www.apa.org/about/policy/sexual-orientation.aspx

Aranda, F., Matthews, A. K., Hughes, T. L., Muramatsu, N., Wilsnack, S. C., Johnson, T. P., & Riley, B. B. (2015). Coming out in color: Racial/ethnic differences in the relationship between level of sexual identity disclosure and depression among lesbians. *Cultural Diversity and Ethnic Minority Psychology, 21*(2), 247.

Assil, S. (2014). Can you work it: Or flip it and reverse it: Protecting LGBT youth from sexual orientation change efforts. *Cardozo Journal of Law & Gender, 21*, 551–581.

B4U-ACT. (2011). *Statement on issues of agreement.* https://www.b4uact.org/about-us/statements-and-policies/statement-on-issues-of-agreement/

B4U-ACT. (2015). *Peer support.* Retrieved March 23, 2015, from http://www.b4uact.org/

B4U-ACT. (2019). *Learn.* https://www.b4uact.org/know-the-facts/

Baiocco, R., Fontanesi, L., Santamaria, F., Ioverno, S., Marasco, B., Baumgartner, E., ... Laghi, F. (2015). Negative parental responses to coming out and family functioning in a sample of lesbian and gay young adults. *Journal of Child and Family Studies, 24*(5), 1490–1500.

Ballard, M. R. (1990). A chance to start over: Church disciplinary councils and the restoration of blessings. *The Church of Jesus Christ of Latter-Day Saints.* https://www.lds.org/ensign/1990/09/a-chance-to-start-over -church-disciplinary-councils-and-the-restoration-of-blessings?lang=eng

Barbara Sinatra Children's Center Foundation. (2016). Protect yourself rules—Introduction [Video file]. https://www.youtube.com/watch?v= RCGPuLur4fk

Barnes, D. M., & Meyer, I. H. (2012). Religious affiliation, internalized homophobia, and mental health in lesbians, gay men, and bisexuals. *American Journal of Orthopsychiatry, 82*(4), 505.

BBC News. (2018, January 15). Bijan Ebrahimi murder: Bristol City Council calls for fresh probe. https://www.bbc.com/news/uk-england-bristol -42696102

Beaber, T. (2008). *Well-being among bisexual females: The roles of internalized biphobia, stigma consciousness, social support, and self-disclosure* [Doctoral dissertation]. ProQuest Information & Learning.

Becker, H. S. (1967). Whose side are we on? *Social Problems, 14*, 239–247.

Beckstead, A. L. (2012). Can we change sexual orientation? *Archives of Sexual Behavior, 41*(1), 121–134.

Beier, K. M., Ahlers, C. J., Goecker, D., Neutze, J., Mundt, I. A., Hupp, E., & Schaefer, G. A. (2009). Can pedophiles be reached for primary prevention of child sexual abuse? First results of the Berlin Prevention Project Dunkelfeld (PPD). *Journal of Forensic Psychiatry & Psychology, 20*(6), 851–867.

Berkwits, M., & Inui, T. S. (1998). Making use of qualitative research techniques. *Journal of General Internal Medicine, 13*(3), 195.

Blanchard, R., Klassen, P., Dickey, R., Kuban, M. E., & Blak, T. (2001). Sensitivity and specificity of the phallometric test for pedophilia in nonadmitting sex offenders. *Psychological Assessment, 13*(1), 118.

Blanchard, R., Kolla, N. J., Cantor, J. M., Klassen, P. E., Dickey, R., Kuban, M. E., & Blak, T. (2007). IQ, handedness, and pedophilia in adult male patients stratified by referral source. *Sexual Abuse, 19*(3), 285–309.

Blanchard, R., Lykins, A. D., Wherrett, D., Kuban, M. E., Cantor, J. M., Blak, T., ... Klassen, P. E. (2009). Pedophilia, hebephilia, and the DSM-V. *Archives of Sexual Behavior, 38*(3), 335–350.

Bogdan, S., & Taylor, R. (1998). Go to the people. In *Introduction to qualitative research methods* (pp. 3–23). Wiley.

Bowen, G. A. (2009). Document analysis as a qualitative research method. *Qualitative Research Journal, 9*(2), 27–40.

Boyle, S. C., LaBrie, J. W., Costine, L. D., & Witkovic, Y. D. (2017). "It's how we deal": Perceptions of LGB peers' use of alcohol and other drugs to cope and sexual minority adults' own coping motivated substance use following the Pulse nightclub shooting. *Addictive Behaviors, 65,* 51–55.

Braithwaite, J. (1989). *Crime, shame and reintegration.* Cambridge University Press.

Brick, J. (Ed.). (2012). *Handbook of the medical consequences of alcohol and drug abuse.* Routledge.

Briere, J., & Runtz, M. (1989). University males' sexual interest in children: Predicting potential indices of "pedophilia" in a nonforensic sample. *Child Abuse & Neglect, 13*(1), 65–75.

Cantor, J. M., Blanchard, R., Christensen, B. K., Dickey, R., Klassen, P. E., Beckstead, A. L., ... Kuban, M. E. (2004). Intelligence, memory, and handedness in pedophilia. *Neuropsychology, 18*(1), 3.

Cantor, J. M., Klassen, P. E., Dickey, R., Christensen, B. K., Kuban, M. E., Blak, T., ... Blanchard, R. (2005). Handedness in pedophilia and hebephilia. *Archives of Sexual Behavior, 34*(4), 447–459.

Cantor, J. M., & McPhail, I. V. (2016). Non-offending pedophiles. *Current Sexual Health Reports, 8,* 121–128.

Carbado, D. (2001). *Black men on race, gender, and sexuality: A critical reader.* New York University Press.

Cash, B. (2016). *Self-identifications, sexual development, and wellbeing in minor-attracted people: An exploratory study* [Master's thesis, Cornell University].

Cass, V. C. (1979). Homosexuality identity formation: A theoretical model. *Journal of Homosexuality, 4*(3), 219–235.

Cass, V. C. (1984). Homosexuality identity formation: Testing a theoretical model. *Journal of Sex Research, 20,* 143–167.

Charmaz, K. (2014). *Constructing grounded theory: A practical guide through qualitative analysis* (2nd ed). Sage.

Chaudoir, S. R., Earnshaw, V. A., & Andel, S. (2013). "Discredited" versus "discreditable": Understanding how shared and unique stigma mechanisms affect psychological and physical health disparities. *Basic and Applied Social Psychology, 35*(1), 75–87.

Chekola, M. (1994). Outing, truth-telling, and the shame of the closet. *Journal of Homosexuality, 27*(3–4), 67–90.

Chenier, E. (2008). *Strangers in our midst: Sexual deviancy in postwar Ontario.* University of Toronto Press.

Child Welfare Information Gateway. (2016). *Mandatory reporters of child abuse and neglect.* U.S. Department of Health and Human Services, Children's Bureau.

Cid, J., & Martí, J. (2012). Turning points and returning points: Understanding the role of family ties in the process of desistance. *European Journal of Criminology, 9*(6), 603–620.

Clark-Flory, T. & Andrews, J. (2016, December 21). Reddit shuts down pedophile community. *Vocativ.* https://www.vocativ.com/386165/reddit-pedofriends-pedophile-shut-down/index.html

CNN. (2019). Transcripts: Mayor Pete Buttigieg (D) presidential candidate fields question at town hall. http://transcripts.cnn.com/TRANSCRIPTS/1904/22/se.05.html

Coast Live. (2019, October 28). An organization that aims to prevent child abuse using puppets on Coast Live. WTKR. https://wtkr.com/2019/10/28/an-organization-that-aims-to-prevent-child-abuse-using-puppets-on-coast-live/

Cohen, L. J., Wilman-Depena, S., Barzilay, S., Hawes, M., Yaseen, Z., & Galynker, I. (2019). Correlates of chronic suicidal ideation among community-based minor-attracted persons. *Sexual Abuse* [Online First], 1–28.

Cole, S. W., Kemeny, M. E., Taylor, S. E., & Visscher, B. R. (1996). Elevated physical health risk among gay men who conceal their homosexual identity. *Health Psychology, 15*(4), 243.

Coleman, E. (1982). Developmental stages of the coming out process. *Journal of Homosexuality, 7*(2–3), 31–43.

Compas, B. E., Connor-Smith, J. K., Saltzman, H., Thomsen, A. H., & Wadsworth, M. E. (2001). Coping with stress during childhood and adolescence: Problems, progress, and potential in theory and research. *Psychological Bulletin, 127*, 87–127.

Connor-Smith, J. K., Compas, B. E., Wadsworth, M. E., Thomsen, A. H., & Saltzman, H. (2000). Responses to stress in adolescence: Measurement of coping and involuntary stress responses. *Journal of Consulting and Clinical Psychology, 68*(6), 976.

Corrigan, P. W., Watson, A. C., & Barr, L. (2006). The self–stigma of mental illness: Implications for self-esteem and self-efficacy. *Journal of Social and Clinical Psychology, 25*(8), 875–884.

Cossins, A. (2000). Masculinities, sexualities and child sexual abuse. In G. Mair & R. Tarling (Eds.), *The British Criminology Conference: Selected Proceedings.*

Couzens, J., Mahoney, B., & Wilkinson, D. (2017). It's just more acceptable to be white or mixed race and gay than black and gay: The perceptions and experiences of homophobia in St. Lucia. *Frontiers in Psychology, 8*, 947.

Critcher, C. R., & Ferguson, M. J. (2014). The cost of keeping it hidden: Decomposing concealment reveals what makes it depleting. *Journal of Experimental Psychology: General, 143*(2), 721.

Cummings, J. R., Allen, L., Clennon, J., Ji, X., & Druss, B. G. (2017). Geographic access to specialty mental health care across high-and low-income US communities. *JAMA Psychiatry, 74*(5), 476-484.

Day, N. E., & Schoenrade, P. (1997). Staying in the closet versus coming out: Relationships between communication about sexual orientation and work attitudes. *Personnel Psychology, 50*(1), 147–163.

Devin, N., & Edwards, E. (2012). *Virtuous pedophiles.* http://www.virped.org/.

Dolan, M. (2019, December 26). California Supreme Court allows therapists

to challenge law on child porn reporting. *Los Angeles Times.* https://www
.latimes.com/california/story/2019-12-26/california-supreme-court
-therapists-child-porn

Drapeau, M., Körner, A., Granger, L., Brunet, L., & Caspar, F. (2005). A plan
analysis of pedophile sexual abusers' motivations for treatment: A qualitative pilot study. *International Journal of Offender Therapy and Comparative Criminology, 49*(3), 308–324.

Eke, A. W., Seto, M. C., & Williams, J. (2011). Examining the criminal history and future offending of child pornography offenders: An extended
prospective follow-up study. *Law and Human Behavior, 35*(6), 466–478.

The Enough Abuse Campaign. (2019). *State laws mandating or allowing
child sexual abuse education in schools.* https://www.enoughabuse.org
/legislation/mapping-state-legislative-efforts/csa-education-in-schools
.html

Erikson, E. H. (1959). *Identity and the life cycle.* W. W. Norton & Company,
Inc.

Erikson, E. H. (1968). *Identity, youth and crisis.* W. W. Norton & Company,
Inc.

Finkelhor, D. (1984). *Child Sexual Abuse: New Theory and Research.* Free
Press.

Forliti, A. (2017, October 2). Supreme Court won't hear Minnesota sex
offender case. *Associated Press.* https://www.twincities.com/2017/10
/02/supreme-court-wont-hear-minnesota-sex-offender-case/

Frable, D. E., Wortman, C., & Joseph, J. (1997). Predicting self-esteem, wellbeing, and distress in a cohort of gay men: The importance of cultural
stigma, personal visibility, community networks, and positive identity.
Journal of Personality, 65(3), 599–624.

Freimond, C. M. (2013). *Navigating the stigma of pedophilia: The experiences
of nine minor-attracted men in Canada* [Master's thesis, Simon Fraser
University].

Freund, K., & Kuban, M. (1993). Toward a testable developmental model
of pedophilia: The development of erotic age preference. *Child Abuse &
Neglect, 17*(2), 315–324.

Gellerman, D. M., & Suddath, R. (2005). Violent fantasy, dangerousness,
and the duty to warn and protect. *Journal of the American Academy of
Psychiatry and the Law Online, 33*(4), 484–495.

GLAAD. (2016). *Media reference guide.*

Glaser, B. G., & Strauss, A. L. (1967). *The discovery of grounded theory: Strategies for qualitative research.* Aldine Publishing Company

Global Prevention Project. (2020). *MAP support.* http://theglobalprevention
project.org/maps

Goffman, E . (1963). *Stigma: Notes on the management of spoiled identity.*
Prentice-Hall.

Goode, S. (2009). *Understanding and addressing adult sexual attraction to
children: A study of paedophiles in contemporary society.* Routledge.

Grady, M. D., Levenson, J. S., Mesias, G., Kavanagh, S., & Charles, J. (2019). "I can't talk about that": Stigma and fear as barriers to preventive services for minor-attracted persons. *Stigma and Health, 4*(4), 400.

Green, R. (2002). Is pedophilia a mental disorder? *Archives of Sexual Behavior, 31*(6), 467–471.

Greene, K., Derlega, V. J., & Mathews, A. (2006). Self-disclosure in personal relationships. In A. L. Vangelisti & D. Perlman (Eds.), *The Cambridge Handbook of Personal Relationships* (p. 409–427). Cambridge University Press.

Greenwood, M. (2018.) *Christian Pedophile: Finding a Way.* https://www .christian pedophile.com/

Halkitis, P. N., Mattis, J. S., Sahadath, J. K., Massie, D., Ladyzhenskaya, L., Pitrelli, K., . . . Cowie, S. A. E. (2009). The meanings and manifestations of religion and spirituality among lesbian, gay, bisexual, and transgender adults. *Journal of Adult Development, 16*(4), 250–262.

Hall, R. C. W., & Hall, R. C. W. (2007). A profile of pedophilia: Definition, characteristics of offenders, recidivism, treatment outcomes, and forensic issues. *Mayo Clinic Proceedings, 82*(4), 457–471.

Harris, K. M., & Edlund, M. J. (2005). Self-medication of mental health problems: New evidence from a national survey. *Health Services Research, 40*(1), 117–134.

Hasin, D. S., Sarvet, A. L., Meyers, J. L., Saha, T. D., Ruan, W. J., Stohl, M., & Grant, B. F. (2018). Epidemiology of adult DSM-5 major depressive disorder and its specifiers in the United States. *JAMA Psychiatry, 75*(4), 336–346.

Haydon, D. (2014). Early intervention for the prevention of offending in Northern Ireland. *Youth Justice, 14*(3), 226–240.

Henderson, K. (2013). Mandated reporting of child abuse: Considerations and guidelines for mental health counselors. *Journal of Mental Health Counseling, 35*(4), 296–309.

Herbert, P. B., & Young, K. A. (2003). Tarasoff at twenty-five. *Focus, 30*(4), 275–381.

Hicks, K. A. (1999). Reparative therapy: Whether parental attempts to change a child's sexual orientation can legally constitute child abuse. *American University Law Review, 49*, 505.

Holohan, C. J., Moos, R. H., & Schaefer, J. A. (1996). Coping, stress resistance, and growth: Conceptualizing adaptive functioning. In M. Zeidner & N. S. Endler (Eds.), *Handbook of Coping* (pp. 24–43). John Wiley & Sons.

Homel, R., Lincoln, R., & Herd, B. (1999). Risk and resilience: Crime and violence prevention in Aboriginal communities. *Australian & New Zealand Journal of Criminology, 32*(2), 182–196.

Ilic, M., Reinecke, J., Bohner, G., Hans-Onno, R., Beblo, T., Driessen, M., . . . Corrigan, P. W. (2012). Protecting self-esteem from stigma: A test of different strategies for coping with the stigma of mental illness. *International Journal of Social Psychiatry, 58*(3), 246–257.

Irwin, J. A., Coleman, J. D., Fisher, C. M., & Marasco, V. M. (2014). Correlates of suicide ideation among LGBT Nebraskans. *Journal of Homosexuality, 61*(8), 1172–1191.

Jahnke, S., Philipp, K., & Hoyer, J. (2015). Stigmatizing attitudes towards people with pedophilia and their malleability among psychotherapists in training. *Child Abuse & Neglect, 40*, 93–102.

Jahnke S., Schmidt, A. F., Geradt, M., & Hoyer, J. (2015). Stigma-related stress and its correlates among men with pedophilic sexual interests. *Archives of Sexual Behavior, 44*(8), 2173–2187.

Jenkins, P. (1998). *Moral panic: Changing concepts of the child molester in modern America.* Yale University Press.

Johns Hopkins. (n.d.). *Welcome to help wanted.* https://www.helpwantedprevention.org/

Kalichman, S. C. (1999). *Mandated reporting of suspected child abuse: Ethics, law, & policy.* American Psychological Association.

Kelly, R., & Lusk, R. (2013). Theories of pedophilia. In W. T. O'Donohue & J. H. Greer (Eds.). *The sexual abuse of children, volume I: Theory and research* (pp. 168–203). Routledge.

Kessler, R. C., Berglund, P., Demler, O., Jin, R., Merikangas, K. R., & Walters, E. E. (2005). Lifetime prevalence and age-of-onset distributions of DSM-IV disorders in the National Comorbidity Survey Replication. *Archives of General Psychiatry, 62*(6), 593–602.

Khantzian, E. J. (1997). The self-medication hypothesis of substance use disorders: A reconsideration and recent applications. *Harvard Review of Psychiatry, 4*(5), 231–244.

Kingston, D. A., Firestone, P., Moulden, H., & Bradford, J. M. (2007). The utility of the diagnosis of pedophilia: A comparison of various classification procedures. *Archives of Sexual Behavior, 36*, 423–436.

Krieger, N., & Sidney, S. (1996). Racial discrimination and blood pressure: The CARDIA Study of young Black and White adults. *American Journal of Public Health, 86*, 1370–1378.

Lasher, M. P., & Stinson, J. D. (2017). Adults with pedophilic interests in the United States: Current practices and suggestions for future policy and research. *Archives of Sexual Behavior, 46*(3), 659–670.

Law, T. (2019, November 19). Why the LDS Church joined LGBTQ advocates in supporting Utah's conversion therapy ban. *Time.* https://time.com/5741789/utah-conversion-therapy-ban-lds/

Laws, D. R., & Ward, T. (2010). *Desistance from sex offending: Alternatives to throwing away the keys.* Guilford.

Legate, N., Ryan, R. M., & Weinstein, N. (2012). Is coming out always a "good thing"? Exploring the relations of autonomy support, outness, and wellness for lesbian, gay, and bisexual individuals. *Social Psychological and Personality Science, 3*(2), 145–152.

Levenson, J. S., & Grady, M. D. (2019a). "I could never work with those people…": Secondary prevention of child sexual abuse via a brief training for therapists about pedophilia. *Journal of Interpersonal Violence, 34*(20), 4281–4302.

Levenson, J. S., & Grady, M. D. (2019b). Preventing sexual abuse: Perspectives of minor-attracted persons about seeking help. *Sexual Abuse, 31*(8), 991–1013.

Levenson, J. S., Willis, G. M., & Vicencio, C. P. (2017). Obstacles to help-seeking for sexual offenders: Implications for prevention of sexual abuse. *Journal of Child Sexual Abuse, 26*(2), 99–120.

Levine, J. (2002). *Harmful to minors: The perils of protecting children from sex.* University of Minnesota Press.

Lewis, R. J., Derlega, V. J., Griffin, J. L., & Krowinski, A. C. (2003). Stressors for gay men and lesbians: Life stress, gay-related stress, stigma consciousness, and depressive symptoms. *Journal of Social and Clinical Psychology, 22*(6), 716–729.

Li, C. K. (1991). "The main thing is being wanted": Some case studies on adult sexual experiences with children. *Journal of Homosexuality, 20,* 129–143.

Link, B. G., Cullen, F. T., Struening, E., Shrout, P. E., & Dohrenwend, B. P. (1989). A modified labeling theory approach to mental disorders: An empirical assessment. *American Sociological Review, 54,* 400–423.

Link, B. G., Mirotznik, J., & Cullen, F. T. (1991). The effectiveness of stigma coping orientations: Can negative consequences of mental illness labeling be avoided? *Journal of Health and Social Behavior,* 302–320.

Lynch, H. F., Joffe, S., Thirumurthy, H., Xie, D., & Largent, E. A. (2019). Association between financial incentives and participant deception about study eligibility. *JAMA Network Open, 2*(1), 1–10.

Major, B., & Schmader, T. (1998). Coping with stigma through psychological disengagement. In J. K. Swim & C. Stangor (Eds.), *Prejudice: The target's perspective* (pp. 191–218). Academic.

Maletzky, B. M., & Steinhauser, C. (2002). A 25-year follow-up of cognitive/behavioral therapy with 7,275 sexual offenders. *Behavior Modification, 26*(2), 123–147.

Malón, A. (2012). Pedophilia: A diagnosis in search of a disorder. *Archives of Sexual Behavior, 41*(5), 1083–1097.

Malone, L. (Contributor). (2014a, April 11). Tarred and feathered [Radio series episode]. In I. Glass (Producer), *This American Life.* Chicago Public Media.

Malone, L. (2014b, August 10). You're 16. You're a pedophile. You don't want to hurt anyone. What do you do now? *Matter.* https://medium.com/ matter/ youre-16-youre-a-pedophile-you-dont-want-to-hurt-anyone-what-do-you-do-now-e11ce4b88bdb

Marsh, J. C. (2002). Learning from clients. *Social Work, 47*(4), 341–343.

Marshall, W. L., & Barbaree, H. E. (1990). An integrated theory of the etiology of sexual offending. In W. L. Marshal, D. R. Laws, & H. E. Barbaree (Eds.), *Handbook of sexual assault: Issues, theories, and treatment of the offender* (pp. 257–275). Springer.

Marshall, W. L., Barbaree, H. E., & Eccles, A. (1991). Early onset and deviant sexuality in child molesters. *Journal of Interpersonal Violence, 6*(3), 323–335.

Maruna, S. (2001). *Making good: How ex-convicts reform and rebuild their lives.* American Psychological Association.

Massoglia, M., & Uggen, C. (2010). Settling down and aging out: Toward an interactionist theory of desistance and the transition to adulthood. *American Journal of Sociology, 116*(2), 543–582.

Maxwell, J. A. (2009). Designing a qualitative study. In L. Bickman & D. J. Rog (Eds.), *Handbook of applied social science research methods* (2nd ed). Sage.

McGarrity, L. A., & Huebner, D. M. (2013). Is being out about sexual orientation uniformly healthy? The moderating role of socioeconomic status in a prospective study of gay and bisexual men. *Annals of Behavioral Medicine, 47*(1), 28–38.

Mickelson, K. D., & Williams, D. R. (1999). The prevalence, distribution, and mental health correlates of perceived discrimination in the United States. *Journal of Health and Social Behavior, 40,* 208–230.

Miller, C. T., & Kaiser, C. R. (2001). A theoretical perspective on coping with stigma. *Journal of Social Issues, 57*(1), 73–92.

Miller, C. T., & Major, B. (2000). Coping with stigma and prejudice. In T. F. Heatherton, R. E. Kleck, M. R. Hebl, & J. G. Hull (Eds.), *The social psychology of stigma* (pp. 243–272). Guilford.

Miller, J. A. (2010). Sex offender civil commitment: The treatment paradox. *California Law Review,* 2093–2128.

Mingus, W., & Burchfield, K. B. (2012). From prison to integration: Applying modified labeling theory to sex offenders. *Criminal Justice Studies, 25*(1), 97–109.

Minton, H. L., & MacDonald, G. J. (1983). Homosexual identity formation as a developmental process. *Journal of Homosexuality, 9*(2–3), 91–104.

Mogul, J. L., Ritchie, A. J., & Whitlock, K. (2011). *Queer (in) justice: The criminalization of LGBT people in the United States.* Beacon Press.

Moser, C. (2016). Defining sexual orientation. *Archives of Sexual Behavior, 45*(3), 505–508.

Morris, J. F., Waldo, C. R., & Rothblum, E. D. (2001). A model of predictors and outcomes of outness among lesbian and bisexual women. *American Journal of Orthopsychiatry, 71*(1), 61–71.

Movement Advancement Project. (2020). *Conversion "therapy" laws.* https://www.lgbtmap.org/equality-maps/conversion_therapy

Murray, C. (2010). Conceptualizing young people's strategies of resistance to offending as "active resilience." *British Journal of Social Work, 40*(1), 115–132.

Murray, C. (2012). Young people's perspectives: The trials and tribulations of going straight. *Criminology & Criminal Justice, 12*(1), 25–40.

National Association of Social Workers: Utah Chapter. (N.d.) *Social workers and the duty to warn.* http://c.ymcdn.com/sites/www.utnasw.org /resource/resmgr/imported /SocialWorkersANDDutytoWarn.pdf

New York State Office of Children and Family Services. (2016). *Summary guide for mandated reporters in New York State.*

Nock, M. K., Hwang, I., Sampson, N., Kessler, R. C., Angermeyer, M., Beautrais, A., . . . De Graaf, R. (2009). Cross-national analysis of the associations among mental disorders and suicidal behavior: Findings from the WHO World Mental Health Surveys. *PLoS medicine, 6*(8), e1000123.

NYC Administration for Children's Services. (2003). *Parents' guide to New York State child abuse and neglect laws.*

Okami, P., & Goldberg, A. (1992). Personality correlates of pedophilia: Are they reliable indicators? *Journal of Sex Research, 29*(3), 297–328.

Pachankis, J. E. (2007). The psychological implications of concealing a stigma: A cognitive-affective-behavioral model. *Psychological Bulletin, 133*(2), 328.

Pachankis, J. E., Hatzenbuehler, M. L., Rendina, H. J., Safren, S. A., & Parsons, J. T. (2015). LGB-affirmative cognitive-behavioral therapy for young adult gay and bisexual men: A randomized controlled trial of a transdiagnostic minority stress approach. *Journal of Consulting and Clinical Psychology, 83*(5), 875.

Peersman, C., Vaassen, F., Van Asch, V., & Daelemans, W. (2012, September). Conversation level constraints on pedophile detection in chat rooms. In *CLEF* (Online Working Notes/Labs/Workshop).

Pendar, N. (2007, September). Toward spotting the pedophile telling victim from predator in text chats. In *International Conference on Semantic Computing* (ICSC 2007) (pp. 235–241). IEEE.

Rabinovich, A., & Morton, T. A. (2016). Coping with identity conflict: Perceptions of self as flexible versus fixed moderate the effect of identity conflict on wellbeing. *Self and Identity, 15*(2), 224–244.

Ricciardelli, R., & Moir, M. (2013). Stigmatized among the stigmatized: Sex offenders in Canadian penitentiaries. *Canadian Journal of Criminology and Criminal Justice, 55*(3), 353–386.

Riessman, F. (1965). The "helper" therapy principle. *Social Work, 10*(2), 27–32.

Robbers, M. L. (2009). Lifers on the outside: Sex offenders and disintegrative shaming. *International Journal of Offender Therapy and Comparative Criminology, 53*(1), 5–28.

Ross, L. E., Doctor, F., Dimito, A., Kuehl, D., & Armstrong, M. S. (2007). Can talking about oppression reduce depression? Modified CBT group treatment for LGBT people with depression. *Journal of Gay & Lesbian Social Services, 19*(1), 1–15.

Rowen, C. J., & Malcolm, J. P. (2003). Correlates of internalized homophobia and homosexual identity formation in a sample of gay men. *Journal of Homosexuality, 43*(2), 77–92.

Russell, G. M., & Richards, J. A. (2003). Stressor and resilience factors for lesbians, gay men, and bisexuals confronting antigay politics. *American Journal of Community Psychology, 31*(3–4), 313–328.

Russell, S. T., Driscoll, A. K., & Truong, N. (2002). Adolescent same-sex romantic attractions and relationships: Implications for substance use and abuse. *American Journal of Public Health, 92*(2), 198–202.

Rutgaizer, M., Shavitt, Y., Vertman, O., & Zilberman, N. (2012, March). Detecting pedophile activity in bittorrent networks. In *International Conference on Passive and Active Network Measurement* (pp. 106–115). Springer, Berlin, Heidelberg.

Ryan, W. S., Legate, N., & Weinstein, N. (2015). Coming out as lesbian, gay, or bisexual: The lasting impact of initial disclosure experiences. *Self and Identity, 14*(5), 549–569.

Samenow, C. P. (2012). Child pornography and the law: A clinician's guide. *Sexual Addiction & Compulsivity, 19*(1–2), 16–29.

Sampson, R. J., & Laub, J. H. (1995). *Crime in the making: Pathways and turning points through life.* Harvard University Press.

Savin-Williams, R. C. (1998). *"—and then I became gay": Young men's stories.* Routledge.

Savin-Williams, R. C., & Diamond, L. M. (2000). Sexual identity trajectories among sexual-minority youths: Gender comparisons. *Archives of Sexual Behavior, 29*(6), 607–627.

Schallhorn, K. (2015, September 21). Salon publishes essay by pedophile: "Before judging me harshly, would you be willing to listen?" *The Blaze.* https://www.theblaze.com/news/2015/09/21/salon-publishes-essay-by -pedophile-before-judging-me-harshly-would-you-be-willing-to-listen

Schmidt, S. (2020, November 19). "Boy Scouts must settle 95,000 abuse claims by next summer —or risk running out of cash." *Washington Post.* https://www.washingtonpost.com/dc-md-va/2020/11/19/boy-scouts -bankruptcy-abuse/

Schrimshaw, E. W., Siegel, K., Downing, Jr., M. J., & Parsons, J. T. (2013). Disclosure and concealment of sexual orientation and the mental health of non-gay-identified, behaviorally bisexual men. *Journal of Consulting and Clinical Psychology, 81*(1), 141.

Schumer, T. (2014). Abusing our LGBT youth: The criminalization of sexual orientation change reports. *Southern California Review of Law & Social Justice, 24*, 53.

Seto, M. C. (2012). Is pedophilia a sexual orientation? *Archives of Sexual Behavior, 41*(1), 231–236.

Seto, M. C. (2017). The puzzle of male chronophilias. *Archives of Sexual Behavior, 46*(1), 3–22.

Seto, M. C. (2018). *Pedophilia and sexual offending against children: Theory, assessment, and intervention* (2nd ed.). American Psychological Association.

Seto, M. C., & Eke, A. W. (2005). The criminal histories and later offending of child pornography offenders. *Sexual Abuse: A Journal of Research and Treatment*, 17(2), 201–210.

Seto, M. C., & Lalumière, M. L. (2001). A brief screening scale to identify pedophilic interests among child molesters. *Sexual Abuse: A Journal of Research and Treatment*, 13(1), 15–25.

Seto, M. C., Lalumière, M. L., & Blanchard, R. (2000). The discriminative validity of a phallometric test for pedophilic interests among adolescent sex offenders against children. *Psychological Assessment*, 12(3), 319.

Seto, M. C., Murphy, W. D., Page, J., & Ennis, L. (2003). Detecting anomalous sexual interests in juvenile sex offenders. *Annals of the New York Academy of Sciences*, 989(1), 118–130.

Seto, M. C., Stephens, S., Lalumière, M. L., & Cantor, J. M. (2017). The revised Screening Scale for Pedophilic Interests (SSPI–2): Development and criterion-related validation. *Sexual Abuse*, 29(7), 619–635.

Sibbald, E. (2019). *Help-seeking and distress: Exploring the attitudes and experiences of minor-attracted people in the UK* [Doctoral dissertation, University of Surrey].

Singh, A. A., Hays, D. G., & Watson, L. S. (2011). Strength in the face of adversity: Resilience strategies of transgender individuals. *Journal of Counseling & Development*, 89(1), 20–27.

Small, M. A., Lyons, Jr., P. M., & Guy, L. S. (2002). Liability issues in child abuse and neglect reporting statutes. *Professional Psychology: Research and Practice*, 33(1), 13.

Solomon, P. (2004). Peer support/peer provided services underlying processes, benefits, and critical ingredients. *Psychiatric Rehabilitation Journal*, 27(4), 392.

Stout, D. (2002, April 16). Supreme Court strikes down ban on virtual child pornography.

New York Times. http://www.nytimes.com/2002/04/16/national/ supremecourt-strikes-down-ban-on-virtual-child-pornography.html

Substance Abuse and Mental Health Services Administration. (2015). Ending conversion therapy: Supporting and affirming LGBTQ youth. *HHS Publication No. (SMA) 15-4928*.

Suh, J. J., Ruffins, S., Robins, C. E., Albanese, M. J., & Khantzian, E. J. (2008). Self-medication hypothesis: Connecting affective experience and drug choice. *Psychoanalytic Psychology*, 25(3), 518.

Talley, A. E., & Littlefield, A. K. (2014). Pathways between concealable stigmatized identities and substance misuse. *Social and Personality Psychology Compass*, 8(10), 569–582.

Taylor, M., & Quayle, E. (2003). *Child pornography: An internet crime.* Brunner-Routledge.

Terry, K. J. (2015). Sex offender laws in the United States: Smart policy or disproportionate sanctions? *International Journal of Comparative and Applied Criminal Justice*, 39(2), 113–127.

Thorstad, D. (1991). Man/boy love and the American gay movement. *Journal of Homosexuality, 20*(1–2), 251–274.

Tourangeau, R., Smith, T. W., & Rasinski, K. A. (1997). Motivation to report sensitive behaviors on surveys: Evidence from a bogus pipeline experiment. *Journal of Applied Social Psychology, 27*(3), 209–222.

Trammell, R., & Chenault, S. (2009). "We have to take these guys out": Motivations for assaulting incarcerated child molesters. *Symbolic Interaction, 32*(4), 334–350.

Troiden, R. R. (1989). The formation of homosexual identities. *Journal of Homosexuality, 17*(1–2), 43–74.

Tumblr Staff. (2018). *Our community guidelines are changing.* https://staff .tumblr.com/post/177449083750/new-community-guidelines

Twitter. (2020). *Child sexual exploitation policy.* https://help.twitter.com/en /rules-and-policies/sexual-exploitation-policy

United States Department of Justice. (2017). *Citizen's guide to U.S. federal law on child pornography.* Washington, DC: Author.

United States Department of Justice. (2018). *Citizen's guide to U.S. federal law on obscenity.* Washington, DC: Author.

Varley, C. (2018, March 7). Is Japan turning a blind eye to paedophilia? *British Broadcasting Company.* https://www.bbc.co.uk/bbcthree/article/ 57eaaf23-0cef-48c8-961f-41f2563b38aa

Varni, S. E., Miller, C. T., McCuin, T., & Solomon, S. (2012). Disengagement and engagement coping with HIV/AIDS stigma and psychological well-being of people with HIV/AIDS. *Journal of Social and Clinical Psychology, 31*(2), 123–150.

Virginia's Legislative Information System (2019). § 54.1-2400.1. Mental health service providers; duty to protect third parties; immunity. Retrieved June 12, 2019, from https://law.lis. virginia.gov/vacode/title54 .1/chapter24/section54.1-2400.1/

Virupaksha, H. G., Muralidhar, D., & Ramakrishna, J. (2016). Suicide and suicidal behavior among transgender persons. *Indian Journal of Psychological Medicine, 38*(6), 505.

Walker, A. (2019). "I'm not like that, so am I gay?" The use of queer-spectrum identity labels among minor-attracted people. *Journal of Homosexuality,* 1–24.

Walker, A., Butters, R. B., & Nichols, E. (In press.) "I would report it even if they have not committed anything": Social service students' attitudes toward minor-attracted people. *Sexual Abuse.*

Walker, E. R., Cummings, J. R., Hockenberry, J. M., & Druss, B. G. (2015). Insurance status, use of mental health services, and unmet need for mental health care in the United States. *Psychiatric Services, 66*(6), 578–584.

Walsh, W. A., Wolak, J., & Finkelhor, D. (2013*). Prosecution dilemmas and challenges for child pornography crimes: The third National Juvenile Online Victimization Study.* Crimes Against Children Research Center.

Wardell, J. D., Shuper, P. A., Rourke, S. B., & Hendershot, C. S. (2018). Stigma, coping, and alcohol use severity among people living with HIV: A prospective analysis of bidirectional and mediated associations. *Annals of Behavioral Medicine, 52*(9), 762–772.

Wells, M., Finkelhor, D., Wolak, J., & Mitchell, K. J. (2007). Defining child pornography: Law enforcement dilemmas in investigations of internet child pornography possession. *Police Practice and Research, 8*(3), 269–282.

Windle, G., Bennett, K. M., & Noyes, J. (2011). A methodological review of resilience measurement scales. *Health and Quality of Life Outcomes, 9*(8), 1–18.

Wodinsky, S. (2018, July 9). Reddit CEO says it's "impossible" to consistently enforce hate speech rules. *The Verge.* https://www.theverge.com/2018 /7/9/17550824 /reddit-ceo-steve-huffman-hate-speech-moderation-nearly-impossible-leaked-chat

Wolak, J., Finkelhor, D., Mitchell, K. J., & Ybarra, M. L. (2008). Online "predators" and their victims: Myths, realities, and implications for prevention and treatment. *American Psychologist, 63*(2), 111.

Wright, R., & Bennett, T. (1990). Exploring the offender's perspective: Observing and interviewing criminals. In K. L. Kempf (Ed.), *Measurement issues in criminology* (pp. 138–151). Springer-Verlag.

Index

Founded in 1893,
UNIVERSITY OF CALIFORNIA PRESS
publishes bold, progressive books and journals
on topics in the arts, humanities, social sciences,
and natural sciences—with a focus on social
justice issues—that inspire thought and action
among readers worldwide.

The UC PRESS FOUNDATION
raises funds to uphold the press's vital role
as an independent, nonprofit publisher, and
receives philanthropic support from a wide
range of individuals and institutions—and from
committed readers like you. To learn more, visit
ucpress.edu/supportus.

Ingram Content Group UK Ltd.
Milton Keynes UK
UKHW010114060523
421313UK00005B/371